It Ain't Over . . .
Till It's Over

Also by Marlo Thomas

Free to Be . . . You and Me

Free to Be . . . a Family

The Right Words at the Right Time

The Right Words at the Right Time, Volume 2: Your Turn

Thanks & Giving: All Year Long

Growing Up Laughing: My Story and the Story of Funny

IT AIN'T OVER . . . TILL IT'S OVER

Reinventing Your Life— and Realizing Your Dreams— Anytime, at Any Age

Marlo Thomas

ATRIA BOOKS

New York   London   Toronto   Sydney   New Delhi

It Ain't Over . . .
Till It's Over

Editor
MARLO THOMAS

Executive Editor
ALISON GWINN

Consulting Editor
BRUCE KLUGER

ATRIA BOOKS

A Division of Simon & Schuster, Inc.
1230 Avenue of the Americas
New York, NY 10020

First Atria Books hardcover edition April 2014

ATRIA BOOKS and colophon are trademarks of Simon & Schuster, Inc.

Certain names and identifying characteristics have been changed.

For information about special discounts for bulk purchases, please contact Simon & Schuster Special Sales at
1-866-506-1949 or business@simonandschuster.com.

The Simon & Schuster Speakers Bureau can bring authors to your live event. For more information or to book an event
contact the Simon & Schuster Speakers Bureau at 1-866-248-3049 or visit our website at www.simonspeakers.com.

Interior design by Dana Sloan
Jacket design by Jeanne Lee and Bruce Kluger
Jacket photographs by Randee St. Nicholas

Manufactured in the United States of America

10   9   8   7   6   5   4   3   2   1

Library of Congress Cataloging-in-Publication Data

It ain't over . . . till it's over : reinventing your life—and realizing your dreams—anytime, at any age / by Marlo Thomas
and Friends ; Marlo Thomas, editor.
        pages   cm
    1. Career changes—United States—Case studies.   2. Entrepreneurship—United States—Case studies.
3. Businesswomen—United States—Case studies.   4. Self-realization in women—Case studies.   5. Success—Case
studies.   I. Thomas, Marlo.
    HF5384.I82 2014
    650.1—dc23   2013045446

ISBN 978-1-4767-3991-5
ISBN 978-1-4767-3993-9 (ebook)

For the women in my family—
Terre, Dionne, Tracy, Kristina, Kate, Gaby,
Annie, Tracey, Mary Rose, Reed, Kenzie—
and the women in your families, who have the
spirit and the courage to embrace change

Contents

CONTENTS

PART SIX

Family Ties

PART SEVEN

Adventurers

PART TWELVE

Giving Back

Acknowledgments

When I sat down to begin work on this book, I was excited and energized. There's nothing I love—and need—more than the reassurance that we can all dream and start over again. The process of gathering hundreds of personal stories, picking the best of the best, nurturing them, and then weaving them into a meaningful whole is both rigorous and delicate. And I knew it would take a good team.

So I am ever grateful to all those who lent their time and talent to the creation of this collection.

As always, my heartfelt thanks go out to the smart and savvy gang at Atria Books—led by Judith Curr and Greer Hendricks—who always provide a warm and safe home for me, embracing my ideas and giving me the freedom to explore them.

I'd like to thank my attorney and friend (and not in that order) Bob Levine, for his wise counsel and unerring compass throughout the creative process, and for his buoyant spirit, which always drives me forward.

I can't say enough wonderful things about the gifted and dedicated writers who helped bring life to the 60 compelling stories you'll read in these pages: Julie Besonen, Jeryl Brunner, Danielle Gasbarro, Katie Hafner, Roseann Henry, Dana Hudepohl, Jamie Malanowski, Jennifer Rainey Marquez, Kate Meyers, Hollace Schmidt, and Nicole Zeman. Also, thanks to Lori Weiss, who helps us tell the "It Ain't Over" stories on MarloThomas.com.

Thanks, too, to my tireless assistant, Amy Novak, for keeping the rest of my life humming smoothly as I buried myself in manuscripts, edits, and re-writes; and to my colleague and pal Dan Sallick, for his ample bounty of killer ideas (and even ampler bounty of friendship and support).

I am deeply indebted to the five dozen women who generously shared their lives with us, in our efforts to tell the larger story of reinvention. Their amazing journeys are the true spirit of this book, and I admire all of them for their determination, their vision, and their courage. I am likewise thankful to those women whose stories ultimately did not make it into these pages, but whose remarkable accomplishments are no less inspiring.

And, of course, to my two comrades in the trenches, Alison Gwinn and Bruce Kluger, who worked with me for 14 months, bringing the kind of creative energy, professionalism, and love of laughter that make working on any project a true joy.

Finally, to my husband, Phillip, with whom it ain't—and won't ever be—over.

Foreword

"Never face the facts; if you do you'll never get up in the morning." That's one of my favorite sayings, and I truly believe it. The facts—polls, statistics, conventional wisdoms—can keep anyone from ever starting anything. Better to create your own facts.

I meet so many women as I travel the country. And wherever I go, I listen to them talk about the dreams they left behind; or the ones they tried to achieve that went nowhere; or the ones they never even attempted. And more often than not, I hear the deep yearning in their voices as they talk about their search for a way to rekindle those dreams.

And their fear is always the same: *It's too late, isn't it?*

Well, now that I've lived a little, I know this to be true: It's never too late. It ain't over till it's over.

These women inspired me to launch my own website on AOL and the Huffington Post in 2010. I wanted to create a destination where women could

gather together, tell their stories, share their passions, and encourage one another to create a new dream—or to go back and pick up an old one.

After a few months online, I began to notice a common theme among the
women who were sharing their stories: They were stuck. Some were stuck
in dead-end jobs that made them feel lifeless inside. Others were new empty
nesters—confronted, practically overnight, with a big, quiet house and a bigger, quieter future. Still others had experienced a life crisis—a divorce, a lay-
off, the death of a loved one—and had fallen into a stultifying funk.

Most were aware that they were at a crucial crossroads, but they had no
idea which way to turn.

Some, however, had a positive response to this defining moment in their
lives. To them, the giant wall that had sprung up in their path was not a bar-
rier, but something to leap over.

I was eager to shine a spotlight on these courageous women, so I created a
weekly Web series called "It Ain't Over Till It's Over" in the hope that others
who were similarly adrift would take inspiration from what these women
had achieved.

And they did. "It Ain't Over" became an instant hit with readers, garner-
ing millions of clicks every week. We had touched a nerve. And that nerve
feels like the beginning of a new generation—the Reinvention Generation—
populated by those who are not daunted by what they haven't done, but,
instead, are empowered by the idea that they can go for it now. They've discovered that it's never too late to step up to the plate. And if life throws you a
curveball, try to knock it out of the park.

As much as I love the Web—its bustle, its ever-changing face—I wanted
to chronicle this remarkable reinvention phenomenon as a book. That way,
women could always have it handy—in their purses, on their night tables,
propped up on the handlebars of their Lifecycles—and draw encouragement

from it. And rather than revisit the women featured on my website, I wanted to comb the nation, interview women, speak with their families and friends, and bring back their stories.

And that's what you hold in your hands now—60 inspiring stories. Some of them feature women who built entire empires out of a single idea—like Veronica Bosgraaf of Holland, Michigan, who wanted to create healthier school lunches for her children, so she whipped up a recipe in her kitchen and called it the Pure Bar. Not only did her kids love it, *everybody* loved it; and today it is sold in stores across the country, earning Veronica millions.

You'll also meet women who found new ways to fulfill themselves after experiencing profound personal loss—like Jane Alderman of Washington, D.C., whose brother perished in the World Trade Center on 9/11. Devastated by his death, Jane chose to rechannel her grief into something meaningful, quitting her desk job, earning her MBA, and—with her parents—launching a global foundation to care for other victims of trauma.

And some women simply rejected their own complacency about their lives and rebuilt themselves—physically and mentally.

Like phone saleswoman Natasha Coleman, whose weight had reached a perilous 428 pounds; a humiliating incident aboard an airplane convinced her to address the problem at long last—and in the process save her own life.

Or Trish B., a 53-year-old English teacher from Maryland, who one day discovered—during a routine trip to the mailbox—that her husband of many years had been chronically cheating on her. Trish was devastated at first, but refused to be a victim. "I knew I was stronger than that," she recalls. And the story she tells—of her emotional torment and her ultimate survival—is both harrowing and inspiring.

Or Diane Dennis, a twice-divorced mother of two, who, at age 50, felt "washed up, middle-aged, discarded. It was like I had an elephant sitting on my chest." So she relocated her life to the banks of the placid Willamette River in Oregon, where she bought a home, took up the unlikely sport of wakeboarding, and learned to breathe again.

Or California music teacher Layla Fanucci, who, confronted with a big, blank wall in her living room, fantasized about filling it with something bursting with color. Having secretly harbored a lifelong dream of being an artist, Layla decided she'd do it herself. "I had all of this inside of me, and it just poured out," she recalls. Fifteen years—and hundreds of canvases—later, Layla's paintings now sell for as much as $100,000 apiece.

Although the women who appear in this book couldn't be more different, what they have in common is that they all dared to dream again—and they all knew that no one had the power to make their dream come true but themselves.

It's in that spirit that I give you *It Ain't Over . . . Till It's Over*, a handbook for a new and ageless generation, starring the remarkable women who have proven that "impossible" is just something that hasn't happened yet.

As I read and reread these stories, it makes me think of something I was told a long time ago: If you want to predict the future, invent it.

New York City
Spring 2014

PART ONE

Moment of Truth

"It was so exciting to hold in my hands what had once just been in my head!"

Solving the Case

Jamie James, 54
North Hampton, New Hampshire

"*Where are my keys?*"

If she'd said it once, she'd said it a thousand times—Jamie James could never find anything.

And it was worst at the grocery store, always provoking sighs and grumbles from the people behind her in line. There she'd be, doing her purse-excavation routine, digging through receipts, reading glasses, and candy wrappers looking for the credit card she'd thrown into the leather abyss after her last purchase.

"I was always moving too fast to stop and put things back in my wallet," Jamie confesses.

Jamie, mother of four and family law attorney, typically blew into the courtroom like a tornado, digging through her oversized bag for a ringing phone, never able to find it. "I felt like a bag lady," she says. "I needed to simplify."

She envied her daughter Kaitlyn, who organized all of her essentials (college ID, credit card, and even a random $20 bill) by tucking them inside the protective silicone gel skin surrounding her cell phone so they were always handy.

But clever or not, Kaitlyn's system wasn't foolproof. "Mom, you're going to kill me!" she moaned one day after losing her credit card—yet again. The problem was that over time, the soft cell phone case would stretch, allowing her valuables to slip out and vanish.

There has to be a better way, thought Jamie. *How great would it be to have one compact, convenient place where I could stow all of my must-haves: cell phone, cash, AmEx, debit card, driver's license, health insurance card, and keys?*

It was an idea that itched at the back of Jamie's mind for months, something she might never even have acted on if not for a sudden tragedy: In November 2009, Jamie's healthy, vibrant mom and dad fell ill with the H1N1 flu, were hospitalized, and died.

"My life came to a stop," Jamie says. "I went to my parents' funerals within 17 days of each other. No child, no matter how old, should ever have to go through that."

Their deaths shook Jamie awake. "I realized that life can change on a dime. I said to my husband: *We need to start new.*" Two months later, they sold their house in Andover, Massachusetts, and settled into a home a mile from the ocean in North Hampton, New Hampshire, where Jamie, her husband, and their four children had memories of many happy summers spent sailing and going to the beach.

The change was good for Jamie and her family; their home life felt comfortable and safe. What wasn't so great was Jamie's work life, as she had to commute back and forth to her office in Massachusetts—an hour each way—every day.

The family law she had practiced for nearly 20 years, in which she dealt with divorces and child custody, was depressing. And now it felt even more so. "It's almost like being an oncologist. I was dealing with the worst time of someone's life every day. I'd go to bed questioning *Is this what I want to do the rest of my life?* Yes, it pays the mortgage and the tuition, but dealing with individuals who are so unhappy is emotionally draining."

That's when Jamie began thinking again about designing a product that busy women like her could use to hold all of their "vitals." "It was almost like, if I could figure this product out, then I could figure *me* out. I needed to do something that was *happier.*"

Jamie knew she couldn't outright quit her career, but she could start taking steps toward creating a business. A month after moving into their new home, she hosted a dinner party for four couples. She cornered her friends' husbands and showed them a prototype of the product that she'd whipped together. It was the very definition of jerry-rigged: She'd cut some slits in the back of a gel skin phone cover that would serve as credit card slots, taped a piece of cardboard on as a makeshift cover, and added a string to form a wristlet. Not much to look at, but Jamie pointedly wanted to get the guys' opinions.

"I knew my girlfriends were more likely to be supportive and say, *Yes, you should do it!*" she says. "But the guys would be brutally honest."

At first, the husbands didn't really "get" what Jamie was showing them, until she asked them a few questions: *Does your wife ever have trouble finding the phone when you call her? Does she always have to root around in the depths of her bag to find her keys? Does she make you carry her phone and ID when you go out?* Yes, yes, and yes.

The men got interested and started brainstorming.

"I always have to carry her lipstick, too!" one said. "Can you add a place for that?"

"I know a website guy!"

They were on a roll—until one husband posed a question that stumped the crowd:

"How are you going to create a product that fits all of the different cell phones out there?" *Ya got me,* Jamie thought. But, undeterred, she went ahead and took her prototype to her tailor along with some fun fabric.

"I was so nervous. I told him, 'This is just between you and me. It's our secret.'" But when she saw the finished product a few days later, her butterflies went away.

"It was so exciting to hold in my hands what had once just been in my head!" she recalls.

To test out her creation, Jamie began using it everywhere—at cash registers, at restaurant tables, at the ATM, in bathrooms, and at her desk. And—bingo!—it actually did what she wanted it to do: made her life *simpler.* But in doing so, it was getting filthy fast. Jamie realized she was going to have to manufacture it in leather. Problem solved.

But other complications kept nagging at her, especially that one husband's question about the product accommodating different-sized phones. Jamie arrived at the answer one day during her hour-long commute. *Velcro!* she thought. *That's it! Velcro! That's what we'll use to stick any phone to it.*

She loved the idea so much that, within days, she applied to obtain a patent for the design. Unlike other cell phone cases already on the market that opened up like a little book, Jamie's cover flipped up and over, like a steno notebook, essentially turning the wallet part inside out, so a user could talk directly into the cell phone without obstruction. Jamie also added a wristlet strap that unhooked so you could attach your keys.

"Everything you needed was in the palm of your hand," she says.

Now all Jamie needed was a manufacturer—and she found one at a horse show, where a vendor was selling beautiful leather goods. They started talking and two months later, Jamie visited the company. "That's when the lawyer in me came out," she says. "I asked the president to sign a nondisclosure agreement so he couldn't steal my idea."

"I was thrilled at his reaction. He took one look at my product, hit his head, and said, 'I can't believe nobody else has thought of this!'" Over the next few months, Jamie picked out her favorite Italian leather and fine-tuned the design, and in January of 2011, production began.

But what to call it? "My friends and family encouraged me to name it after myself, but then someone said to me, 'Someday you'll create another invention and what are you going to call that? You want Jamie James to be the name of your *company,* not your *product.*'" On a long drive home from a ski trip, Jamie, her husband, and her daughter Kaitlyn (via speaker phone) spitballed names and came up with the winner: the Cellfolio.

When the first 600 Cellfolios were delivered, Jamie was ecstatic. She was also overwhelmed by what lay ahead. "That's when the real work came. I had this product that I had borrowed thousands of dollars against our retirement accounts to make, and now I had to figure out how to get it out there."

Kaitlyn helped her map out a strategy. She suggested that they immediately set up a website—nothing fancy, just a landing site that would provide information and facilitate orders—and then got to work spreading the word.

"I know all my friends will want one," Kaitlyn told her mom, "so let's get the product into their hands. And they'll get them into their moms' hands. And their moms will get them into their friends' hands."

That's how their grassroots campaign began. Next, they passed out batches of the Jamie James Cellfolios to college kids across the country, offering to give them a cut if they sold any. She also gave them away to real estate agents, lawyers, and doctors.

"During that first month," Jamie recalls, "someone from Colorado ordered 15 of them off the website; I called and asked, 'How did you hear about us?' She said, 'I was at a medical conference in Florida and one of the doctors showed me his, so I decided to buy one for everyone in my office.' I was elated."

Then, Jamie doubled down on social media, setting up a Facebook page, Tweeting, and blogging. "I had to learn a whole new language," she says. She also signed on to be a vendor at gift shows in seven states.

"It was a huge step out of my normal box, but it was also uplifting. For the first time, I had a smile on my face while I was working."

Soon, the Cellfolio began dominating her thoughts, no matter where she was. "Whenever I walked into my law office, before asking my assistant if any clients had called, I'd ask, 'Where did the orders come in from today?'" And when she'd spot women using the Cellfolio at restaurants or in line at the coffee shop, she'd get an instant lift. "You see somebody holding a product that you made and you realize that you actually did something to change their day-to-day life."

Today, Jamie, who hasn't used a purse in three years, has sold so many Jamie James Cellfolios that she has been able to repay the retirement funds she'd tapped to get her invention off the ground. "The goal now is to get to a financial place where I can get out of law completely and just do this thing I love," she says.

In February 2013, after the Cellfolio was mentioned in a Los Angeles magazine, it was chosen to be included in the gift bag for the Academy Awards—and Jamie got to fly out for the ceremony. She also streamlined her inventory by creating a Velcro-free design made solely for iPhones. "When I did the market research, I found out that 70 percent of people in the U.S. carry an iPhone."

For all her success, Jamie has just one regret: that her parents didn't get to see the fulfillment their daughter found with her "fifth baby."

"It's almost been like a rebirth," she says. "I was lucky that I was only 50 when all of this came into being. I still had time in my life to be something else. I know they would have been really proud of me."

Match Game

Lori Cheek, 40
New York, New York

How many times have you locked eyes with an intriguing stranger on a train, in a café, or at the beach, and wished you could see him again? Over the years, Lori Cheek had had her share of such fleeting, *what-if* moments.

But then one night she was grabbing a bite to eat with a guy pal. "I'm the exception to the rule that you can't be friends with the opposite sex," she says. "My guy friends are some of my best girlfriends." At one point, Lori excused herself from the table; when she returned, her friend was scribbling a note— "Want to have dinner?"—on the back of his business card, which he slipped to a woman at the next table as he and Lori left the restaurant.

"I loved it," Lori says. "No *what-if* for him."

The more Lori reflected on the card-passing encounter, the more she became convinced that such old-world pickup lines were just what the online dating world needed. *There's so little mystery in this too-much-information age,* she thought. *Wouldn't it be great to create a website that combined newfangled technology with good, old-fashioned flirting?*

The thought excited Lori, a single New Yorker who had worked in architecture and interior design for 15 years. "I had a good salary and was able to afford an insane amount of designer clothes," she says, "but I found it beyond frustrating to always be building someone else's dream. I had a burning desire to do my own thing."

For a year, Lori explored her dating website idea with friends. "Then I talked to two guys who showed me how to write a business plan and patent a trademark and offered to partner with me in the business." Their support convinced her to give it a go.

So Lori quit her job and poured her entire savings—$75,000—into launching the site, but the partnership quickly proved less than ideal.

"Finding the perfect partner in business is almost like getting married," she says. "Both parties have to be equally involved and bring different skills into the relationship." What she realized was that she and her partners had similar expertise, but all three lacked the know-how to build a website. Before they could even get it off the ground, Lori had gone through all of her $75,000 investment.

Lori was devastated but determined to start over, this time flying solo. "I'm an all-or-nothing kind of gal," she says. To replace the money she'd lost, she sublet her apartment, sleeping on friends' couches and living out of a suitcase. She hawked her designer clothes at consignment shops and on eBay. And she earned money by participating in focus groups, guest bartending, and selling off her electronics on Craigslist and Amazon. It was tough, but her sacrifices raised another $75,000, and in May 2010 she launched her new dating site, called Cheek'd.

The service costs $20 to join; for that fee, members get a deck of 50 black calling cards printed with different messages like "I saw you checking me out" or "Let's meet for a drink" or a basic "You're hot." See someone you like? Then hand them a card, and a code on the back will direct the recipient to your page on the Cheek'd website, where they'll find your bio and contact information. To keep the code active, members pay $9.95 a month.

Lori viewed Cheek'd as a huge improvement over the popular online dating site that she had once briefly tried years earlier. "It took me forever to fill out the profile on that site, and immediately one of my architecture clients popped up. I didn't like mixing my personal life with my business life—or having him know what I was looking for in a mate. I also felt that shopping for the love of your life in solitude was kind of creepy. It lacked the natural chemistry that can happen in real life. Cheek'd encounters begin in the physical, not virtual, world."

As soon as she launched Cheek'd, Lori promoted her new business relentlessly. "I'd carry three cards in the morning and three at night," she says. "If I was on the train and saw a guy reading a book, I might slip him one, so that he could use it when he saw someone he wanted to connect with."

That kind of guerrilla marketing has continued to be Lori's main tactic for getting the word out. She'll slip cards into people's pockets ("Tag. You're It"), shopping bags, and wallets ("Emotionally available")—even between the pages of dating advice books at Barnes & Noble ("Need a date for my sister's wedding"). She'll plaster them on the insides of subway cars and bathroom stalls, on movie ads and street art. She'll hide them in the sugar stacks at Starbucks. Or she'll chalk "Have you been Cheek'd?" on the sidewalks outside events and parties.

New York's Citi Bike bike-sharing program became another vehicle for promotion: Lori printed a batch of cards that read "My bike likes your bike" and dropped them in bike baskets all over town, driving more traffic to her website.

Lori is also a walking billboard for her brand. Her iPhone and laptop sport Cheek'd wallpaper, she has "Cheek'd" fake-tattooed on her left arm at all times (reapplied every week), she carries a branded Cheek'd backpack, and she often wears a Cheek'd T-shirt bearing various come-on lines. Her favorite is a black one that says "My AmEx is also this color."

Every little bit helps: Lori says a day doesn't go by without someone asking her, "What's Cheek'd?"

Cheek'd now has about 10,000 subscribers, 51 percent of them female and 49 percent male. The average age is 32 to 35. Stacks of little black cards have been shipped to 47 states and 28 countries, translated into German, Swedish, and Russian. "We just sent some to a guy who lives in a forest in Washington State. Just think how hard it is for *him* to make a connection." Lori is launching a mobile app that will allow users to "flick" virtual Cheek'd cards with icebreaking pickup lines to a hottie nearby. And in 2013 she was listed by American Express Open Forum, which helps power small-business success, as one of the top CEOs to watch.

For all the connections Lori made for others, there was one that was still missing.

Until summer 2012.

"I was sitting alone at a crab shack in Montauk, New York, with no phone signal. I tossed my iPhone into my beach bag and when I looked up, a gorgeous man in Ray-Bans and a baseball cap sitting next to me said, 'Nice tattoo.' It was my fake Cheek'd one. I handed him the card that reads 'Let's meet for a drink.' We did—and we got engaged almost seven weeks later."

His name is Sebastian, and he's an actor and personal trainer. Lori no longer lives on friends' couches; she now lives with him on the Lower East Side.

And the proposal?

"I'd had a tooth pulled," Lori says, "so I was sedated and spent the entire day in bed. That night I went down to our local bar to meet him for a glass of wine. He was shaking and nervous and I thought, *Oh my God, is he going to ask me? If he asks me to marry him right now, without a tooth, he loves me.*" He did, and he does.

Score one for the Cheek'd team.

Losing to Win

Natasha Coleman, 35
Panama City, Florida

At five feet nine inches and just over 400 pounds, Natasha Coleman was, amazingly, unconcerned about her weight.

Her entire family was obese, including her parents and three older sisters. Overeating fattening fried foods and sugary desserts was just normal for them; exercise was not. And they weren't unusual—most everyone in Natasha's tight-knit African American community in Panama City, Florida, where she still lives, was heavy.

"Obesity was never a big deal. It was just accepted," Natasha says. "My sisters and I always had nice hair, nice clothes, and a lot of friends. We were known as the heavy, pretty girls." And she never wanted for boyfriends. In 1997, Natasha married her high school sweetheart, David, a six-foot, 280-pound guy, and they had three great kids.

Despite her size, Natasha had always had a sense of confidence. In 2009, she entered the American Beauties Plus pageant—for women size 14 and up—

and placed first. As part of the competition, each contestant had to declare a cause they were passionate about; Natasha's was fat acceptance.

"There are a lot of preconceived notions about overweight people, including that they're lazy and stupid," she says. "I wanted to stand up for plus-sized women."

Of course, there were aspects of being big that bothered her. "It got on my nerves when people told me I had 'such a pretty face.' *What about the rest of me? I'd think.*" Natasha spent a lot of time and money on clothes, which she either special-ordered or sewed herself. "Looking back, I think I was hiding behind all the makeup, outfits, and jewelry."

Naturally competitive, Natasha outperformed her coworkers in phone sales, where her job was to persuade people to switch their cable and Internet service. She was so good at closing deals, her company regularly awarded her with luxury trips for being a top performer. It was on one of these trips, in February 2010, that she had an experience so mortifying it changed her life.

"The company was flying my husband and me to Mexico first class, which we were so excited about," recalls Natasha. "But when I got to my seat, I couldn't maneuver my body into it. I was just too big." As a flight attendant tried to help, the other passengers began to stare, and what she saw in their eyes cut her to the bone. "The looks these people were giving me were cruel and judgmental, as if they were saying, 'How dare you be so fat that you hold up this plane?'" Told she'd have to move to a special seat at the very back of coach, Natasha walked down the center aisle of that plane feeling huge and humiliated. To make matters worse, when she arrived at the extrawide seat, the seat belt wouldn't fit around her middle, so she had to flag down the flight attendant again and ask for an extender.

As she sat alone in what felt like exile for the long flight, her embarrassment hardened into determination. "It was that competitive part of me that swore this would never happen again. I was *going* to lose weight."

Natasha's resolve doubled when she returned home and went to see her doctor about a chronic sinus problem. Weight had been a regular topic at previous visits, with her doctor suggesting both prescription weight loss pills and gastric bypass surgery. Natasha had even tried two commercial diets, losing an unsatisfying 20 pounds on each, then quickly regaining the weight.

On this visit, with the scale under Natasha's feet reading 428 pounds, her doctor said that weight loss was now a necessity, not an option. "She showed me my chart, and I had gained each year since my first baby was born. At the rate I was going, she said, I wouldn't be able to walk by the next year." Her doctor recommended that she get gastric bypass surgery immediately, but the risks frightened Natasha.

"I thought, *What if I lie down on that table only to never wake up? What would happen to my family?* I asked her to just give me a chance to lose the weight on my own. 'Tell me what to do,' I said. 'Tell me where to start.'"

Natasha's doctor advised her to stop drinking soda and handed her a sheet of paper with meal ideas for a 1,500-calorie-per-day diet. She said to come back in three months—if Natasha was unable to shed pounds the hard way, surgery would still be an option.

"I leapt out of that office ready to get my mind right. I was a star at work, a decent wife, a really good mom. I had had twins without an epidural. I was a superwoman. I could do this."

But once Natasha began reading stories about people who had managed to lose hundreds of pounds, she was disheartened by how slow the process was. "It could take years. I'm a typical American—I want it now and fast," she says. That's where her fierce drive helped. "I looked in the mirror and saw my only competition. I'd already beaten a lot of other people in my job. Can I beat *her*?"

At the time, First Lady Michelle Obama was launching her Let's Move campaign, and Natasha was angered by statistics revealing that nearly half of all African American children were obese. Her 14-year-old son and 8-year-old twins (a girl and a boy) were also overweight and steadily gaining.

"I started getting mad at food, mad at being surrounded by unhealthy options, mad at my lifestyle." At every event she went to in her community, tables were groaning with platters of fried, sugary, fattening foods. It seemed like overeating was practically part of her culture. But Natasha was horribly conflicted given her recent public stance on fat acceptance.

"I felt pulled two different ways. On the one hand, I thought, 'You're fat— accept it.' On the other, I told myself, 'You don't have to be this way; you can change.'"

Without saying a word to her family or friends, Natasha stopped eating fried food, junk food, and sugar of any kind except for fruit. "It was very, very, very, very hard. I had to force myself to avoid whole aisles of the grocery store because just looking at junk food made my mouth water. But I found that if I only put healthy food in my fridge and cabinets, that's what I would eat. Things were harder to control at work—there were boxes of doughnuts, vending machines full of goodies, fried fatty foods for breakfast and lunch—it was everywhere. I hid at my desk, feeling isolated."

Of course, there were some weak moments. "One Saturday, after cutting off all of my hair and panicking about what I'd done, I went to Burger King, ordered a Triple Whopper and ate it so fast I think I bit my finger. Twenty minutes later, I had to pull over by the side of the road to throw up. My stomach couldn't handle the grease. Since then, I've had small slipups, but nothing like that."

When Natasha went back to the doctor three months later, she had dropped

60 pounds. Her doctor was shocked and delighted. "She joked, 'Let me see your stomach to see if you went to Mexico and had gastric bypass surgery without telling me.'" As Natasha continued losing, her doctor kept asking for before-and-after photos to use as inspiration for other overweight patients.

At around 370 pounds, Natasha gathered the strength to start exercising. In just a few weeks, she lost five quick pounds by taking a 20-minute daily walk around a small park. Encouraged, she decided to start going to the gym. "All of the machines had warnings that they were for people 350 pounds or less, but I figured that was just an estimate and it wouldn't be a problem."

On her second day using the treadmill, disaster struck. "I noticed that the treadmill was starting to tilt forward, and it must have been making noise, but I had my headphones on so I didn't hear it. The next thing I knew, the machine cracked apart, the monitor went flying off, and I was rolling on the floor. I was so embarrassed, I left there as quickly as I could."

For the next four days, Natasha just sat on her living room couch, feeling really down on herself. "I couldn't believe it. I was even too fat to exercise." But she was determined to keep exercising, so she ordered some exercise DVDs; at first, she just watched them. Finally, she got up and followed along for a few minutes, then a little longer, and a little longer, until she was doing entire workouts.

Over the next several months, she lost 30 more pounds. Then a friend introduced her to Zumba. "My first instructor was a size zero and moved way too fast for me to keep up. Plus, I had read a tip about Zumba that you should stand in front so you can see the instructor and watch what you're doing in the mirror, so that's what I did. At the beginning of one class, a woman rudely asked me if I could move to the back because no one could see around me. I was so angry, but I just swallowed, gave her a look, and said, 'No.' I danced through the whole class trying to hide that I was crying."

As she had before, Natasha used the embarrassing experience as motivation. She found a better Zumba class taught by a teacher who was more her speed, and started going four days a week while continuing to walk on weekends. She dropped down to 290, then hit a frustrating plateau. Knowing she had to do more, she gave up her favorite indulgence—peanut butter—and forced herself to go back to the gym. This time, she used the elliptical machine, and though she found it boring, she loved the way it melted fat from all the right places on her body. "It whittled my waist and made my thighs and hips more toned," she says.

Two years after starting what she calls her "fitness journey," Natasha weighed 280 pounds and felt amazing. "I went on a plane and was able to use the regular seat belt without an extender. That was a mind-blowing moment for me—to just sit down and buckle up like everyone else. I was so proud, I cried."

Now closing in on her goal weight of 170 pounds, Natasha has added stair-climbing and weight lifting to her fitness routine and remains extremely disciplined about what she eats.

"My kids are eating better, too," she says. "They drive their grandmother crazy when they look at the food labels on snacks she gives them and say, 'This has too many carbs!'"

Natasha gets additional motivation from a weight-loss support group she started. "I began blogging about my weight loss on Facebook and, for the first year, no one really commented. But when I started saying I'd lost 75 pounds and posting pictures, a lot of people asked me for advice. I decided to hold a onetime meeting at my church to answer everyone at once. Then word spread and I started getting more questions. I figured it would be easier to hold a weekly meeting. We started with 12 women and it quickly grew to 30. We have a sisterhood. It motivates me because I can't tell people to keep pushing themselves if I'm not doing it myself."

Natasha's weight-loss success also gave her the confidence to try for a sales

position at her company that she had long coveted. Because the job involved face-to-face meetings, she had always assumed her weight would get in the way, but this time, when a position opened up, she applied. "I went on three interviews and blew them away. I got the job, beating out candidates with more experience, and I tripled my salary."

It's hard for Natasha to describe how it feels to have gone from a size 32 to a size 10. "It's surreal to not break the heels off a pair of shoes after wearing them for only two weeks, to walk into a store and buy a dress right off the rack, to wake up and find that my hands and feet aren't swollen, to have so much energy that I can't fall asleep at night because I'm so excited about my new life."

Natasha is a new woman—someone she doesn't always even recognize herself. "The other day, I was walking past a building when I saw a normal-sized woman wearing the same orange-colored shirt that I had on. Then I realized it was *my* reflection!"

Whispers in the Night

Trish B.,* 53
Hagerstown, Maryland

Vince was late again. Trish had asked him to be home tonight on time so she could get to her book club, but it was getting close to six and he was still MIA.

He'd been doing this a lot lately—coming home late, or showing up only when one of their young sons had a game or practice. It was starting to feel like he didn't want to come home at all.

As Trish waited, she went out to collect the mail. Flipping through the usual assortment of ads and bills, she came across an envelope with a return address she didn't recognize.

At first she thought it was a thank-you note from a wedding she and Vince had attended many months earlier, when his assistant from his former job had gotten married. The cover of the card was a cut-out photo of Vince and the bride.

* The subject has chosen not to use her real name.

22

"I remembered the picture being taken," says Trish. "All of the men were lined up and the bride lay across their arms, and everyone was laughing. Vince was in the middle, holding her at the waist."

But the photo on the card showed just Vince and the bride. Everyone else in the group had been cut out; the bride seemed to be floating horizontally in midair.

"Then I read the inside," Trish says. "At first the words didn't make any sense. There were allusions to Bill Clinton and Monica Lewinsky, which had just come to light in the news. There were also references to Moby-Dick and 'Dick-tation.'" The card was signed "Loosey," which Trish initially thought was a strange typo for Vince's nickname for the bride, "Lucy."

Trish read the note several times as she walked from the mailbox back to the house. "I kept looking at the picture—him holding her, all the rest of the men cut out, the strange message. And then it hit me," she says. "It was one of those moments when the world starts spinning, and you're thrust into an alternate reality. I got dizzy."

In a flash, Trish found herself connecting the dots. Since he'd changed jobs recently, Vince had stopped wearing his wedding ring (he said it interfered with his golf swing). He hadn't put Trish's photo in his new office, and had begun snapping at her whenever she asked for news about people from his old job. He never wanted her to go with him on any of the business trips his new job required. She'd been troubled by the distance that seemed to be widening between them.

She knew something was wrong, but she'd never suspected *this*.

It was 6:45 when Vince came home from work, too late for her to make it to her book group. She showed him the card.

"I waited for him to deny it, but he just looked at it for a long time, then turned red," Trish says. "I started to cry, and I begged him to tell me what it meant. He didn't answer. He just stared at me with teary eyes and said, 'I'm sorry.'

"I began shrieking, 'Did you sleep with her, did you sleep with her?' " Trish recalls. "And he said, 'Just once.' I ran up to our room and hid in the bathroom, breathing fast and not knowing what to do. I was crying and kept saying, over and over, 'I don't believe it.' Vince followed me upstairs, warning me that the boys could hear me, and asking me not to scream. But I wanted to scream. I wanted to break the door down. I wanted to punch him so hard."

Vince kept apologizing, but insisted it wasn't an affair. He said that he and Lucy had had a one-night stand after an office party, and that the real reason he'd left his old job was to avoid a scandal. He said he loved Trish and wanted to save their family. Trish wanted to believe that, but the past few years had been tough on her, and she wasn't so sure Vince loved her at all anymore.

This was not what Trish had hoped for in her marriage. As a child, she would fall asleep at night to the sound of her parents' murmured bedtime conversations. Those comforting "whispers in the night," as she called them, assured Trish that all was well. She'd wanted that deep connection, too. That real intimacy.

Vince and Trish had shared some of that as newlyweds, but those days were long gone. Trish, an English teacher with a master's degree, had stopped working after the children were born. The young family had moved from the city to the suburbs, where as a stay-at-home mom, she felt increasingly isolated. The marriage felt strained. Then came the bombshell in the mailbox.

"I'm not sure he ever understood how wounded I was by his lie," says Trish. "It was the worst thing I could imagine. I alternated between sadness and anger after that, questioning every late night, every golf date, every moment when I felt that we had lost control of our marriage. But in some weird way, it was a relief. At least now I knew."

Life went on, but things changed. Trish was clingy and defensive, needing to know Vince's whereabouts at all times. On the surface Vince was a model husband, coming home from work when he said he would, spending time with the boys, even wearing his wedding ring again. But he had shut down emotionally, and didn't want to talk to Trish about anything except the boys. He traveled often for work, and Trish tried to get used to sleeping alone. There were no more whispers in the night.

In 1999, both Vince and Trish turned 40. The birthdays were joyless, the year grim. But on New Year's Day—the first day of the new millennium—things got even worse.

"Lucy called our house to see if Vince was okay," says Trish. "She said he had called her the day before from a park and told her he was going to kill himself. She told me Vince loved her and wanted to be with her, but that he didn't want to leave his family."

Trish hung up and ran to the garage, where Vince was getting the boys ready for sledding. "I was crazy, shouting things like, 'So I guess your midlife crisis has blond hair!' I was livid."

This time Vince didn't deny anything. He didn't want to argue in front of the boys, so he took them and left the house. After he was gone, Trish called Lucy back.

"'That's when she told me everything," says Trish. "She told me that they had never stopped seeing each other, and that he had left his first job so they could be together. She had been traveling with him on his business trips. She and her husband had split up, and now she was living in an apartment that Vince paid for. He had promised her marriage, a home. He'd told her he was living in another wing of our house—I had to laugh at that one; there was no 'other wing'—and that I was aware he was seeing her, which I wasn't; and that we were not sleeping together, which we were. And he said the only reason he was staying was for the boys."

Both women had to confront Vince's lies, but it was Trish's whole world that was shattered. Even as Vince was acting the part of the devoted husband and denying he'd even had an affair, he'd been continuing to see Lucy. He'd been living a double life, one with Lucy and another with Trish and the boys. Trish was more than a woman scorned now. She was a wife and a mother, deceived, betrayed, and humiliated.

"I knew nothing about her, but she knew everything about my life," says Trish. "She knew our floors were being redone, that my mother had been in the hospital, that my sister had had a miscarriage. And worse, she'd even been to my house, when I was visiting my sister in Florida, and she and Vince had shared a bottle of wine and a tryst in my basement while the boys slept upstairs."

That was the last straw. Trish drove two hours to her mother's house, where she broke down. Her stepfather handed her a blank check and said, "Do what you have to do." Trish knew what that was: She used the money to hire a lawyer and file for divorce.

Trish's attorney advised her to get a job, and she went to work at a local bookstore while she looked for a teaching position. "It was something to do to get out of the house and stop wallowing in my sorrow," she says. "There, busy working in a stockroom, I was able to put the angst of the divorce aside. The perpetual knot in my stomach would subside for a few hours, and I just became Trish."

Slowly, very slowly, Trish began to rebuild herself—at first from the out-side in. She got a new haircut. She lost a little weight. Then the hard work began: She joined a support group for separated and divorced Catholics, where she met others who were struggling to reclaim their lives. They were all facing the same question: Who are you when life as you knew it is over? Trish knew she had to decide who she was going to be when she emerged, alone, from the divorce.

"My 'outing' as a victim helped me to acknowledge that I really didn't want to be one," says Trish. "I knew I was stronger than that. Each public step I took away from the marriage made it clearer to me that I was better outside of it than I was in it.

"It took a lot for me to admit that my marriage was over," she says. "But I wasn't sour on marriage. I had made a bad decision and would make a better one someday. I craved intimacy, I wanted a partner, but I knew that I had to become a whole person first before *I* could be a partner."

During the difficult months of this transformation, Trish got a lot of support and advice from her mother. When Trish's mom was widowed at just 48, she'd felt robbed of her happiness. But she had regained her footing, restarted a career, and learned to live on her own. After a while, she met a widower, married him, and took control of her life—and recaptured her happiness.

Trish had also been robbed, but she was barely 40; she had a lot of life ahead of her, and her mom encouraged her to embrace it.

"She wanted me to go for that second chance someday, if it came around," says Trish. "She warned me not to let the rest of my life become a shrine to my failed marriage."

Trish treasured time on the phone with her mom, much of it catching up on news from the neighborhood. One "poor kid" from Trish's childhood, a man named Eddie, was also reeling from a failed marriage, her mom told her. His wife had walked out on him, taking their son with her, and was now making big financial demands on him.

Trish knew that "kid"—she'd dated him once, pre-Vince. And what a date it was. Trish blushed just thinking about it, because that evening had ended with what she calls "the perfect kiss": sitting on Eddie's lap in his parked car, under an overpass, making out. Even now, she felt a tingle of excitement just thinking about it.

Would he look back on that night as fondly as she did? With her mom's encouragement, Trish decided to take a chance and call him. Just hearing Eddie's voice on the answering machine made her feel good and comfortable, and she left a hurried message. Eddie called back and said he would love to reconnect.

Over the next week they had several phone conversations, catching up and comparing notes on what it felt like to be "left." Those chats were long and easy and soothing, and Eddie seemed genuinely interested in what Trish had to say. They agreed to meet in the city the following week.

"When Eddie met me at the car, I knew right away that things would be all right," Trish says. "I felt an instant attraction—a connection—and I could tell he felt the same way." The evening ended on Eddie's terrace, where the two talked about their marriages, their sadness about their shattered dreams, their hope about the future. Throughout it all, Trish was keenly aware of how Eddie was looking at her—*really* looking at her—taking in her every word. It was what she'd been craving all along, that sense of engagement, of connection.

"At some point in the evening, I thought, *Even if there isn't any physical contact between us, it doesn't matter,*" says Trish. "That's because Eddie had shown me that I was interesting and vital. I didn't want the night to end, but it had to. And then we kissed—and it was exactly as I had remembered."

Five years later, after "lots and lots of therapy to help me get over my fear of abandonment and learn to trust again," Trish and Eddie were married. Surrounded by family and lifelong friends, the bride and groom felt an overwhelming sense of peace. "And both of us kept hearing the same thing all day," Trish says. "'I've never seen you so happy.'"

Trish was that happy, and remains so today. But looking back, she knows that she'd never have reached this place had she not first done the hard work of rediscovering who she was.

"I didn't like who I became when I was married to Vince," says Trish. "I had changed from being an independent person to being a whiny wimp. Now I try to maintain a vision of myself as someone who's healthy and strong, and not think of myself only as someone's wife. And I have a husband who values that. We have common interests, and things to talk about. We are honest with each other. And everything I needed but didn't get from my first marriage—security, intimacy, faith—is all there."

Trish's mom died a year after the wedding, but her spirit lives on: Trish and Eddie now share those whispers in the night. And Trish no longer tells people that her first husband left her for another woman.

"I knew I was better when I stopped saying that," she says. "Instead I started saying, 'I threw him out because he didn't deserve me.'"

Must Love Dogs

Heidi Ganahl, 46
Denver, Colorado

When Heidi Ganahl was in her early twenties, she seemed like one of the lucky ones. Most of the big building blocks of her life were set firmly in place: She and her husband, Bion, were young, in love, and living an adventurous life in Colorado, where he was finishing his degree in business, and she had a good job as a pharmaceutical rep.

They even had a dream for a business they wanted to start together one day: a day-care center for dogs. Heidi and Bion loved their dogs, and hated leaving them behind when they traveled, but they never had much luck finding a good boarding facility for their two mutts, Winnie and Mick.

"You could either take your dog to a kennel, where all they had was a drab concrete run, surrounded by a chain-link fence," Heidi says, "or you could take them to a vet clinic, where they'd be kept in a little box in the back. It was just horrible."

The camp for dogs that Heidi and Bion imagined was spacious and clean, offering loads of room for pooches to run and play together. The idea seemed so promising that they even wrote up a business plan for it. "We were both very entrepreneurial, very creative," says Heidi. "We knew we didn't want to have boring eight-to-five jobs, and what could be better than working together to build a business we loved?"

They each had nonboring ideas for fun, too. So for Bion's twenty-fifth birthday, Heidi's family treated him to a private flight in an open-cockpit "Snoopy" stunt plane. "Bion had such great energy and spirit, and normally, I did everything with him," Heidi says, "but that day I stayed back home to help with a community garage sale, so my parents went to watch. As the pilot was doing a flyby, so that my folks could take pictures, the plane suddenly dove into the ground—right in front of them. I still remember the moment I heard the news: My brother was the one who had to come tell me that Bion had been killed."

The marriage, the friendship, the dream—it was all gone.

Three months later, Heidi received a $1 million settlement as a result of the crash. "I come from a lower-middle-class family," she says, "and that was a lot of money to me. At first I thought, *What good is this money if it can't bring Bion back?* But it also gave me some solace, because I didn't have to think too far ahead: *Okay, at least I don't have to worry about working—I can just take care of myself.* But then it became stressful, because people were asking me for loans. I also felt guilty about having it. I kept thinking, *This isn't the way I wanted to make money in life,* you know?"

It was a rough time. "After Bion's death, I was in a daze. I made a lot of bad decisions," Heidi says. Seeking comfort in a relationship, she married again within two years and gave birth to her daughter. But the marriage didn't last—and Heidi began struggling with what to do professionally.

"I really wanted to see through the idea that Bion and I had come up with, but people around me kept saying, 'That will never work. You'll just waste all of your money. Do something practical.'"

So Heidi complied, launching a few conventional businesses—a high-end baby-bedding catalog and a financial-management firm—but neither idea really clicked. By the fall of 2000, she was a single mother with only $83,000 of the original $1 million left in the bank—and hobbled by a growing sense of desperation.

Enough was enough, she decided. And that's when she finally dusted off the business plan she and Bion had written a decade earlier.

"As I paged through it," Heidi remembers, "I thought, *Man, this is good!* In every bone of my body, I knew it was exactly what I was meant to do. Ever since getting my first dog, Daisy, for my third birthday, I have always loved dogs. They don't play emotional games—they just love you, love you, love you. They make the world a better place."

Driven by a new energy, Heidi began to flesh out the idea. The name she came up with—Camp Bow Wow®—seemed perfect, and she started to visualize the space. Dogs would need to have both indoor and outdoor areas to play and socialize, places to run and places to rest. There would be separate spaces for the younger dogs to romp, while the older ones could just hang out and snooze. Also, there would be special areas for the 15-pounds-and-under set, so they wouldn't feel overwhelmed by their larger mates.

Then Heidi hit on an ingenious idea—not for the dogs, but for their owners: She'd set up webcams throughout the facility so they could check in on their pets whenever they chose.

"We wanted to create a place where a dog could be a dog," she says, "and where owners could feel less guilty about leaving them with us. By going online, they could watch their dogs having fun."

Tapping into what was left from the crash settlement, Heidi opened her first facility near downtown Denver, initially attracting clients by going to local parks with her young daughter and handing out flyers to dog owners that offered a free day at camp—enticingly accompanied by dog biscuits.

Within nine months, Camp Bow Wow® was hosting more than 40 dogs a day—and gaining citywide notice. Not all of it was a marketer's dream: When a Denver newspaper reporter dropped by to do a story on the business, he walked in just as Heidi's brother was admonishing one of the dogs: "Hey, no humping allowed!"

"What do you think they wrote as the headline on the story?" Heidi recalls with a sigh. *"No Humping Allowed at Camp Bow Wow."*

Flea-bitten journalism notwithstanding, Heidi had clearly found something that filled a niche—and she wanted to take it to the next level.

"There's a term for the space between $1 million in revenues and $10 million," Heidi says, "and that's called no-man's-land. Nothing gets you through that except tenacity and commitment."

Over the next few years, Heidi guided Camp Bow Wow® through a rapid expansion. "There were a lot of tense moments," she says. "I wound up going through the entire $83,000 left from the settlement, plus $150,000 from two lines of credit that I had—plus, I maxed out a couple of credit cards. There were a few times when I didn't think I was going to make payroll. But I was so completely committed that we survived all our close calls. In fact, the one piece of advice I would give to anyone thinking about starting a business is this: Make sure that it's something you are truly passionate about, because you will eat, live, and breathe it 24/7."

Today, Heidi is remarried (her husband, Jason, is a chef on the professional barbecue circuit) and she's feeling blessed by her professional success. The business idea she and Bion had dreamed up all those years ago has gone well beyond the $10 million mark they had fantasized about. Now a $60 million business, Camp Bow Wow® is the largest dog-care franchise in the world, with 150 camps in 40 states and Canada. The company has also added a home-care service, dog training, and an animal adoption service.

"It's been a long, tough road for me," Heidi reflects, "but life wasn't meant to be stagnant or easy. When you go through difficult times, you really learn who you are, who your friends are, and how to find your passion in life. I've had my share of ups and downs, but I'd rather have had the highest of highs and lowest of lows than a boring, uneventful life. The getting-through part—that's what has created my resilience and my belief in myself.

"And I've known love. A lot of it. From my children, my husband, family, and friends—and from a dear man I will never forget, who dreamed this dream with me so many years ago."

PART TWO

Dreamers

"That trip was the number one thing on my bucket list. But life gets in the way."

The Wild Ride

Kathleen Dodds, 49
Portland, Oregon

Cowboys had always been her weakness. As a six-year-old, watching a Western on TV with her dad, Kathleen Dodds was so smitten with the guys riding the range that she announced, "I want to ride a horse across the country!"

Some dreams never die.

As an adult, Kathleen began training horses, teaching riding, and fantasizing that one day she'd take a trip like the early American settlers. "I was always so interested in the pioneers. They were so brave," she says. "They left everything they knew behind for a chance at a new life. So that trip was the number one thing on my bucket list. But life gets in the way. . . ."

Fast-forward to 2007, when Kathleen had to travel to New Delhi to have a grapefruit-sized fibroid removed from her uterus, a surgery she'd been unable to afford back home in Oregon. During a post-op checkup, she was stunned when her doctor told her: "If you had waited another month, you would have had uterine cancer. You are one lucky lady."

That's when a voice inside her head whispered—shouted, actually—"Take that trip!" It was time.

Her dad didn't like the idea one little bit. No matter that she was an adult—she'd be a woman traveling more than 2,500 miles *alone*. What if she lost her way, became hypothermic, or was the victim of an attack? "This from a guy who'd been a scoutmaster," says Kathleen, "taking me and my five siblings on camping and canoeing trips, teaching us how to start fires by rubbing two sticks together or use landmarks to find our way in the deep woods."

But Kathleen was unfazed. Without a husband or kids to tie her down, she was raring to go.

The first order of business: getting in shape. Her clients pitched in and bought her a gym membership. She also started walking—four miles uphill to the barn every morning and four miles back down to her house every afternoon. Trotting at her heels was her 12-year-old Australian cattle dog, Solo—as in Han Solo—who had been with her since he was seven weeks old, so attached he refused to eat when she left him with a sitter. She had tossed and turned for months trying to decide what to do with the old guy.

"I knew if I left him, he would probably starve himself," she says. "I didn't think he could make it across the country, but he was never happier than when he was following me on a horse." With the vet's blessing, it was decided: Solo was going, too.

Kathleen ended her lease, sold her washer and dryer, and stored her furniture, car, and all her other belongings at a friend's house. She asked her top student to take over her clientele, still worried that some students might defect. "I was torn about leaving my business behind," she says. "I had worked really hard to get it to where it was."

At dawn one day in May 2010, with Solo by her side, Kathleen quietly slipped out of Oregon City, wearing a black, floppy-brimmed Aussie hat and hiking boots and riding a ten-year-old Appaloosa mare named Mystic. With a cell phone tucked in her pocket and a sleeping bag bungee-corded to the saddle, she had everything she figured she'd need: a tarp, inflatable mattress, change of clothes, underwear, jerky, granola bars, water bottles, $1,000, a hatchet, and a loaded gun (just in case she came face-to-face with any grizzlies). She also had grain and a first-aid kit for her horse: disinfectant, bandages, and Super Glue that she figured would heal up any of her wounds as well.

The first few days through Oregon, she tried to stick to a schedule, pushing herself to get from one campsite to the next. But at the first town, she threw away her intricate topographic maps, bought a regular state map and decided to also just stop people on the street, asking for the best way to get across the state. "I didn't want to always be worried about making a deadline," she says. "It was more fun to meet people."

From then on, that's how she rolled, using the local wisdom as her compass. There were only a few towns on her must-see list, like Punxsutawney, Pennsylvania (*Groundhog Day* was a favorite movie), and Upper Sandusky, Ohio, to visit a friend. Otherwise, she was all about the direct route. By now, Mystic's four-year-old filly, Delightful, had also joined them to help carry gear (a friend had delivered her by trailer).

When there weren't rural roads, the rustic travelers had to ride on highway shoulders—an odd sight with cars whizzing by at 70 miles an hour. Some would slow to a crawl and pull off the road in front of her. "I had to stop and ask what you're doing," they'd say, some slipping her 20 bucks before speeding off.

The travelers covered 20 to 25 exhausting miles a day. "There were times when I would just stand there staring around me, not remembering why I stopped because I was so tired," Kathleen says.

Sometimes, she'd pass the time by shooting the breeze with her horses, using one accent for her part and another for their reply. "If anyone had seen me, they would have thought I was insane," she says.

She sang, too, trying to piece together the full lyrics to John Denver's "Country Roads" or Kris Kristofferson's "Me and Bobby McGee." One day, listening to the clip-clop of the horses' hooves on the pavement, the Rolling Stones' "Painted Black" came to her and she couldn't stop humming it—*for three days.* "To get it out of my head, I had to go through the entire '99 Bottles of Beer on the Wall' four times in a row!" she says.

At lunch- or dinnertime, they'd stop in flyspeck towns with names like Point of Rocks (Wyoming) or East Palestine (Ohio). Some were so teeny it seemed that within a half hour of her arrival, everyone in town knew who Kathleen was and what she was doing. Newspapers even featured her on their front pages. Local families were so intrigued they invited her into their homes—for a hot shower, a warm meal, or a soft bed.

When Kathleen began her lone-wolf journey across the country, she never envisioned that her days would be far from lonely. Her new acquaintances started calling their friends in the next towns ahead on her route telling them she was coming. "I'd get to a town and go buy grain and the feed store would donate it to me or I'd go buy lunch at a café and somebody had already paid for it," she says. "It's humbling to know how kind the people of this country really are. They will help a total stranger."

Some she'll never forget. Like Brooks, a leather-faced, soft-spoken, real-life cowboy nearly 80 years old whom she met in a Rocky Mountain pass; he called every rancher he knew for 100 miles ahead and told them to keep an eye out for her.

The great thing about moving three miles an hour, Kathleen discovered, is that she had plenty of time to take in the roadside attractions: the family of black bears in Oregon (thankfully a half mile away); the minerals weaving pretty patterns in the desert sands of Wyoming; the pastel wildflowers speckling the cornfields of Nebraska; the white Indiana farmhouses that were so tidy they looked like paintings; the leaves changing to fall rusts, oranges, and yellows along the winding rivers in Ohio.

"Every state has something pretty about it," she says. "You don't notice that kind of stuff when you're flying by in a car."

But at times, it still seemed like the Wild West. In Idaho, she was cornered by a skinhead, who told her that a woman shouldn't be out on the road alone and that he'd show her what a woman should be doing. One look at her loaded gun put an end to that conversation.

Kathleen pressed on, and just before Thanksgiving, after a half year on the road, she stopped traffic—literally—as a police cruiser escorted her across a bridge from Pennsylvania to New Jersey. As she arrived in Green Village, New Jersey, where she was to spend her last night, she was still wearing the hat that had shielded her from sun, rain, and wind for six months. Now it was a faded brown.

"I felt like Superwoman," she says. "It was the hardest, most painful, most fantastic thing I've ever done."

But the triumph of her adventure was not without its costs. Most devastating was losing Solo, who died of a heart attack two weeks into the trip. She also discovered that while she had been away, her rent had doubled while her business had dwindled to a half-dozen clients.

But given the chance, she'd do it all again. Maybe someday she will.

"I gave up everything to do this trip, but I gained so much," she says. "I was beaten down emotionally and physically when I left, and now I love who I am. I know I can do anything I put my mind to."

Spoken like a true pioneer.

From Hiding to Soaring

Tina Reine, 47
Palm Beach Gardens, Florida

"The elephant man."

That's how Tina Reine says she felt as a child in Evansville, Indiana. Born with severe facial deformities, including a cleft lip and palate, Tina was bullied mercilessly by her classmates for years.

"I had things thrown at me. Kids made faces at me," she says. "One time a boy told me I looked like I had been hit by a Mack truck." It was hard, but throughout the years of torment, Tina's staunch defender was her older brother, Mike.

"He would stand up for me and get into fights with the kids who bullied me," Tina says. "If it hadn't been for him, I don't know what would have happened."

Although she had undergone a series of corrective surgeries starting at six months, the deformities were still obvious.

"I knew I didn't look normal," says Tina. "And nobody ever let me forget it." Feeling like a complete outsider, she escaped into her own world. "I didn't really have friends, so I'd play by myself and pretend I was someone else. I

43

loved to dance, sing, and put on plays in my room for all of my dolls. They were my only friends and they made me feel safe."

Tina remained tucked inside her own shell, isolated though protected, until her freshman year in high school, when tragedy befell her family: Her big brother and guardian angel, Mike, was killed in a car accident.

"I was devastated," Tina recalls, "as were my parents. My extended family kept telling me that, as the only child left, I had to be strong for them. So I did my best. Mike had always been super-involved in school and extracurriculars, so I decided to put aside my own insecurities and take up that same role. I didn't want my parents to worry about me, and it also gave me a distraction from my own grief, so I just threw myself into every single activity that came my way."

Among those self-assignments was auditioning for the school play, a production of the musical *Mame*. Tina was selected for the chorus; it was the first time she'd ever performed in front of a real audience.

"It might have seemed like a small thing to other people," Tina recalls. "After all, I was just in the chorus. But for me, it was huge. I had been hiding myself all those years for fear of being made fun of, but now here I was, standing in front of everyone, self-confident. I don't know whether it changed the way my classmates saw me, but it definitely changed the way I saw myself."

When her parents came to see her perform, Tina remembers, "they were floored. I seemed like a totally different person." From that point on, Tina knew she wanted to continue being onstage.

But her self-consciousness about the way she looked held her back.

"I was passionate about performing, but I still felt that I looked too different to make anything of it," she says. "After my surgeries, I figured I had gone from 'the elephant man' to 'somewhat normal,' but I still had some underlying issues with the bone structure of my face. I knew I wasn't beautiful, so as much as I wanted to be back up on that stage, I kept trying to squash that dream."

So she stayed away from theater, and tried to find other activities that engaged her. After high school, she studied Japanese at a small private college near her home, earning scholarships to pay her way. After graduation she held a series of jobs, at one point teaching English in Japan, a job that allowed her to save up the money she needed for what she hoped would be a final, life-changing surgery.

"I had heard about a bone-grafting procedure that could fill in the places in my face where the bone had never grown in properly," she says. So she sought out the surgeon who created it; and in 1990, at age 24, Tina flew to Texas by herself for the ten-hour procedure.

"When I woke up, I felt like my face was covered in Silly Putty. It took awhile for the implants to settle and feel normal. There were so many screws in there that if you took an X-ray of my face it would have looked like a hardware store. But when I looked in the mirror afterward, I couldn't believe it! It was the first time in my life I felt that I looked not just normal, but even attractive."

Still, it took awhile for Tina's self-image to catch up with her outer image. "I did feel more self-confident, but only up to a point," she says. "Those years of bullying and name-calling were still inside me—they weren't so easy to erase." But her transformation did give her the courage to try to tackle her longtime dream: moving to New York City, the world capital of theater.

"Like most hopefuls, I got a job as a waitress and started taking dance classes," Tina says. "Musical theater, jazz, Bob Fosse–style, you name it." She also entered into a serious relationship for the first time, and eventually married (though the marriage ended amicably a few years later). "I had met him right after the surgery, and he encouraged me to believe in myself. He played a huge part in helping me catch up to my new looks."

Before long, Tina found herself with enough confidence, and dance ability, to begin auditioning.

"My goal was to try out for a Broadway show," she says. "Not even to get the job, just to audition." And she surpassed that goal, landing dance roles in a few off-Broadway productions and even a stage show in Las Vegas.

But dance and waitressing weren't paying the bills in an expensive city like New York. So, taking advantage of her time spent in Japan and her knowledge of the language, Tina started a business exporting American designer clothes and jewelry to Tokyo.

"I knew there was a lot of demand there for American brand names and designer goods," she says, "and the exchange rate was great, so I could make a nice profit."

Inspired by her business success, Tina applied to Columbia University, with the goal of becoming a Wall Street trader. "I knew I had a head for numbers and the ADD-type brain that could follow the constantly changing market dynamics." And after graduation, she did find her niche on Wall Street, as a carbon trader. "I still loved the performing arts and always made time to take a class or see a show," she says, "but it was exciting being in a field in which I was thriving."

But all of the good fortune came to an end in 2009, when the financial markets crashed. Tina knew it was time to make yet another change.

"I had loved living in New York for 18 years," she says, "but I was a huge wimp about the cold winters. I wanted to be somewhere warm, near the beach." So she convinced one of her JP Morgan clients, a company based in Palm Springs, Florida, to create a position for her there as a carbon trader.

"I was all set to move," she says, "and decided I'd treat myself to one last show in New York. I never imagined that buying that one ticket would change my life."

The production Tina chose was the Cirque du Soleil, the world-renowned stage extravaganza that features high-flying acrobats, including aerialists suspended on ribbons of silk. Tina had never seen anything like it before, and she was mesmerized.

"It was so elegant, like dancing on air," she says. "And you could tell it took so much skill. But what really struck me was how breathtakingly beautiful the dancers were."

Even after she got to Florida, Tina could not get the Cirque aerialists out of her head, and she wasted no time searching for a school that could teach her how to perform on silks. Amazingly, she found a weekend class in Miami—a 90-minute drive away—and she immediately signed up.

"It was like I was leading this double life," she says. "Monday through Friday I was working hard at the new trading job, but as exhausted as I was by the end of the week, I'd also be pinging with excitement about taking the silk class."

At age 43, Tina was nearly two decades older than everyone else in the class, which required a level of physical fitness she had never encountered before. "The amount of strength it takes just to pull yourself up on a silk is crazy," she says. "Still, I was so happy to touch the fabric, to learn how to wrap my feet around it, that the energy just exploded out of me. And it's so rewarding when you finally get that first move down, and then another, and then another.

"Imagine being 35 feet up in the air," Tina explains, "then twisting yourself up in the fabric and suddenly unrolling your body in a dramatic drop. The first time I learned how to drop, I screamed all the way down!"

Tina's training was grueling, and after only a few weeks, other students in her class began dropping out, one by one. But that only pushed Tina to become more dedicated—and she threw herself into learning arabesques and swings, splits, and twirls.

"I took every bit of it seriously," she recalls. "My single driving thought was: I've got to get good at this so I can perform!"

Six months into her training, Tina's teacher asked her to join a small group of students who were performing at a city street festival. "I instantly said yes," Tina recalls, "even though I was really nervous. But once I got up and started doing the tricks, I was in a complete state of bliss."

That one festival energized Tina's ambition, and she soon began choreographing her own routines to pop and classical music. She even did a full-length solo performance (five to seven minutes—"but it feels way longer when you're doing it!") at the famed Art Basel venue in Miami. "That was the crowning achievement," she says.

Although she continues to work in finance to pay the bills, Tina still performs regularly at clubs or corporate and charity events—anyplace that will allow her to once again experience the unchecked joy of dancing on the air.

"I've performed on golf courses, with my silks hanging from trees, and in art museums suspended from the ceiling—you name it," says Tina, who also designs her own costumes. "On silks, I feel like I'm doing something so unique, so transfixing, that people are just blown away. And when I tell them I didn't start learning until I was in my forties, they're blown away even more. I feel like I'm an inspiration to people my own age."

The most rewarding part, Tina says, is teaching kids. "It's touching to watch a student master a move, and then see her feel so proud. I think about everything I went through as a kid and I know that there's incredible value in teaching young girls to be strong emotionally, and in helping them believe in themselves. I want them to learn to persevere, in the studio and in life, just as I have."

Lovin' the Beat

Heather Femia, 48

Great Falls, Virginia

Heather Femia was excited as she headed to her first deejay gig—and she looked fabulous. The stay-at-home mom of three spent most of her days in the kind of casual clothes you'd wear to the supermarket, but as the former corporate fashion director of Nordstrom, she still had what it took to rock a great look: on this night, the baggy jeans then being shown on the runways, a spaghetti strap tank, and, thrown over her shoulders, a leopard-print shrug with "a beautiful lavender silk lining."

As great as Heather looked on the outside, inside she was torn. Her youngest, four-year-old Joey, hadn't felt well all day and she worried about leaving him at home. But she'd promised a friend she'd deejay her fortieth birthday bash. "She was counting on me. I *was* the music for her party." With her husband assuring her they'd be fine, she picked up Joey to kiss him good night—and he promptly got sick all over her. Not *exactly* how she'd pictured launching her glamorous new career.

As outlandish as it might seem for a 40-year-old minivan-driving mom from suburban D.C., becoming a deejay was not some kind of weird midlife crisis for Heather. It was a leap that she had finally, after years, gotten up the nerve to take.

Heather had collected music for as long as she could remember. As an only child in the seventies in Virginia Beach, Virginia, she says, "Music was like the sibling I never had." As young as six, she'd tag along with her dad to Woolworth's to pick out a record from the 99-cent rack: Sonny and Cher, Three Dog Night, Rod Stewart. "I remember my mom and grandma cooking and I'd be by myself with my grandfather's very old record player, dancing around the living room and looking at album covers. I can still tell you what those record labels looked like."

By high school, she'd developed a passion for fashion as well. Voted "Best Dressed" her senior year, she'd wait eagerly each month for the next issue of *Vogue*. Saturday mornings, she was glued to CNN's *Style with Elsa Klensch*, which not only gave her a peek at high-end fashions from around the world but also introduced her to the chic electronic European dance club music playing in the background, so different from the songs—Hall & Oates, Lionel Richie—she was used to hearing. "It was the coolest thing ever," she says.

After earning a two-year degree in art and design, Heather spent more than a decade working her way up to become head style guru for Nordstrom, where she coordinated the company's high-profile fashion shows, including the music. Heather was fascinated by what the deejays did after she gave them a song list—editing and mixing the music, then adding a light show to create a mood for an event. "Someday I'm going to have *your* job," she'd tell them.

"I wanted to be the one pushing the buttons," she says. "I wanted a more intimate relationship with the music."

But other things came first. By 1998, Heather was married with a four-year-old daughter, Natalie, and was traveling a lot: heading to New York City every season to pick the latest trends, presenting her findings at Nordstrom's Seattle headquarters, going to store openings across the country, and, during the holidays, heading back to New York to be interviewed on air about the hottest styles for the upcoming year.

"It was super flattering and exciting. But it got to the point where Natalie would throw herself on the floor when I pulled out my suitcase. She would cry, 'I don't want you to go!'"

And Heather and her husband, who has a construction management and real estate development company, wanted more kids. "I knew I couldn't handle any more on my plate," Heather says. "Looking back on it, I feel like that whole 'you can have it all' thing is a misrepresentation. Something had to give, and as much as I loved my job, that something ended up being my career." In 1998, she resigned.

After what Heather dubbed her "detox" year ("I took yoga, did projects around my house, cooked healthy meals"), she felt ready to try for another baby—then promptly had two, a daughter and a son, exactly 12 months apart.

So, suddenly, the former glitzy fashionista was spending her days buried under laundry, diapers, and doctors' appointments.

"I was always lugging a double-stroller, snacks, drinks, wipes, and tissues. The basement looked like a preschool that had exploded—trains, books, and dolls everywhere. And try grocery shopping with two kids under three. I could barely keep my head above water."

Heather's savior was music. Whenever she could catch a break, she'd stop into a CD store, slip on headphones, and listen to the latest tracks. Or she'd wait until her husband got home and the kids were tucked into bed and go out to clubs with former coworkers, not only to dance but to watch the deejays in action. "I had so much admiration for how they created that sweeping, uplifting mood through music," she says.

Her husband was totally supportive. "He knew I felt like I was losing a sense of self." So in 2005, she and a girlfriend celebrated her fortieth birthday by going to Ibiza, whose nightlife draws world-famous deejays and music enthusiasts.

"It's a Disneyland for deejays," Heather says. They were even on the beaches. At dusk, "they would literally play a soundtrack to the sunset, timing it so the final piece had this big crescendo as the sun made its last little dip into the water. It was an art form. People applauded when it was over."

When Heather left Ibiza, she needed a separate suitcase for all the music she bought.

"I thought, *If I can bring just a tiny bit of this back home, I'll be offering something special.*"

Heather knew good music. But the mechanics of a deejay's work? That she had to learn. For example, deejays create special effects to rev up a crowd, repeating a cool section of a song over and over or pulling out the bass for an uplifting beat. Most challenging is transitioning from one song to the next, matching the bass beats for a seamless sound. "When you do that wrong, deejays call it 'boots in the dryer' because it goes *ba-bump, ba-bump,*" Heather says. "If you've got a dance floor going and you mess up a mix, everything stops. Managing a dance floor is high pressure."

Next, Heather bought a sound-mixer with two CD players for $200, but they sat in the box for six months. "I was totally intimidated."

Finally, her friend said, "I'm having a fortieth birthday party and you're deejaying it!"

With only two weeks' notice, Heather started figuring out how her mixer worked. She deejayed the party, and though her skills were basic, her set was a hit. "And I was hooked," she says.

Heather finally got a break at a hip Georgetown sushi lounge. The owner put on one of her mixes and a woman in the crowd, who happened to be a young, hip deejay, loved it. "That was huge for me," Heather says. "She was telling me *I've* got good taste."

Over the next year, Heather learned how to use professional equipment and met deejays, who would invite her to come to shows and sit in their booths. While she did have some screwups ("I had my share of 'boots in the dryer' "), her new career steadily flourished. By day, she was a full-time mom. But at night or on weekends, with the help of babysitters, her husband, and her mom, who took turns watching the kids, she was usually booked several times a week—a coup in an industry dominated by guys in their twenties. She has spun music in Times Square windows, at parties at the Smithsonian, and at trendy dance clubs all over Washington.

Every gig is different. "One year I did a party at the Jefferson Building here in D.C. They wanted the music to reflect the nature of the classical architecture, so I chose house music with beautiful strings and piano woven in with dance beats. And for a dinner party at an art gallery, the client wanted music that simulated a heartbeat. I did all this research and used American Indian and aboriginal drumbeats. It was challenging, but it was fun to stay on theme."

Not bad for a woman who is inching her way toward 50.

"When I get my mind set on something I'm just not going to give up," Heather says, even if that means that along with her fabulous outfit she has to wear reading glasses to see her song list under a club's dim lights.

"It took a lot of guts to do this at my age, but it comes from an authentic place. I love the music I play."

The Cupcake Couple

Kristi Cunningham Whitfield, 43
Washington, D.C.

Five months after Kristi Cunningham and her boyfriend, Sam Whitfield, started dating, he proposed—a business idea, that is.

"We were cooking dinner and having one of those 'How was your day?' conversations," Kristi recalls, "when suddenly he turned to me and asked, 'What would you think about opening a cupcake truck?'" Kristi recalls.

"A cupcake truck? You're a lawyer, and I'm in transportation logistics. What do we know about cupcakes? Or trucks?"

Sam told Kristi that he and his fellow attorneys had been craving cupcakes that day but no one felt like trekking to a bakery across town to get any. "What if we started a business to bring cupcakes to customers' neighborhoods?" he asked.

"I actually thought it was a pretty great idea," Kristi says. "And my mind started whirring: How would it work, exactly? What kind of truck would we get? What flavors of cupcakes would we sell? We just started creating the business in our imaginations."

The more they brainstormed, the better the idea seemed: There was just one other food truck in all of D.C., and cupcakes seemed like a perfect "truck stop" food: easily portable impulse buys that wouldn't need a full kitchen setup onboard.

"We had taken a trip up to New York, where cupcakes seemed to be *everywhere*. I figured the cupcake trend would trickle down to D.C. and take off here, too."

Kristi wasn't exactly looking for a new career; she was doing well in her corporate job. But after a few months of fantasizing, Kristi and Sam couldn't let the idea go.

"I remember the distinct moment when Sam looked at me and said, 'Are we really gonna do this?' I think we both understood that we weren't just talking about the business; we were also talking about our relationship. We were in love. If we did this together, how could it not be awesome? So we said, let's go for it."

Their first step was to recruit friends and coworkers for a little market research. "We weren't really worried about whether people would like cupcakes. The real questions were: Would you be willing to eat them off a truck? How much would you pay for a cupcake? And how far would you walk to get it?" The friends were skeptical—but intrigued.

But if they were going to do it, Kristi wanted to do it fast. "I was so nervous that someone else was going to beat us to it, and I was laser-focused on being the *first* cupcake truck—not the second, not the third."

Since food trucks weren't common in D.C., there was no well-established playbook for how to get this off the ground. So they cobbled one together. "I was navigating the Department of Health, filling out a million forms, waiting for licenses. And the people who worked at the Department of Consumer and Regulatory Affairs practically thought I *lived* there."

57

After learning that the city required the truck to be a certain length and width, Kristi came across the perfect vehicle for sale in Florida. The couple bought a one-way plane ticket, drove the truck around the block twice, bought it, and then drove it home.

"That trip made the business real. It's one thing to fill out the paperwork to incorporate a business, it was another to fly to Florida and buy a truck!"

After that, says Kristi, "it was like filling in a Mad Libs business plan: *What color should the truck be?* Pink! *What should the logo look like?* A cupcake on wheels! *Should we bake the cupcakes ourselves?* No, let's hire a professional."

As the business started to take shape, some friends and family began expressing their doubts. "There were a lot of 'Are you out of your minds? How are you going to support yourselves?'" says Kristi. "We were launching at the beginning of a recession, and people assumed we'd lost our jobs. They couldn't fathom that we were quitting our careers to start this whole new endeavor."

Kristi says, "I knew it was crazy, but we just did it anyway." Still, she admits there were wobbles along the way. "We were learning about each other and each other's work styles at the same time. Sam's more methodical and likes to plan things out; I'm more flexible and fly by the seat of my pants. But we've figured it out and adapted, both personally and professionally."

Six months after Sam first brought up the food truck idea, the pair were ready to debut their cupcakes with a stand at the city's popular H Street Festival. Though they made some rookie mistakes ("We charged $2.75 each, which meant we needed gobs and gobs of change—after that we raised the price to $3"), they sold out of the 600 cupcakes that they had brought. Three months later, once the truck was outfitted with a vending window and had passed inspection, Curbside Cupcakes set out on its first route.

And a few weeks after that—one year to the day after they started dating—Sam proposed again. This time, he meant marriage.

"In the beginning, it was just the two of us, plus the professional baker we hired," says Kristi. "Every morning, Sam would drive to the commercial kitchen, pick up the cupcakes, and head out in the truck, while I managed planning and marketing."

Within a couple of months, it was clear the truck was a hit. "We were a novelty, so people would see this bright pink truck and follow it just to see what it was," she says. Sam would make four scheduled stops a day, plus a "wild card" location based on the number of requests they received via Facebook and Twitter.

As Curbside Cupcakes began taking off, selling out hundreds of cupcakes each day, Kristi and Sam realized it didn't make sense to continue outsourcing the baking—it was eating up too much of their costs, and the baker wasn't always available. So, you guessed it: Kristi took over cupcake-making duties, too.

"I was nervous. I know what tastes good, but I'm not a culinary school graduate—this was a business idea. So I started in my home kitchen with one recipe—for chocolate cake. And after thousands and thousands of batches, which Sam and I taste-tested, we hit on a winning recipe." Then they tackled Curbside's other bestselling flavors, like carrot cake and red velvet.

Today, Curbside Cupcakes operates three trucks, a kiosk in D.C.'s Union Market, and has a new commercial kitchen with a small café. The business sells hundreds of $3 cupcakes a day in 37 flavors—from key lime to peanut butter cup to dulce de leche—and caters special events, like the time Ford Motor Company bought 1,400 cupcakes in one day.

And two years after they married, Kristi and Sam welcomed another addition to the Curbside Cupcakes family: a baby boy. "The first three months after Drake was born, I would wrap him up in a carrier and bake with him sitting on my chest," she says. "I'm deeply grateful to be my own boss, to be able to be with my kid and never have to explain my choices to anybody."

But with all their success, becoming a part of their customers' lives is their greatest reward.

"We make cupcakes. And that means we get to be involved in people's celebrations—their birthday parties, their bar mitzvahs, their weddings, their special moments," including a marriage proposal one guy planned around a special Curbside Cupcakes delivery.

"Back in the early days, when Sam and I would spend hours fantasizing about how exciting it would be to open our own business, we dreamed big. But this is bigger than anything we ever imagined."

And that's the icing on the cupcake.

The Healer

Gaylee McCracken, 61
Cleveland Heights, Ohio

When Gaylee McCracken was just seven years old, her mother was diagnosed with breast cancer. Even at that tender age, she felt drawn to caring for her mother. She also felt scared. Helpless. But she remembers feeling something else: curiosity.

Other children might have reacted to surgery scars and hair loss with an emphatic "Yeccch!," but Gaylee was fascinated by how the body worked. Soon she was envisioning herself wearing a stethoscope and white coat like the doctors who cared for her mother, and she began to fantasize that she, too, might one day go to medical school.

But when she shared this with her father, an Italian gentleman of the old school, his response was discouraging. "Don't be a doctor," he told her. "Marry one."

Dad wasn't expressing a chauvinistic attitude, Gaylee believes, but rather the simpler, harder view that life was tough and seldom very kind to dreamers. "He came from a poor immigrant family and had to drop out of school himself," she says. "In his mind, dreams were for rich people. People like us had to be practical."

So practical she became. Gaylee devoted her energies to her studies, winning a scholarship to Bowling Green University, where she majored in English and art. After graduation, she applied for a job as an in-house graphic designer at Case Western Reserve University, where her husband was beginning law school. "I was one of five finalists for the position," Gaylee recalls. "Our test was to design a brochure. I wanted to distinguish myself, to set myself apart. So I rewrote it." Gaylee's display of chutzpah was rewarded: She got the job.

Gaylee liked being a graphic artist for the university, and developed a clever method for working with the many departments. "If the Electrical Engineering Department needed a poster," she says, "I hung around with them for a while to get a feel for what they did." One day she was asked to develop some materials for the medical school, so she went over to the school to hang out and absorb the vibe. Immediately the visit rekindled her childhood desire to be a doctor. The atmosphere, the subjects, the classes—as sure as Gaylee had ever been about anything, she knew this was where she was meant to be.

What she doubted, however, was that she was at the right moment of her life to go there. By now she was the mother of two small children, her husband was launching his law career, her mother's health was still fragile. No, she decided, this was not the time.

The dream may have been deferred, but it would not be denied. It stuck with her. Finally, she began to share her feelings with her friends and family. The reaction was unanimous: "Do it!" they said.

But *could* she do it? Her doubts persisted. She would have to attend four years of medical school, followed by two years of an internship and two years of a residency, before she would be allowed to practice medicine—and all of that *after* she had successfully completed 42 hours of undergraduate course work in math and science.

Then she had an epiphany. "I'm going to be 50 someday anyway," Gaylee thought. "I may as well be 50 and be a doctor. If I don't do this now, I will always regret it."

The road wasn't easy—"calculus almost killed me"—but at age 42, Gaylee was accepted to medical school at Case Western. It didn't hurt that she had designed the school's brochures years before, or that the school had a strong belief in admitting "untraditional" students—namely, people who were older or who had prepared differently for the program. She was one of five students in her class who were over forty. All were women. All passed.

At one point in her cardiovascular class, Gaylee studied herself into what she thought was a heart attack. It turned out to be a *panic* attack, not uncommon for stressed-out med students.

And then there was the weirdness: At one student party, Gaylee looked up and was surprised to see her 21-year-old son—who was visiting—kissing one of her class-mates, who was around 25 and thought he was Gaylee's brother. "Everyone had a good laugh," she recalls.

Gaylee graduated from medical school when she was 47. Whatever difficulties she faced along the way, being older was not among them. In fact, she believes that her age was a positive. Her children were old enough not only to support her decision, but to step up and take responsibility for managing the household so she could concentrate on her studies.

Moreover, Gaylee saw that her accumulation of life experiences helped her keep perspective and manage the challenges of med school in ways the younger students could not.

"Hey, my husband and I lost all of our worldly possessions in a fire while we were undergraduates," she says. "Once you get through something like that, being assigned to read a couple hundred pages by next Wednesday isn't something that's going to freak you out."

Most important, from the moment she entered med school, Gaylee was bolstered by the conviction that she was meant to be a doctor. Today, as an internist practicing antiaging medicine, she sees a through-line connecting her experiences.

"From taking care of my mother to being a mother, everything I've done has helped prepare me for this life," she says. "I was meant to be a healer."

PART THREE

Escape

"I started to realize that perhaps 'settled down' isn't all it's cracked up to be."

A Dream for Her Daughter

Maria Figueroa, 52
Fort Myers, Florida

Every time Maria Figueroa pushed her cart of cleaning supplies into an office, she'd play out a fantasy in her mind. An immigrant from Peru, Maria was working as a bank janitor—the latest in a series of menial jobs she'd held over the years—but in her dreams, she was a professional.

"As I went about my work, I'd imagine myself sitting behind one of those big desks as a manager. That's where I wanted to be, not cleaning," says Maria, who often had to bring her then-ten-year-old daughter, Melissa, with her on her evening rounds. "I would sit Melissa down and say, 'This is why you need to study hard, so that you can have an office like this one day, not a job like Mommy is doing.' And she would say, 'I promise, Mommy, I will.'"

As a child in Peru, Maria had been a dedicated student. Schoolwork, especially math, came naturally to her, and she always brought home good grades. When she was a teenager, her father, a college-educated high school teacher, told her, "I don't have enough money to send you to private university, but you've got to continue your education. If you earn your degree, that will be yours forever."

So in 1980, Maria enrolled at one of Peru's free public universities, studying accounting.

"I had a godmother who was an accountant, and I used to beg to visit her at work. She would joke, 'Okay, you can visit, but I'm going to put you to work for me!' She had three boys, and I remember that even after she lost her husband, she never had any worries about providing for them on her own. That taught me a lot about what having a profession could mean."

But two years after Maria started college, the Peruvian government, facing economic problems and a violent guerrilla insurgency, began shutting down its public universities, including the one Maria attended.

"At first, they said the schools would be closed for just a few months, but it turned out to be years," says Maria, who found secretarial work at city hall while she waited to resume her studies. When the university finally reopened in 1985, Maria was devastated to learn that all of her academic records had been lost. *That's two years of my life just thrown away.*

Maria decided to take some time to consider her options. "My grandparents were living in New Jersey, and my grandfather had just passed away. My grandma needed someone to help her for a while, so I told my parents I would go, and I got a visa."

Over the next few years in the States, Maria picked up any kind of work she could find: answering phones for her aunt's mortgage business, babysitting a neighbor's kids, cleaning offices. Often, the work was part-time or temporary, so she moved around a lot, cobbling together a living. Although she missed her parents desperately, Maria couldn't imagine returning home. "There were no opportunities for me in Peru that seemed worth going back for."

In 1993, Maria married a man she'd met through friends in Peru. Americo was a college graduate who had worked as a P.E. teacher in their home country; though he had his green card, his English wasn't very good, so his opportunities in the States were limited. After they wed, Maria got a green card, too, and three years later Melissa was born. Soon after, she and Americo moved to Florida, both for the weather and for the prospect of better schools for Melissa.

But in Florida, Maria and Americo could find jobs only in a factory making plastic bags. "It was awful," says Maria. "Florida is so hot in the summer, and I was working in this cramped area with big loud machines and no air-conditioning. I felt like I was in a sauna."

After a few months, Maria couldn't take it anymore. She had to find something—anything—else. So once more, she began looking for work anywhere she could find it: housekeeping at a nursing home, cashiering at a local supermarket. She even found a contract job delivering mail for the U.S. Postal Service.

"I spent so many years hopping from job to job, and even though some of them were enjoyable, they never felt like something I wanted to do forever," she says.

Maria often met other immigrants in the same situation—overqualified for the low-skill work they were doing. "But they all seemed to be resigned to it," she says. "No one ever expressed wanting to move on, to become a professional. But I just couldn't imagine spending my entire life like this.

"I'd always told Melissa how important it was to get her education, but I had the same goal for myself. I thought that someday I'd finish my studies, but it just never seemed like the right time to go back."

Then, in 2009, Maria took a job as a pre-K teacher's aide. A coworker who wanted to improve her English asked Maria to go with her to visit nearby

Hodges University. When they arrived, the admissions officer asked, "Why are you two looking for English classes? Your English is good! You need to come to college and get a degree!"

"As soon as she said that," Maria says, "I got excited. I thought, *Maybe now is the time.*" Melissa was just starting high school, and Americo had recently been promoted from head custodian to building supervisor at his school, which meant he could be home when Melissa got out of school every day.

The admissions officer told Maria and her friend that they'd need to come back and take an entrance exam, similar to the SAT. The following week, Maria arrived ready for the test, but her friend never showed. "I think she was scared," says Maria, who admits she was a little intimidated herself. "The test was three hours long, and every hour that passed, my headache grew bigger and bigger. I was freaking out, thinking, *I should have studied more! I can't remember anything from my time at the university all those years ago!*"

The most challenging part of the test was the essay. The topic: Why do you want to go back to school? "I wrote about how I wanted to be an example for Melissa," says Maria. "I wrote, 'If I can show her that *I* can do this, she will see that she can do it, too.' It was the first time I'd ever really expressed this goal for myself out loud, other than to my husband."

A few days later, Maria got a phone call—she'd passed.

"I couldn't believe it! Just about every night since I had left college all those years ago, I had dreamed that I was back in a classroom with my old classmates from Peru," she says. "Now, in just a few months, my dream would be real."

In January 2010, Maria started an associate's degree program in accounting, taking classes in the evening while continuing to work as a teacher's aide.

(A financial aid package covered most of her tuition and books; loans took care of the rest.) "The first day, I was giddy," she says. "I thought, *This time, nothing will keep me from finishing.*"

Still, balancing her job, studies, and home life was often exhausting. "I would work from 8:30 a.m. to 3:30 p.m., then do my homework in the afternoon. My classes usually started at six p.m., and I'd get home around ten." Although her classes met only two or three nights a week, "I'd lie to my family and say I had class every night. I can't get anything done at home—there's always someone who needs me to do something for them—so I was able to spend my off-nights studying on campus."

Maria's favorite classes were those in accounting, where she consistently earned As. "I already had a strong foundation from my time at university in Peru, and I felt like, *I can do this! I understand!*" she says. "I'm even able to help a lot of my classmates, which is a good feeling."

Other classes, like English composition, were tougher. "I explained to the professor, 'I have my ideas, but I get blocked when I try to put them down on paper. I still think in Spanish, and it's hard for me to switch over and write in English.' The professor was from Russia, so she understood, but she told me, 'You need to forget Spanish when you're in my class.'" Maria got a tutor, and ended up getting a C, "but I didn't care. When I saw the grade, I was so relieved: I passed."

In the fall of 2013, Maria completed the last two classes she needed to finally earn her associate's degree. But she isn't done. "All along, my goal was to get a bachelor's degree. I can't imagine stopping now."

Maria knows that in finishing her degree, she's proven something to herself—and to her daughter, who joined her mom as a college student, enrolling at Florida Gulf University after graduating summa cum laude from her high school last spring.

"I started this whole journey because of her, to show her that I could do this," she says. Last summer, Melissa visited family in New York City; afterward, she told Maria, "You know, Mom, my cousins have finished college and they have great jobs—they can buy anything they want!"

"I told her, 'That professional life, the independence, is your reward for the hard work you put into your studies. That's going to happen to me when I finish my degree, and it's going to happen to you, too.'"

Her only wish is that her father, who had always encouraged her to earn her degree, had lived to see her receive her diploma. "He never gave up this dream for me, even after so many years," says Maria, her voice breaking. "He would be so proud."

Don't Ask Why
I Didn't Leave Him

Kit Gruelle, 59
Haywood County, North Carolina

"*Why didn't you leave him?*

We need to stop asking that question and instead ask the men: "Why do you put your hands on her? Why do you intimidate her?"

I always wonder what would happen after a bank robbery, if the police went to the bank president and asked, "Why did you keep all that money here? What's wrong with you? We've been out here four or five times already and you're still operating this bank here. You must like getting robbed."

That's what it's like to be a battered woman and get asked repeatedly why you didn't leave. It's like being held hostage—you can't "just leave." People fixate on wanting to see black eyes and broken noses and cracked ribs and that sort of thing, but the most important thing is the stuff that no one ever sees. Domestic violence is really about the coercive tactics that an abuser uses. The

73

physical violence is the punctuation mark, what he uses to enforce the control he feels entitled to.

That's just what it was like with Jack. I was only 22 when I met him, recently separated from my first husband, and with a little boy. Jack was from the mountains here in North Carolina, just like me, but he'd been gone for a long time and he was a bit of a local legend. He was stunningly handsome, the most handsome man I'd ever seen in my life. He was incredibly physically fit. And unbelievably charismatic. He just swept me off my feet.

I know now he was mainly interested in me because my family had money. I had been adopted as a baby into the Gruelle family—my grandfather was Johnny Gruelle, who created Raggedy Anne—so we were well off. My dad wanted kids, and so did Grandmother Gruelle. But growing up, I always sensed my adoptive mom didn't want my brother and me, something she confirmed to me when I was 35, after I'd found my birth mother. I think that helps explain why I grew up feeling completely unlovable and unattractive. So when Jack came along and turned on the charm, I was terribly vulnerable to it.

I had heard stories about Jack's childhood—his father left when he was ten and his mother had her own issues. He'd been sent off to reform school when he was 12 and then joined the marines and went to Vietnam. When I met him, I thought he just needed someone to understand him, someone to give him the kind of love that he'd never experienced.

Not long after we started seeing each other, he moved into my house, which my father had given me. It wasn't long before Jack started to assert his control and dominance in our relationship, and establish that I was his property.

That's what abusers do: They use various tactics that, in effect, disable women. They sweep them off their feet first, and that way, when the control and the coercion and intimidation start, the woman remembers who he was when they first met, and she can't reconcile that with who he is now. The problem is that who he was early on in the relationship is not who he authentically is. Abusers have dual personalities; they can turn the control and the intimidation on and off, depending on the occasion and the goal.

Like every other battered woman I've talked to, I would always think back to how Jack was when we first got together. I never hated him; I just wanted the violence to stop.

Jack would go into town and pick up women and bring them to the house and have sex with them. He would make sure that I was awake upstairs and hearing what was going on. Then he'd take the women back into town, return to the house, and have me get up and fix him a full meal. And I'd have to sit there and listen to him talk about what he did with those women and how they were so much better sexually than I was.

That's what it's like: The things an abuser does to a woman don't necessarily violate any law, but they go a long way toward him exercising and maintaining complete control over her. For example, Jack had started lifting weights when he was in Vietnam and he had become a power-lifter. He was trying to take in a lot of protein to gain weight. One of the things he wanted me to do was prepare protein-rich foods for him. Every night, before he went to town, he would have a bowl of ice cream with peanuts on it (peanuts are very high in protein), but he did not want salt on the peanuts because salt would cause him to "retain fluid." So when I went to the grocery story, he insisted that I buy salted peanuts, bring them home, rinse them off in a colander, and pat them dry before I put them on his ice cream. Then, if I had not done a satisfactory job washing the peanuts, he came after me and screamed at me and grabbed me by the throat for not "getting it right." So every night I would put the peanuts in the colander, rinse them off, pat them dry, and hope that I "got it right" and that he didn't find any salt on his peanuts.

Jack punched me in the face only one time. But he put his hands around my throat almost daily. He would pick me up, hold me against the wall with my feet off the ground, and say, "I could break your fucking neck if I wanted to." He reminded me routinely that he had been trained by the marines to hunt down and kill people. He told me that if I ever tried to leave him, he'd hunt me down and kill me.

This is the crazy thing that battered women get into. We engage in all this magical thinking, like, *If I just wash the peanuts good enough,* or *If I just fix him fried chicken the way he likes it,* or *If I just hoe the garden like he wants,* it will all get better.

I guess that's why I went to Hawaii with him and married him. Jack had a piece of property there, and he wanted us to live and work on it. But what he really wanted was to get me away from everybody and everything I knew. It seems crazy, because I was terrified of this man all the time. But I was pregnant again and I thought, *Well, if we get married maybe the violence will stop.*

I did leave him a few times after that, when we'd moved back to North Carolina. Jack called these my "disappearing acts." I had a good friend who was like a brother to me. He had been with Jack in Vietnam, but at the time he lived up in Michigan. So whenever things would get really, really bad, I would take the boys and run up there. I knew Jack wouldn't come after me if I was with somebody who would stand up to him. I'd stay gone for two or three days and then return. He'd know that he had to kind of dial things down a bit, so he'd mellow out for a little while. But then he'd start up again.

I moved out four or five times. That's typical—battered women leave their abusers an average of five to seven times before they stay gone permanently. What women tend to do is run out the door with a kid under each arm and the clothes on their back, and that's it. They flee to a shelter, or to a friend's or family member's house. Then he promises to change: *It's never going to happen again; I'll go to church; I'll go to A.A.*— all these bullshit promises. Then she goes back and it starts again.

The last time I left, I had taken the boys and gone up to the Northeast. I was going to hide out and change my identity and relocate permanently. About five days after leaving, I called home and learned that Jack and his friend Kenny had gone out of state to look for a job, so I came home. I had the phone number changed and filed separation papers. About two weeks later, I got a call at two a.m. from Kenny's mom. She kept saying, "I don't know how to tell you this . . ." I said, "What? Tell me!" She said, "Jack's dead." He had been killed in an accident on an offshore barge.

I was sure it was my fault. I thought, *Oh my God, I willed this to happen. I willed for this man to die.* A few weeks earlier I had tried to kill myself, because I knew it was going to have to be either him or me. That was the only way it was going to end. And now it had ended.

When Jack's body came back from Louisiana, I went to the morgue. Even though he was dead and I touched him and he was cold and hard, like the steel table that he was on, I still imagined that he was going to come up and put his hands around my throat and strangle me again.

His body was covered with this muslin sheet. I pulled the sheet off and sat there for about an hour, just looking at his entire body from the top of his head to the tip of his toes. I thought about how we needed to make his face look as good as it possibly could, because I knew that some of his girlfriends would be coming to the funeral home and he should look nice.

I looked at his hands and I thought about how those hands had been around my throat so many times, but also how he taught me to garden. I

raised my first organic garden with him. I looked at his chest and remembered that he had worked so hard to be so strong, and now here he was, 29 years old and dead. And it was this whole huge waterfall of different emotions that all blended together. That's the way it is for victims of domestic violence. It's not a clean thing. It's this complex, multilayered thing.

Today I train police officers about how to handle domestic violence. One of the main things they must understand is that battered women are like benign hostages. A woman may not have a gun held to her head all the time, but that doesn't mean that she's not a hostage. She's living with a set of rules and expectations that she must fully adhere to. If she doesn't meet those exacting standards—and by the way, the standards change all the time—then she thinks she's going to get either beaten up or killed. And then if she does the most revolutionary thing she can do—leave—she stands a good chance of being stalked and murdered.

We still don't have a clear sense of what battered women are up against in this country, and we need to change that. Then maybe people will stop blaming the victims for the abusers' violence and stop asking us why we don't just leave.

Highway Heaven

Doreen Orion, 54
Everywhere, USA

D oreen Orion thought her husband was nuts. And she's a psychiatrist. Then again, he's a psychiatrist, too.

Tim, a car enthusiast who could spend hours browsing through the mechanics magazines at his local newsstand, had picked up one called *Bus Conversions,* about people who strip down and remodel tour buses and turn them into homes on wheels.

His proposal: He and Doreen take a sabbatical, convert a bus, and travel the country.

Her reply: "No way! Why can't you be like a normal husband in a midlife crisis and have an affair or buy a Corvette?"

Doreen, who had just turned 40, was content with her life. She was living in a big house in the mountains of Colorado, had her own private practice that was fulfilling both financially and emotionally, and still had plenty of time to indulge her love of shopping (and had the gargantuan walk-in closet to prove it).

"We thought we were living the American dream—nice house, good careers, settled and secure," she says. "I was content to just read, hang out, and watch movies. I was comfortable." She knew that Tim felt burned out at work, and couldn't see why he didn't just slow down. "I didn't see why *my* life had to be upended," she says.

Over the next few years, Tim persisted—and what he said started to resonate with Doreen. She began to notice how often her older patients would lament putting off their dreams until retirement, only to realize it was too late.

In 2003, Doreen finally gave in. She and Tim would buy a bus, remodel it, and hit the road. The caveat: After their year of living peripatetically, they'd sell it and resume their old lives. Deal? Deal.

They packed, pared down (after all, they were going from a 4,500-square-foot home into a 340-square-foot tour bus), and plotted. Doreen, they decided, would step down from her practice and shift toward doing online insurance work that she could do from the bus; Tim would temporarily give up both his medical director's job and his private practice. "We didn't want him to have to do temp work," Doreen explains, "because that would mean having to stay in one place for at least a month at a time, and that wasn't the plan."

Then two months before their planned departure, they decided to take a three-week "shakedown cruise" to get acquainted with piloting their 40-foot, 20-ton home on wheels.

But the first day out proved to be a bumpy one.

While backing down the driveway, Tim almost ran over Doreen.

When they were on the highway, going 60 miles an hour, the bus door flew open and Doreen thought she was going to be sucked out.

Near Rock Springs, Wyoming, they drove into a hailstorm so severe that even the truckers were pulling over.

When Doreen and Tim got to their first overnight truck stop, it was so full they had to drive around in the rain to find another place to park. When at last they settled in to sleep—in the parking lot of a Wyoming community college—they discovered that one of their cats had been so freaked out by the storm she'd peed on their mattress.

Things could only get better.

But they didn't. As they were about to leave a gas station in Reno a few days later, the door lock—the same one that had let the door fly open on the highway—got stuck. Doreen and Tim were left standing outside the bus in 100-degree heat; their poodle and two cats were locked inside with no air-conditioning.

While waiting for the locksmith to get there, Doreen had a meltdown.

"I felt stuck," she says. "We had already rented out our house for the whole year and there was no turning back." She was so miserable, Tim actually offered to turn around, go home, and live in a rental until they could get their house back. But Doreen agreed to give it some time. "I knew it was very important to him," she says.

Besides, she *was* looking forward to escaping the winter cold—and, as the saying goes, they had places to go and people to see.

After they got back from their test run, they put their plan into motion. Musts on their itinerary: Mount Rushmore in South Dakota; the Mall of America in Minneapolis ("my Mecca," says Doreen); and then they'd "meander East for a while," just in time to chase the fall colors down the coast.

"Our lives had been so planned out that we really wanted to wing it as much as possible," Doreen says.

So off they went. It didn't take Doreen long to fall in love with the carefree lifestyle. "Two months in," she says, "we were in New Hampshire about to drive up Mount Washington. It was a gorgeous New England fall day in the

middle of the week. I remember thinking, *I wouldn't have this day if I were still living in Colorado and going to the hospital. What a gift this is.*"

During their year on the road, they traveled more than 20,000 miles to 47 states, including Alaska (where, it turned out, Doreen didn't get much work done since their satellite Internet and cell phones couldn't get reception).

If they liked a place, they stayed longer; if they felt like moving on, they did.

On Amelia Island, Florida, they walked four miles on an almost empty beach, watching dolphins frolicking offshore. In San Francisco, they played tourist, grabbing lunch in Chinatown and dessert at Ghirardelli Square.

"After 4 years of college, 4 years of medical school, 4 years of residency, then 15 years of private practice—all in their predictable order, with their predictable schedules—I didn't realize how much I needed to take a leap into the unknown," Doreen says. "My life had become routine. I started to realize that perhaps 'settled down' isn't all it's cracked up to be."

Not that life on the road was always smooth. In Virginia, faulty wiring caused flames to shoot out of the bus roof. In Arizona, they encountered an armed robber at a burrito joint. In California, they accidentally stumbled into a nudist RV park. "All the new experiences, even the bad ones, challenged me in a way I never would have imagined," she says. "They brought a certain aliveness back that I hadn't even realized was missing."

And Doreen felt more connected to Tim than ever before. "Getting through all the disasters boosted my confidence in us as a team," she says. "It gave me the feeling we could handle anything." Back home in Colorado, they would plop down in front of the TV after work to eat dinner. On the bus, they grocery shopped together, flirting in the aisles, and listened to music while Tim cooked.

"We had always had a good relationship, so I was surprised at how much closer we grew," she says.

The travels also gave Doreen time to look within herself, "instead of focusing on external things, like maintaining a dream house or having a shoe collection worthy of Imelda Marcos," she says. "It made me realize that collecting experiences is more important than collecting stuff."

Doreen even started a blog chronicling their adventures, which she turned into a personal memoir: *Queen of the Road: The True Tale of 47 States, 22,000 Miles, 200 Shoes, 2 Cats, 1 Poodle, a Husband and a Bus with a Will of Its Own.*

When the year was up and they returned to their house and to reality, Tim and Doreen couldn't bring themselves to sell the bus. So even as they resumed their jobs, they rearranged their schedules so they could take winters off and hit the road to warmer climates.

"But every time we returned home, we missed life on the bus," she says. So in 2012, they went all the way: They sold their house and most of their possessions, and the day before Doreen's fifty-third birthday, they embarked on a permanent road trip. They work just enough at their telecommuting jobs to support their scaled-down "explorer's life."

"When fellow travelers ask us where we're from, we always answer nowhere—and everywhere. Not a day has gone by that we don't look at each other and marvel at how lucky we are to be living this new life. Literally and figuratively, it has taken us places I've never been. When your surroundings are downsized, your horizons are endless."

Lift Ticket

Lynn Douglas, 52
Tahoe City, California

Lynn Douglas walked into her boss's office and, exhibiting the same strength and conviction that had catapulted her up the ladder during her 17-year career at the company, abruptly quit.

"It was the first time I'd ever done something so impulsive."

Lynn's career had been her life. She was so dedicated to her job, she'd made a conscious decision not to get married or have kids. And through the nineties, that single-minded devotion to career paid off: She thrived on the challenge of working on contracts with booming Silicon Valley high-tech companies.

"It was like solving a puzzle," she says. "And because I was a broker, I was the middleman, talking to both the client and the company, so there was this wonderful personal interaction." To top it off, her coworkers were young and fun—and she was pulling in six figures. What was not to like?

But in 1999, her firm was swallowed up by a bigger company, Marsh & McLennan. The result: more bureaucracy, more managerial duties, and less time for personal attention to her customers. "I didn't feel like I could make a difference anymore in this big pond," she says, "so I lost the drive."

To get it back, Lynn decided in early 2001 to take a three-month vacation to reinvigorate her spirits. And what better place than a ski cabin near Lake Tahoe? She'd learned how to ski at age five, taken childhood ski trips to Yosemite with her family every Christmas and Easter, and skied through high school and college. Then life—in the form of her first real insurance job—intervened. Working late into the evenings and many weekends for more than a decade, she'd had no time for the slopes.

But when she was 35 and her friend Danna offered her a spot in a cabin at Squaw Valley, "I immediately took to skiing again," she says. She'd go bell to bell—from the moment the lifts opened to the last chair of the day. "I loved the adrenaline rush," she says, "the freedom from unleashing all the pent-up energy and frustrations of a desk job." She'd fly down the mountain runs, feeling confident and strong. "I had defined myself by my job titles and responsibilities," she says. "Now I was liberating myself from them."

Driving up Squaw Valley Road on Friday evenings, Lynn would often roll down her window to let the absolute stillness surround her. "It's what you *don't* hear that is remarkable," she says. "I could feel the serenity."

It was that peacefulness she was after during her work break in January 2001. Lynn and a girlfriend skied and skied. She was happy, but torn. Though she wanted this life in Tahoe, she told herself, "You can't have it. Don't get attached. You have to go back to work."

And she did go back to her life in San Francisco and her job at Marsh that April, recharged and ready to bury herself over the next six months in a big project: the company's internal audit.

Two women from Marsh's New York audit department arrived in San Francisco on September 10, 2001. The next day, driving in to work and anxious to hear the audit results, Lynn turned on the radio to breaking news: Two airplanes had just crashed into the World Trade Center. It was so shocking that Lynn didn't believe it at first.

But what startled her more was her reaction as she arrived at her eerily quiet office and everyone was being told to go home.

"I thought, 'How is this going to affect all the work I put into this audit?'" Lynn says. "I mean, really: 'How is this going to affect *me*?'"

When the office reopened the next day, Lynn found out that all 300 Marsh employees on floors 93 through 100 of the Trade Center's North Tower had been killed. Lynn had briefly met only a few of the victims, but as the announcements came over her email, listing name after name of lost peers, "that's when the wave of tears came," she says. She realized how selfish she had been, how insignificant she, and the work she had done for the audit, truly were. "That was a turning point," she says. "I knew I needed to change."

Lynn looked hard at her own life. The last six months, pouring all of her time and energy into prepping for this audit, why did it matter?

Did she love what she was doing? No. Was it important to her? No. Was she happy? No.

Lynn couldn't quiet the noise in her head.

So three months later, when her boss called her into his office to ask a routine question, she didn't even sit down before blurting out, "I can't work here any longer." He didn't act surprised, nor did he try to convince her to stay. Meanwhile, running through her mind was: *How could I have done this?* She didn't have another job lined up. What exactly was she going to do next?

But over the next two weeks, as she finished up projects and cleaned out her desk, she felt her body unclench. "I knew I had made the right decision," she says.

Lynn had saved enough money that she didn't have to work again right away, so she headed back up to Tahoe. Three months into her new life, she met a guy on the chairlift named Dave. Fresh off a divorce, he had also left an unfulfilling career to take time off and refocus on his future.

"He had integrity, the kind that comes from really caring about more than just himself," she says. "I wanted to be around that type of person; I wanted to learn from him." And it got even better: He was an avid cook, and when she opened his freezer, she found containers filled with single servings of food he had put away for the week. "He was comfortable being on his own, and I admired that about him," she says. "I knew he was a keeper." Three dates later, she moved in with him.

Just who *was* this unpredictable woman in the 40-year-old body? Lynn didn't know, but she sure liked her. "Instead of waking up every day with

a feeling of dread, I woke up and thought, 'I can't wait to start my day,'" she says. "All of a sudden I'd become this other person, and I'd never been happier."

But part of the old Lynn was still in there. She took a job at the Squaw Valley Ski School, first to teach beginner kids and later adults. But then that old competitive drive started thrumming: She wanted to instruct the *experts*. To do so, she'd need to take a certification exam that had a passage rate of only 15 percent.

Lynn trained for five years, learning to ski anywhere, in any conditions, at any time of day. She studied the physics, physiology, and biomechanics of skiing. And in 2011, at age 50, she aced the test.

Lynn and Dave married; today he works part-time as a consultant and she teaches most winter days when the weather allows. For so long focused on her own success, she now finds joy in watching her students light up when they learn a new trick.

The healthiest she's ever been—on the slopes for six-plus hours at a time, running, and doing CrossFit—she can't imagine still sitting behind a desk. She can barely last an hour in her home office these days before the sparkling white view through her window beckons her back outside. She plans on skiing, she says, until she can no longer walk.

"I have changed so much, and I would never have thought that something as simple as skiing could do that for me," Lynn says. "Letting go of everything I had worked so hard to attain was a huge risk, but the alternative of staying was an even bigger one. I learned to trust myself."

Woman of the World

Karen Schaler, 49

New York, New York

For as far back as Karen Schaler can remember, she was glued to the news. Watching TV with her mother in their apartment in Everett, Washington, she was fascinated by the stories of people in distant places who were caught up in dramatic circumstances and had to overcome hardship, prejudice, and danger. And there was something about the journalists she saw covering the stories. They were at the center of things. By the age of ten, when people asked her what she wanted to be when she grew up, Karen would tell them she wanted to be a news reporter.

That answer might have seemed a bit precocious, the kind of thing kids soon outgrow. But by the time she was 14, an age when some kids are still trying to remember the combinations to their lockers, Karen was poring over college catalogs, and one—California State University at Fullerton, with its state-of-the-art broadcasting program—really captured her heart.

There was only one problem: how to afford the tuition on her mother's income as a public school teacher. Working with her high school counselor, Karen developed an audacious plan. Instead of finishing high school in Washington, she would eventually move to California, enroll in school there, and take a job as a live-in babysitter for a family in Calabasas.

"It was such a huge adjustment," Karen recalls. "Not only were these people total strangers, but I had never even lived with other children, let alone cared for them, and I had never been outside of Washington."

But the plan worked perfectly, and after a year, Karen was eligible for the much lower tuition rate offered to state residents. Four years later, she graduated with honors.

At one point during her undergraduate career, Karen saw Peter Jennings, the anchor of *World News Tonight* on ABC, speak at a conference. "I remember it vividly," she recalls. "He said, 'You are the watchdogs of society. Whenever something happens, whether it's at the local school or at the White House, people depend on journalists to keep them informed about what's important in their lives.' Some people thought that was kind of clichéd, but I found it inspirational. Empowering."

After graduation, Karen landed an on-air job at a tiny station in Billings, Montana. "I wanted to cover any and all stories," she recalls, "but because I was ambitious and worked hard, I kept getting the top story to report every night, which was often hard news. By the time I realized I was constantly covering death and destruction, I was already hooked on the adrenaline rush."

Karen thrived on the intensity, sharpening her skills and developing an impressive reel full of hard-hitting pieces that kept carrying her to better jobs in larger markets.

But there was a cost. "I was living for my work," Karen recalls. "That wasn't hard, because I really did love it. I always filled in when somebody was out, always worked holidays. I worked 18 Christmases in a row! As a result, I seldom saw my family, didn't get married, never wanted to get that close to a man who could tie me down. And I wasn't doing it for the money. The jobs in these small markets pay under $25,000 a year. I just loved the work."

But there were also rewards: three regional Emmys, respect, wider exposure, more challenging opportunities. In the nineties, while working for a station in Salt Lake City, she became the first reporter in the world to be embedded with troops in Bosnia. "With the career I had built," she says, "I hoped it would help get me closer to my dream of landing a job at one of the networks and being a full-time foreign correspondent."

Then things began to turn. Karen joined another big-market station in Dallas. As she had done elsewhere, she volunteered to work on Christmas and was scheduled to anchor the broadcast. That's when she got a call from her father: Karen's beloved grandmother, long ill, had taken a turn for the worse and was near death.

"I told my supervisor that my grandmother was dying and that I needed to go," Karen recalls. "He said that I couldn't, that everyone else was gone. So I stayed and anchored the broadcast, and my grandmother died without my being able to say good-bye. It was then that I began to have doubts about my career. I'd already given so much to this profession, but look what I'd lost."

But she continued working and soon moved to a station in Phoenix, where she was assigned to be embedded with an Apache helicopter unit in Afghanistan. "One day I was doing a live-shot report," she recalls, "and a bomb exploded a couple hundred feet away. There was noise and chaos and ambulances. I was hustled into a bunker with a bunch of soldiers, and for two hours we hunkered down there while a loudspeaker kept blaring 'This is not a drill! The base is under direct attack. Mass casualties have been reported. This is not a drill!'"

Karen later learned that 26 people had been killed in the explosion. "People always ask me if I had been afraid of dying. I can honestly say I wasn't. All I could think about was 'Have I told everyone I love that I love them? Have I done all I can to make a difference? Am I happy?'"

Back in Phoenix, Karen finished a documentary she'd been working on and began preparing to return to Afghanistan, a promise she had made to the troops with whom she'd been embedded. Then she received some shocking news. The station had decided not to send her back. For several days, Karen vehemently appealed the decision, but the news director was adamant. "The decision is final," he said, "and there's nothing you can do about it."

Something inside Karen had reached its breaking point.

"Yes, there is," she answered calmly. "I quit."

Moments later, she called her mother, who didn't believe what she was hearing. "You quit your job?" she asked.

All at once, Karen began thinking of all the hours she had put in, the holidays she had missed, everything she had sacrificed—the husband, the kids, the life outside work.

"Not just my job, Mom," she said. "I quit my career."

But now she had to find something else to do. Karen remembered that when she was in the bunker, some of the soldiers got to talking about what they wanted to do when their tour was over. Visit family was a frequent answer. Take the wife to Hawaii. Take the kids to Disneyland. Karen was struck by how many of them wanted to travel, intuitively recognizing that in going somewhere new, they would be revived, restored, reinvigorated.

"For almost two decades as a reporter, I had been doing what Peter Jennings told us to do, which was to give people information that was important to their lives. I had focused on crime, scandal, war. But suppose a person needed to know how to restore her spirit, or recover her energy, or develop a more positive outlook on life? And that's when my idea of Travel Therapy was born."

Karen had given herself a new assignment. She would build a Travel Therapy Trips website and write a book that would help people inspire and empower themselves through travel.

It wasn't easy to make the transition. Karen's finances had taken a hit when she quit, but she felt she needed to take the plunge. "After I built the website, I sold my car and cashed in my 401k," she says. "Then I bought a one-way plane ticket and took a one-year lease on an apartment in New York City, where I knew almost no one. That's where I wrote my book, *Travel Therapy: Where Do You Need to Go?*, featuring trips to take based on whatever you're going through in life."

Using her skills as a reporter and a communicator, Karen tells her website audience about spas, resorts, beaches, and other destinations and activities.

"I'm not literally a therapist," she says, "and the closest I get to writing a prescription is when I say 'Take two vacations and call me in the morning.'"

What separates Karen from other travel reporters is that, while she's writing about adventure trips, family vacations, or romantic excursions, she maintains her focus on the things that help restore and maintain peace of mind.

And just as her audience is on a journey—both inward and outward—so, too, is Karen. "I'm different now," she says. "I make sure that I have more balance in my life. The truth is, to be good at my job, I had to become numb to the horrors I was covering. But the problem with going numb is that you can't decide when to turn it on and off. I found that I had become numb in my personal life, too.

"I want to feel joy, to experience beauty, to be in touch with my spirit. You know you're doing the right thing in the right place if it gives you the courage to go forward. I can't wait to see what's around the next corner."

PART FOUR

Body Works

*"There wasn't anything even remotely
appropriate to try on. . . . It made me
feel so bad about myself."*

Perfectly Suited

Robina Oliver, 53
Puerto Vallarta, Mexico

"My butt looks huge!"

"My thighs are so jiggly!"

"My boobs need a lift!"

Every day, Robina Oliver listens to women put down their bodies as they stare into the mirrors of her swimsuit shop. "It's really difficult to hear," she says, "because that used to be me."

Rewind to 2003. A size 16 Robina was vacationing with her husband in Puerto Vallarta, Mexico, browsing for a new swimsuit. Each one she pulled off the rack was skimpier than the last. A string bikini? Get serious. A one-piece with cutouts on the sides? Like *that's* gonna hide love handles. A crocheted thong bottom? Not on your life.

"There wasn't anything even remotely appropriate to try on," she says. "It started to get really depressing. It made me feel so bad about myself—even worse than I normally did."

Robina had struggled with weight her whole life. "I've always been big," she says. Growing up in Connecticut, she had a tumultuous home life. Her parents divorced when she was two, her dad moved to the Cayman Islands when she was nine, and her mom remarried, had two sons, then divorced again when Robina was 15. Robina sought comfort in eating. She'd binge on bologna, mayo, and white bread sandwiches, eating one, then another, then another. "It was a way to fill the void," she says. "Then, after food, I turned to other things."

Namely, men. "I was always looking for male approval and attention," she says. "If they liked me, that was enough, even if they were jerks. I was using them to escape."

At age 19, Robina wound up in Austin, Texas, following a guy she'd met while waiting tables back home. Soon after, she found out she was pregnant. "He didn't want children," she says, "and I just let myself go along with it. So there I was all by myself." Too far along for an abortion, she decided she'd put the baby up for adoption and, after giving birth six months later, held her little girl for only a few minutes before doctors took her away. "I never saw her again," Robina says. Refusing to let herself get emotional, she blocked out most of what happened that day. "It was the only way I could deal with it. I stuffed it all away. It was something I just needed to get through; I never really faced it."

Austin, with its lively nightlife, was an easy place not to face problems. Working as a waitress and hostess, Robina earned a reputation as a sassy, loud-mouthed party girl. "It was fun, but I was just drifting. I drank away my pain."

In 1989, Robina decided it was time for a change. She moved cross-country from Austin to San Francisco, where a year later she found work as a waitress at the city's hip Zuni Café. Six years after she landed the job, a new dishwasher arrived from Acapulco. His name was Carlos, and it wasn't long before he was smitten with Robina.

"He would follow me around like a puppy," she says, "begging in broken English, 'Give me a chance.'" Though she had sworn off men after moving to California, Robina says, "He wore me down." One date turned into moving in together after three months—and eventually into real love.

"He's very even-keeled, very calm," she says. "Again and again, he proved to me that he would always be there. I knew I could believe in him."

Most important, he loved her for exactly who she was, full figure included. "It was definitely easier to accept myself because he accepted me," she says.

They married in 2001. Carlos was now a runner and busboy at another upscale restaurant, but after more than 20 years, Robina was burned out on the business—and the drug- and alcohol-fueled lifestyle that went along with it. "We were working late nights, going out afterward, and then crashing into bed at six in the morning. It was a blast, but you get older and you're like, 'Now what?'"

The answer came during that 2003 vacation to Puerto Vallarta. Sitting at the pool after her disastrous swimsuit shopping excursion, Robina couldn't get the negative self-talk out of her head: *I'm so fat. I can't fit into anything.*

But then she started to look around her. "It was all these middle-aged women, some bigger than me," she says. "Carlos was lying next to me, and I said, 'What if all these women want to buy a bathing suit? It can't be just me.' Then, it was literally like, 'Bing! You know what they need here? A plus-size bathing suit shop!'" And Robina knew that *she* was the one to open it. She and Carlos could sell their condo and relocate to Puerto Vallarta year-round.

Carlos was skeptical. He'd moved from Mexico seeking opportunity in America, and he'd found it. "He envisioned us living in a shack, eating beans and rice." But Robina wouldn't let it die ("I'm really dogged when I get an idea"). She knew it would be the fresh start they needed. She told Carlos, "I need you to do this for me."

Eventually he relented, but he made her promise that they would come back if things didn't work out. That was Robina's green light. With their savings, she began buying hundreds of bathing suits in sizes 12 through 40, storing them in boxes around their apartment. And she came up with a name for her store: Curvas Peligrosas, meaning "dangerous curves," a reference to both her imagined full-figured clientele and the mountainous roads leading into Puerto Vallarta.

It took three years before Robina and Carlos were able to sell their San Francisco condo, but finally in 2006, they took off for Mexico in a Chevy pickup with a camper top, pulling a five-by-eight-foot trailer filled with bathing suits. What they didn't have: a real business plan. "I'm impulsive. I just said, 'I think we can make this work. Let's do it.'"

And they did—though "to say there were hiccups along the way is an understatement," Robina says. The biggest adjustment was settling into the slower pace in Mexico. "I'm very type A, so at first it was hard," Robina says. "*Mañana* means 'tomorrow' in Spanish but not in Mexico. Here, when a person tells you *mañana*, it could mean something will happen tomorrow, but it could also be the next week—or never. I had to learn to go with the flow."

It took a year to complete their many to-do lists, which started with finding a storefront (located not far from the very shop Robina visited on that first trip) that Carlos and a team of contractors remodeled. "They spackled, painted, fixed the ceiling, built dressing rooms, put in electrical and lighting," Robina says.

She had to learn to do business the Mexican way, which meant jumping through hoops to get permission to hang an awning over the shop (only to take it down a few months later when a new mayor banned them). Or standing in lines all around the city to pay the water, electric, or tax bills. "You can't just drop the bills in the mail with a stamp because they may or may not get there," she says. "And if they do, it could be who knows when?"

Carlos's fluent Spanish proved invaluable, and Robina made it a point to brush up on her language skills as well, particularly swimsuit vocab: *Queda apretado* ("Does it fit tight?") or *Tenemos de todas las tallas* ("We have all sizes").

In its first six years, Curvas more than doubled its sales, and it did even better during the busiest winter months. But Robina isn't focused on the dollars and cents—she shortens the store hours during the quiet summer months so she and Carlos can actually enjoy living in a vacation destination.

"We didn't come here to become millionaires," she says. "We came here to live."

And it's a beautiful life. The home they share with their two dachshunds has views of the mountains and a banana tree in the backyard. Carlos now works as a general contractor, managing crews that do everything from installing tile to building furniture, a business he came up with while remodeling the shop.

And for Robina, Mexico has been just the fresh start she wanted. Since moving there, she "just stopped" drinking and doing drugs. "It was about facing underlying causes," she says, including coping with her decades-old guilt over giving up her baby. "I always wondered where she was and thought about how she was growing up." So before moving to Mexico, Robina found her daughter, then 23, through the adoption agency and flew to meet her in Texas. "We both cried," says Robina, who was overwhelmed to see bits of herself in this young woman. "She has my freckles and she's built like me. We keep up online and get together whenever I travel to Texas."

With a marriage that's stronger than ever, a new relationship with her daughter, and a successful business, these days Robina says, "I'm the happiest I've ever been."

The shop has also turned into an embodiment of Robina's new self-embracing attitude, its Facebook page filled with jokes ("Calories—tiny creatures that live in your closet and sew your clothes a little bit tighter every

night") and inspiring quotes ("Confidence will make you happier than any diet ever will—so embrace your body").

"Now I'm the cheerleader, the positive one," Robina says. When she hears women complaining about how they look, she says, "Stop! Would you say that to your friend? Then don't say it to yourself!"

What makes Robina happiest are the women who appreciate their reflection in her shop's mirrors. One in particular stands out: This 19-year-old girl was a size 30, so Robina pulled out suits up to a 40. "She was beside herself that I even had suits in her size," and when she came out of the fitting room, she had a huge smile on her face. "Oh my God," she said. "This has never happened before. This suit is too big on me!"

Recalling that story, Robina chokes up. "It was the coolest thing in the world," she says. "When I have days like that, it reaffirms that everything I am doing is good."

Sex Sells

Sue Rhea, 71
Lebanon, Tennessee

When Sue Rhea throws a party, she always invites Bob. Several Bobs, in fact. The more Bobs, the better. Bob is *very* popular.

Bob, you see, stands for Battery Operated Boyfriend. He's a vibrator.

Through her 25-year-old company, Surprise Parties, Sue sells 25 different kinds—from small, beginner-sized models like the Mini-G (for "vibrator virgins") on up to the McDreamy, the Aquasaki, and the Lotus Flutter—"arousal for you, arousal for two, arousal for him," Sue says.

And that's not all that Sue sells. She also markets the Love Glove (for massages), Nude Body Shave, fur-lined "love cuffs" (in black or pink), "cock tail shakers," and Chocolate Pens ("write love notes on your sweetheart's body, then lick them off"). And she has made a fortune at it.

It was clear from early on that Sue had inherited the retail gene. "When I was little, our house was right off the bus line, so in the summer I would sit on our porch and sell Kool-Aid or homemade pot holders," says Sue, whose dad was a successful Ohio car dealer. "I was a go-getter. I wouldn't take no for an answer."

But Sue's precocious business skills took a detour when she was 18; she married, had two children within four years, and was divorced by 30. "I had to make a living," she says, and that often meant working two or three gigs at a time, from a $15-an-hour job as a receptionist at a busy Nashville medical practice to selling Avon products to running a dollar store out of a six-foot truck.

"I'd see these people with baskets of food they bought with food stamps, and I'd think, *That will never, ever be me.* I budgeted myself $12 a week for gas and food."

In fact, it wasn't until age 46, after Sue's two sons were grown and out of the house, that she had time to find her true calling. "I always felt there was something bigger and better out there for me," she says. "I'm not a big dreamer, but I wanted to have my own business."

It was her second husband, Joe, who came up with the perfect idea. "We were living in Mount Juliet, Tennessee, and he saw this television ad for adult stores," she says. "You know, windup penises, can toppers that looked like boobs."

They thought the items were funny—and, from her work in the medical office, Sue knew that women could really use a boost in the bedroom. "People have always opened up to me, and one of the things women like to talk about is sex—if they're getting some, any, or none," Sue says. "And I could tell many women didn't know A from Z about their bodies." Sue thought she could fill that niche.

After taking out a credit line on her house, she invested $4,000 ("a huge sum to me at the time") and filled her laundry room with 75 products, from arousal lotions to lingerie to "pants enhancers." Now all she had to do was sell them.

So she placed an ad in a local newspaper: "For women only. I bring all the products. An evening of fun and laughter in your own home."

"We have an expression around here: 'Funny is money,'" Sue says. "I have a very outgoing personality, and I've always loved making people laugh. We were in the middle of the Bible Belt, and I thought, *If I can get this started here, I can take it anywhere.*"

Sue's guests that first night were just regular working-class women, but there was no doubt that they wanted to buy what she was selling. "I wouldn't have made as much in a week at my receptionist job as I made in that one night." Thanks to that first party, Sue quickly booked a half dozen more.

Pretty soon, Sue was doing five to seven parties a week, often taking in $300 to $500 a pop. "The women didn't know how to ask their husbands to please them—or how to please their husbands," Sue says. "And they couldn't believe the products would work. But they were too embarrassed to go into an adult bookstore, so we were their only source.

"I had grown up in a house where there was no introduction to sex or sexuality," Sue says. "People just didn't talk about things then. So I wanted to help women remove that stigma. I'd bring articles from magazines to the parties that quoted ob-gyns. I wanted to give interesting, educational presentations where a woman could realize 'Oh, it's okay to have these feelings.'"

Most of all, Sue wanted to make sex fun: "It's a girls' night out: The women are getting together, having a glass of wine, letting their hair down."

Sue would get the party started by passing out "penis erasers," a perfect icebreaker for lending some levity to the proceedings. Then she'd announce: "Tonight we're going to be showing you beautiful lingerie and novelties, lotions and potions for licking, rubbing, smelling, and tasting. . . ."

She knew just how to hit the right notes. "I'd say, 'Hey, girls, you know when you're lying back and counting the dots on the ceiling and just waiting for something to happen, and the kids are banging on the door trying to get in? Well, it doesn't have to be that way.'"

Then she'd pass out her products: fishnet suspender panty hose, Guava-lava Body Mist ("to moisturize and invigorate"), flavored and unflavored lubricants, the Venus Butterfly (a "mega-powered partner ring that vibrates"), Nipple Nibblers, then forge onward to Ben-Wa Balls.

"I'd make a joke out of them," she says. She knew that most women were multitaskers, right? So, with the Ben-Wa Balls, Sue said, they could take care of business *and* get the laundry done. "I'd tell them to go down to the basement, close the door, get on that washing machine, and ride it till they were done."

For the first year and a half after launching Surprise Parties, Sue kept her day job, spreading her message at night and on weekends. But fairly quickly, she was able to expand the business, putting an addition on her house, then enclosing her two-car garage to make it into a warehouse. By 1991, she'd hired other women to do the parties (training them at seminars and through DVDs) and had grown enough to move the business out of the house. Sue's current warehouse is 20,000 square feet, and she has more than 1,300 reps selling her products in 42 states and Canada.

"Some people have said, 'You sell what? Oh my God!' But I say, 'God intended us to make love.'"

Since opening her business, Sue has passed on her message of sexual empowerment at parties in banks, hotels, apartment complexes, and church basements. "Everybody has sex, kiddo," she says. "What we're preaching is self-esteem, sensuality, and sexuality."

And Sue practices what she preaches. After her second husband, Joe, died in 2001, Sue agreed to a date with a former car dealership general manager named Dean. They're now married. "He's funny, he's caring, he has a good outlook on life, and he adores me," she says.

And what does husband number three think of her business?

"He *loves* it!" Sue says. "He likes to tell everybody that he works for the company in testing and product development."

Success for Dummies

Judi Henderson-Townsend, 55
Oakland, California

Hang out with a roomful of dummies, and you might just come up with a brilliant idea.

For Judi Henderson-Townsend, that epiphany came in 2001, when she was trying to locate a female mannequin to mosaic and display in her back garden as a symbol of fertility and Mother Earth.

"I know that sounds pretty California woo-woo," says Judi, who considers herself more practical than earthy. Still, it was something she had wanted to do for a long time. "I loved the idea."

An ad on Craigslist led Judi to an industrial neighborhood in San Francisco and a gritty warehouse filled with dozens upon dozens of mannequins of every size and shape, some of them missing arms, legs, heads, or torsos. "It was definitely creepy," Judi recalls. The mannequins' owner told Judi she was lucky to have found him when she did, because he was about to close his business and move to New England. That would leave the Bay Area without a place to rent or buy a mannequin.

Standing there surrounded by naked dummies in various states of dismemberment, Judi made the impulsive decision to go for something, well, completely different. "It was a *ding-ding-ding* moment," she recalls.

Judi started peppering the mannequin man with questions about his business and clientele. Before long, she was asking if he would sell her the entire lot, along with his customer list. Sure, he said. "If I didn't buy them, he was going to try to sell them off one by one," she says. "And those that didn't sell would end up in a landfill."

They agreed on a price of $2,500 ("If he'd said $5,000, I wouldn't have done it"), but Judi had to move quickly, as he was leaving within the week.

At first glance, starting her own business didn't make much sense. After graduating from college, she'd mostly played it safe, climbing various corporate ladders as a sales executive at big companies like Johnson & Johnson and United Airlines, and she now worked for a dotcom start-up. Judi was also haunted by her one and only attempt at entrepreneurship: In her thirties, she had tried to start her own business as an agent for photographers and illustrators. She had failed—miserably—and the experience had damaged her financially while also sapping her self-confidence.

"I worried that this might be history repeating itself," she says.

And *mannequins*? "If I'd had time to think about it, I probably would have talked myself out of it," she says.

But Judi held out hope that this time she could make her own business work. Within a few hours of her close encounter with the mannequins, she had buy-in from her husband, Jay, and a few days later, all 50 torsos showed up at their front door.

From a practical standpoint, the timing was good. Because the couple had just refinished their floors, Judi and Jay had removed all the furniture from their living room, and that's where the mannequins took up residence. "That was key," Judi says.

Also, she had recently taken a 14-week class in entrepreneurship, and felt more prepared to start a business than she ever had.

"I was ready," she says. "Whether it's mannequins or widgets, many of the same business principles are at work, like managing cash flow, marketing, finances, and inventory. All of that is important no matter what you're selling."

Choosing a name for her venture was among the easiest early tasks. Once she discovered that the domain name for her first choice, Mannequin Magic, wasn't available, Mannequin Madness quickly popped into her head. "It was perfect," she says. "Either I was a little crazy or this was a crazy niche, but the name worked either way."

Judi's first setback came when the man she bought the mannequins from failed to follow through on his promise to send her his client list, which meant she had to generate business from scratch—and in the visual merchandising industry, no less, in which she had no experience.

So Judi started cold calling—tirelessly. She spent weekends driving around the Bay Area, leaving her card at Macy's, Nordstrom, Sears, and other department store chains. If people came in asking where to acquire a mannequin, she said, send them my way.

Around the same time, Judi built a website for the business. This, too, turned out to be crucial. "I got a call from someone in Canada who had seen the website and was coming to San Francisco for a ski trade show and needed to rent a mannequin. That was a big 'aha' moment for me. I thought my customers would all be local, but now I realized I'd been thinking too small!"

Business began to take off as Judi rented out the mannequins or resold

them to smaller stores, dressmakers, and hobbyists. Then, in late 2001, the dot-com she was working for went under.

"That made me do some real soul-searching," she says. So instead of looking for another conventional job, Judi decided to go into the mannequin business full-time.

The national trend toward recycling helped. Unless a mannequin gets re-used or recycled, retailers toss them out as they get damaged, or as trends change, which shortens a mannequin's life to as little as two years. The general shape, of course, doesn't change—it is always young, tall, and thin. But one year, heads might be in vogue, while the next, heads come off.

"I couldn't stand that these beautiful mannequins were ending up in landfills," she says.

Within six months, Judi's inventory had ballooned from 50 to 500, after a merchandiser from Sears who had held on to Judi's card called to say the chain was getting rid of all its mannequins. If Judi could haul them away from the dozen or so Sears in northern California, he said, they were hers to keep.

"Jay and I cleared out the entire basement and turned it into a mannequin warehouse," she says. Word spread that Judi had become the go-to gal for mannequins past their prime, and soon more companies—Nike, Nordstrom, Ralph Lauren, and Bloomingdale's—were offering their stock. The garage grew engorged with mannequins, and there still wasn't enough space. So Judi and Jay pitched tents for the overflow in the backyard. And when the shipment from Nike arrived in coffin-shaped boxes, the neighbors looked on with amusement.

In 2007, Mannequin Madness moved to a 1,300-square-foot warehouse in Oakland. Two years later, Jay was laid off from his job at a nonprofit and joined Judi full-time. Now they sell mannequins, rent mannequins, broker mannequins, repair mannequins, blog about mannequins, and even deliver them. "We're the FTD of mannequins," Judi says with a laugh. Annual revenues for the company are just shy of their goal of $1 million. "Every year, we get closer," she says.

When Judi tells people what she does for a living, she gets her share of raised eyebrows and outright laughter. But she has learned to take it all in stride.

"I couldn't have done this in my twenties," she says. "When I was younger, I needed the validation of a big company. Now I'm happy to talk about my mannequins. I'm here to show that everything is possible."

As for that garden art project, she never did get around to it. She got too busy.

Going Commando

Kerry O'Brien, 43
South Burlington, Vermont

Wherever Kerry O'Brien goes, there she is, checking out other women's bodies. "I notice every pinching panty line or suffocating bra strap," Kerry says. And when she spots a problem, as she invariably does—muffin hips, pooch-y waists, droopy bottoms—it makes her smile. "It reassures me that my company is on the right track."

Kerry founded her company, cheekily named Commando, in 2003 out of a belief that what lies beneath—seamless, body-smoothing undies and tanks—is what makes whatever is on the outside *truly* ogle-worthy.

Turning lumpy into luscious is a talent that has always come naturally to Kerry. "When my friends and I were single and in our twenties in New York, we all wanted to wear these cute fashions, but often they were made of unlined fabrics or had odd necklines," she says. "If you wore just any old bra and panties with them, they would completely ruin the look, not to mention make you feel self-conscious and uncomfortable."

Kerry couldn't stand that feeling—the awkward, distracting sensation of panty elastic digging into her skin, hose slip-sliding down her legs, a bra that felt like a boa constrictor wrapped around her chest. "I'm not actually obsessed with underwear," she says. "I'm obsessed with *comfort*. When underwear would dig into me, it made me feel bad about myself, even if I was in good shape. It could ruin my whole day."

So whether dressing herself or playing stylist for a friend, Kerry became a MacGyver of undergarments, using any and all tools at her disposal. "I would hand-stitch a bra into a strapless dress, make a friend wear a swimsuit under a low-backed top, use double-sided tape to affix straps in place. I even applied duct tape to my skin—I wouldn't necessarily recommend it, but it worked pretty well!"

Duct tape? That ugly, gummy stuff favored by furnace repairmen? Yup. As Kerry says, "My favorite place to look for style solutions used to be the hardware store."

And Kerry's innate problem-solving ability was just as effective in the boardroom: By age 28, it had catapulted her to senior VP at one of the biggest financial P.R. companies in the world, doing media relations for Fortune 500 companies. "After college, I sprinted to excel in my career, and I did very well," she says, "but I started to burn out. By the time I was 30, I wasn't excited about my work anymore. I didn't want my boss's job or my boss's boss's job."

Then came September 11. Kerry and her husband were living in downtown Manhattan when the planes hit, and she knew she'd never be the same again. "I needed a change, and there was no reason to wait." On September 12, she quit her job.

"Everyone said, 'Give it some time, Kerry, don't do this now,'" she recalls. "But I wasn't going to change my mind, and I wasn't worried. I've always thought that if you're really good at one thing, you can be just as good at something else.

"I'd always wanted to be an entrepreneur. When I was a kid in Vermont, my dad helped my sisters and me start a lawn-mowing business. I also had my own enterprise: picking corn from my family's field, then selling it at a stand, ten ears for a dollar."

Kerry's first idea after quitting her job—writing a short advice book on getting over breakups called *Hit the Road, Jack*—went nowhere. She intended her next book idea—*Rack Management 101: What Every Woman Needs to Know about Bras, Chicken, and Duct Tape*—to be a primer on, among other things, clever undergarment solutions. But a few chapters in, she thought, *Why am I writing about this? I should start my own underwear company!* If someone can build a better mousetrap, she thought, I can build a better pair of panties.

Kerry already had a ready-made focus group: her friends. "I'd call them up and invite them over for dinner, but only if they would bring three ideas on a certain lingerie topic," she says. "And like me, they had *a lot* to say about how our panties, bras, and hose were failing us."

Kerry wanted to launch her new business with something simple that wouldn't require a huge investment. "I'm not a big gambler," she says. "Everything I did, I did in a measured way. I never took any big financial risks."

Her first idea was bra inserts—soft pouches that could instantly turn an A cup into a B or even a C. But she wanted them to be pretty, even sassy—nothing like the sad-looking "chicken cutlets" that lingerie departments kept hidden behind their counters. "I wanted to call my inserts Takeouts—and, for fun, I came up with the idea of putting them in a pink cardboard Chinese food take-out container," she recalls.

"I had a prototype made by a company that manufactures silicone breast implants, worked with a graphic designer to create a logo, and went to Kinko's to print out and assemble my first and only take-out carton.

"When I took one look at that prototype, my toes tingled. It's this euphoric sensation I have always gotten when the right combination of factors come together and I know something is going to be great."

Those tingling toes were right. When Kerry, by now six months pregnant with her first son, waddled into the president's office at the posh New York

department store Henri Bendel ("I had called a friend of a friend of a friend and managed to get the meeting") and put the falsies in the take-out carton on his desk, he howled.

"'I love it!' he said, and placed an order on the spot. I thought, *Oh my God, this is exciting!*"

With just a few months until her due date, Kerry recalls, "I quickly flew to the West Coast with my husband, and he drove me to all the hip boutiques I could find from San Francisco to L.A. I would show up unannounced, holding my tiny Chinese take-out container, and ask to speak to the manager." The buyers all loved it.

In between stops, Kerry frantically made calls trying to nail down packaging, distribution—and details like how to get a UPC code. "It was hard, but I just made one phone call after another until I found people who knew how to get stuff done."

Then a lucky break: Soon after Takeouts debuted at Bendel's, Kerry got a call from a wardrobe stylist on the film *The Stepford Wives*. "They needed us to FedEx dozens of Takeouts to the cast. A week later, they needed dozens more." With her background in P.R., Kerry immediately recognized a golden marketing opportunity. "I called *People* magazine, told them what had happened, and they did a little write-up about it. After that, orders started pouring in."

With a budding business and a baby on the way, Kerry and her husband moved to South Burlington, Vermont, where Kerry had grown up and where most of her family still lived. "My husband, who's a banker, wasn't working at the time," she says. "We figured we could move back to New York any time. But the next thing I knew, things were taking off, and he and I were working together to make a go of the business in Vermont."

And that meant expanding their offerings. Soon Takeouts were joined by Low Beams, little adhesive nipple cover-ups. Now Kerry was ready to tackle the all-time peskiest underwear problem: visible panty lines.

Why, Kerry wondered, did panties have to have ugly seams and elastic trim? "Every manufacturer I called told me that fabric would unravel if I didn't have them, but I refused to accept that. Even though I didn't have a technical background, I felt sure there was a way to cut the right fabric in such a way that it would hold together. I was bumped from one expert to another to another. And I didn't stop until I found what I wanted."

And that was a way to make a thong with no waistband, no trim, nothing but soft, stretchy, comfy microfiber that laid perfectly flat against the skin and seemed to disappear beneath clothes. Kerry dubbed her panty Commando, with the slogan "Better Than Nothing," and introduced it to the marketplace—and the tiny, barely-there undies proved to be another big hit.

Kerry and her husband began scrambling to expand their enterprise: find an office-warehouse, file for patents, manage delivery schedules, and hire staff. It was all new to them, but they just hammered away at their never-ending to-do list. "We decided to do as much as we could right in South Burlington, from quality assurance to distribution, even some manufacturing. We now work in the same building where forklifts move around boxes of bras and underwear, and it's just a mile and a half away from the house I grew up in."

Being in her hometown has set the tone for how Kerry does business. "I don't want to work myself into the same burnout situation that I did before," she says. "We appreciate the quality of life here. There's no reason to put unnecessary stress on everyone by insisting the company grow at triple digits." Yes, she takes emails and calls around the clock, but she still manages to get home by 3:30 p.m. four days a week to be there when her son, now ten, and her twin daughters, five, get back from school.

Kerry's company continues to grow at a steady pace. The original Commando thong spawned panties, boy shorts, high-rise briefs, camis, tanks, bras, slips, shapewear, hosiery, and reversible swimwear, all designed with ultra-comfy, invisible edging.

Commando products are now sold in 1,000 stores and boutiques across the country, including Bergdorf Goodman, Neiman Marcus, Saks, Nordstrom, and Bloomingdale's. "A year ago, I became one of the few lingerie designers invited to be part of the Council of Fashion Designers of America," says Kerry. "That's unbelievable considering I didn't go to school for fashion design. When I got the call, I cried.

"Today, when I walk into a store and see a woman looking at Commando products, I walk up to her and tell her I own the company and I'd love to help her find the perfect underwear. I just can't help it."

There's the Rub

Carol Oswald, 59
Gahanna, Ohio

"What would you do if you won the lottery?"

When that question would come up around the watercooler at work, IBM manager Carol Oswald always had a ready reply. "I'd open a massage parlor!" she'd say, drawing out the word "paaaaahlor" to give it a bawdiness that made her coworkers laugh.

Truth was, Carol had understood the healing power of massage from an early age. Her older brother contracted polio as a young child, leaving his legs so weak that he needed braces and crutches to walk. As a teenager laid up in bed after one of his many surgeries, he'd ask Carol to rub his back the way the nurses in the hospital had. Carol, who adored her big brother and was proud of how accomplished he was despite all he'd been through, happily obliged. "I wanted to help make his life easier in any way I could," she says. "I think I always had a caregiver side to me."

Carol took that hands-on approach with her to Wittenberg University in

Springfield, Ohio, where she became the go-to girl on her dorm floor for any-one who needed a neck rub after a marathon study session. Freshman year, a friend even hung a plaque on Carol's door that read "Madame Sophie's Mas-sage Parlor."

But that wasn't her only talent: Carol was also a math whiz. So she was thrilled when, the Monday after graduation, she was able to turn her mathe-matical prowess into a position at IBM.

"The day I got the job offer was so exciting for both my mom and me," she says. Her mother had been a huge fan of the company ever since she'd worked as a white-gloved "systems support girl" in its Lansing, Michigan, office in the 1940s, giving up her job only because of an IBM policy favoring returning World War II veterans.

Like her mom, Carol fell in love with Big Blue, learning the business inside out, from parsing the technicalities of how its computer systems worked, to helping clients figure out what hardware and software they needed, to helping them install it. "That was part of what I liked about working for IBM: learning about a lot of different things," she says. "And I felt respected, supported, and challenged by both management and my coworkers. It was like a family."

But then in 2001, things at IBM took a bad turn, and for the first time, Carol, who'd always prided herself on her problem-solving and communica-tion skills, had a sales quota.

"I was supposed to be calling on customers and closing business. It was not my strike zone. I didn't enjoy sales because there's lot of rejection. You have to be built of Teflon."

IBM also began thinning its ranks, and as a manager, Carol was often the one delivering the grim news to fellow employees. Then, in October, she got a new list of people who were to be offered buyout packages. This time, Carol's name was on the list. "I felt like I'd been punched in the gut," she says.

She was only 46, six months shy of her twenty-fifth anniversary at the only company she'd ever worked for. IBM made a big deal out of its quarter-century employees, honoring them with a special luncheon. "I had done several of the lunches for other people, and I was looking forward to my own. I loved the company; it meant a lot to me." But now, it seemed, there would be no twenty-fifth anniversary for Carol—only anxiety over her next move.

She did the math. If she took the package IBM was offering, she and her husband, Denny, who was ten years older and a retired computer programmer, had enough saved for Carol to take a year to figure out her next move. Or she could stay at IBM and take a job in a different department.

"I looked at those positions, but it felt like jumping from the frying pan into the fire. Like, 'You thought *your* job was stressful? Try this one on for size!'"

The last thing she needed was more stress; she wasn't taking care of herself as it was. "I was eating at my desk or in the car when I was running late for a customer meeting. And I'd often stop for sandwiches from a fast-food place to eat at eight or nine at night. I also wasn't getting out to exercise. Sure, I'd squeeze in a yoga class every once in a while, but work took priority."

Slowly, the idea of massage crept into the back of her mind. Though Carol loved getting professional massages, she treated herself only every six months or so. But every time, she'd end up quizzing the masseuse: How did you get started? What classes did you take? How did you get licensed? One masseuse told Carol she worked in IBM's marketing department. "I nearly fell off the table," she recalls. "She said she went to school at night and was working at the massage clinic on weekends. That was inspiring."

Denny inspired Carol, too. His hobby of tinkering with old bicycles had morphed into a small bike repair shop in their garage. "He was doing something he was so passionate and happy about. I wanted to have that kind of feeling myself."

So Carol made the leap and took the buyout. "I thought, *This is exactly what you've been waiting for.* Sometimes life conspires to say, 'If you're not going to go do this yourself, I'm going to give you a boot and *get* you to do it.' "

Feeling that boot on her own backside, Carol enrolled in a one-year program to become licensed as a massage therapist. "And once I started school, studying massage techniques, anatomy, and physiology, I knew I was where I belonged. I was on the edge of my seat, soaking it all up."

Going from cold computers to warm bodies might seem like a 180-degree turn, but the two fields turned out to be more similar than Carol had ever imagined. For instance, to computerize medical records in her old job, she first had to understand the process—how papers moved from the admissions desk to the doctor's office to the radiology department to the lab—before she could figure out how to make everything flow smoothly on a computer.

"What I discovered is that our bodies have processes, too," she says. "If you understand them, you can follow the chain of symptoms back to the root cause." Take stress. Scrunched-up shoulders lead to a tighter neck, which leads to a headache, and so on. "Once you know physiologically what is happening in someone's body, then you can deal with it," she says. "It's in your control. It's a freeing feeling to say, 'I *can* do something about this.' "

Carol also found that, after spending her entire career in one industry where she was supposed to know all the answers, it was liberating to be able to ask her instructors as many questions as she liked without feeling stupid. "I could explore and be curious. It was invigorating."

But here was the clincher: At a party one night, she overheard a friend ask Denny, "How is Carol's new venture working out?" Denny replied: "I haven't heard her laugh this much in years."

"That made me tear up and think, 'Oh my God, what kind of grouch have

I been?' It was such a pure acknowledgment that I'd made the right decision for me *and* for him."

In 2003, Carol opened a massage clinic called A Quiet Space with a woman she'd met in class, a former accountant who'd needed to get professional massages to make it through tax season every year. And Carol began making house calls to businesses to give chair massages to stressed-out employees. "I could completely relate to that kind of tension," she says. "I had lived that life."

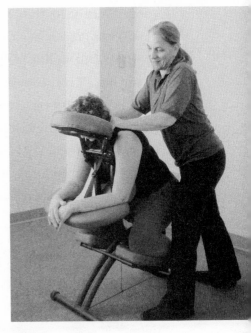

The house calls business took off, so in 2011 Carol decided to close the clinic to focus on corporate massage. She loved the freedom of it—a far cry from being stuck in an office all day. Toting a massage chair and new-age CDs in the trunk of her car, she makes regular visits to companies large and small. One might hire her to reward employees at the end of a big project; another might invite her to set up shop in its conference room, dimming the lights and unplugging the phones so employees can get ten-minute stress-busting sessions; she also works in doctor's offices, treating nurses to half-hour decompression sessions.

And she logs in fewer hours than she once did. She's earning only a fifth of her IBM salary, but she and Denny don't miss the extra cash. "We both drive cars that are more than ten years old and live well within our means as far as our home and travel," she says. "We find we don't want or need much 'stuff' anymore."

Instead, she considers herself rich with time to do things she enjoys. "I am volunteering, exercising, visiting friends and family, serving more home-cooked meals. As they might say in that commercial, 'Lower income in exchange for greater health and happiness . . . priceless!'"

Best of all, unlike her IBM clients, her current customers are always happy to see her. "I come walking in the door and they say, 'Oh, Carol's here! It's massage day!' It's very rewarding."

Sometimes when a customer first sits down in Carol's chair, it's like looking at her old self: cold hands, a sign of poor circulation, or fists clenched in anger or frustration. As soon as she places her hands on their shoulders, she can tell how bad their day has really been. "Sometimes their muscles are as hard as rocks."

If they're quiet, she stays quiet. If they start venting—"My husband really irked me today!" "I'm having a hard time with my mom." "My boss is driving me crazy!"—she lends a sympathetic ear. "People open up quite a bit. Just by listening and saying 'I had a similar experience and it worked out' helps them."

As Carol kneads their shoulders, their breathing slows and their muscles soften. "When they walk out of my massage, they know they can handle anything. And I love knowing that I am helping to relieve people's pain, just as I did with my brother all those years ago."

PART FIVE

Relentless

"I have never given up. You get knocked down, you get stepped on, you get up, you brush yourself off, and you keep going."

Changing the Pattern

Sue Rock, 51
Brooklyn, New York

When Sue Rock opened the door to her apartment building that afternoon, she was stunned. Staring at her from a funeral notice posted on the glass was the face of Tyleasha, a woman she knew from the neighborhood.

She couldn't believe it—she'd just seen Tyleasha a few weeks before. Shocked, she rushed over the next day to see Tyleasha's mom to offer her condolences. The grieving mother hugged Sue and whispered in her ear, "Her husband did it. He took himself, too."

"My blood turned to ice," Sue recalls.

Then Sue began reading news accounts of the killing. The week before her murder, Tyleasha had applied for a protection-from-abuse order, telling the police that her husband had beaten her, choked her, and threatened her with a knife—all in front of her children. Eight hours after the judge granted the order, neighbors reported seeing a man dragging a woman into the house during a violent argument. Tyleasha's husband stabbed her more than a dozen times, then called her mother to say, "I just killed your daughter," and, as security guards approached the house, shot himself in the head. Tyleasha's nine-year-old daughter answered the door.

Tyleasha's death haunted Sue for months, coming at a time when she was just recovering from her own family tragedy: Three years earlier, during his college spring break, her 18-year-old son had ended up in the hospital with end-stage liver failure. He died three days before his nineteenth birthday.

"It was horrifying," Sue says. "I knew I could either grieve for my son and never come back, or try to find a way to live a life without him. It took me three years."

Then Tyleasha's death. "It gave me a sense of urgency. I, too, could be gone at any moment, so any good I could do with my life, I wanted to do it."

Memories of Tyleasha came flooding back, only now Sue saw them in a new, grimmer light. "I began to remember pieces of the times I had seen Tyleasha. Late at night just arriving at her mom's. *Was she running away from her home?* In sweats. *Was that all she was able to leave with?* And I hadn't seen her in a while. *She must have gone back to him.*"

The shocking murder had awakened her to a somber reality: Women escaping domestic violence flee with only the clothes on their back. *How brave they are,* Sue thought. *But how do they even begin to start a new life?*

An idea began to percolate. *The first thing they need is clothes,* Sue thought. *Maybe this is the good I can do in the world.*

And Sue knew about clothes. She had grown up knitting and crocheting, and her husband, Jerome ("Rock"), was a trained tailor. For a year, they had been collecting fabric and other sewing treasures that were literally being given away.

"The garment industry in New York City was in sharp decline," Sue explains, "and free fabric began to flood the market." And not just any fabric: Sue and Rock gathered cotton jersey, silk charmeuse, even leather, rescuing the precious materials before they went into the garbage.

They had been brainstorming about how to put the fabric to use. Jobs were hard to come by in the hospitality industry, where Rock had been working as a sous chef. So with a daughter and young son still at home, they got creative about how to use their talents to make money.

The couple came up with a plan: Sue would continue her nine-to-five job to make ends meet, while Rock would use the reclaimed fabrics to make easy-to-wear women's clothes. They'd call their small clothing line Sue Rock Originals and try to sell them to boutiques and online.

But with Tyleasha's murder, and their business plan in place, they decided that in addition to creating a contemporary eco-fashion line, they would also launch a clothing charity for women who were victims of domestic abuse.

"The idea was to find hundreds of regular folks like me—volunteers who knew how to sew, knit, weave, and crochet—and provide them the materials to make clothing for people in need." The more she thought about the concept, the deeper the connection she felt to the women who would be wearing her clothing.

Sue researched her idea online and was shocked to discover how desperately her charity was needed. Crafters were already supplying preemies with caps, the homeless with scarves, and dogs and cats with fluffy beds. But nothing for women!

Sue and Rock decided that their charity would be funded in part by the clothing line. They would also change the name of the charitable arm to Sue Rock Originals Everyone Inc.—signifying that *everyone* in the community could participate, using their hands, not just their wallets, to make a difference.

Sue began advising her team of volunteers on what kinds of items women in shelters could use, like tank tops or hoodies.

"I felt inspired by how effortless it was," Sue says. "Nobody said no. Fabric samples began pouring in from places like Liz Claiborne, Marc Jacobs, and Van Heusen. Everyone wanted to help. One day my husband even found a sewing machine by the door. And when we would hand out pieces to the women at the domestic violence residences, they were overwhelmed. It was a delicious, life-affirming sensation."

Having started out with three local shelters, Sue's outreach quickly grew to ten more shelters, along with another half-dozen national and international agencies that distributed the goods they made to women in need everywhere.

"Once we got started, we were on a roll," Sue says. "We are get-to-work kinds of folks."

Sue moved her headquarters from her cramped hallway to a 1,200-square-foot studio filled with 45 sewing machines. And she created a three-month program to train domestic violence victims, so they, too, could craft their own possessions. "When a new woman would come to the program," says Sue, "I'd ask, 'Do you want to make a leather coat to go with your wool slacks?' And that would empower her. A woman who has done something as extraordinary and courageous as starting a new life deserves that kind of empowerment."

Transforming the lives of others has transformed Sue, too. "I have created this new person in me who is vital and feels a sense of urgency toward what's good in life. I'm making it up as I go along, but I'm doing it fearlessly."

Laura's Yarn

Laura Zander, 39
Reno, Nevada

Call it pluck. Call it enterprise. Or call it desperation. But when Laura Zander was six years old and living with a single mom chronically strapped for money, she was determined to get an allowance any way she could. So she went door to door in their large apartment building in Raleigh, North Carolina, asking residents if there was a chore she might do in exchange for pay. For 25 cents, she would vacuum, do their dishes—or just keep them company while they watched TV.

So disarming was this small child's request that people invariably took her up on her offer. To Laura's young mind, she was raking it in. She hoarded her earnings, spending only a little, very occasionally, on candy.

Laura always knew how to take care of herself. When she attended North Carolina State, she paid her tuition by waiting tables and doing dorm security. After a year, she transferred to Sam Houston State in Huntsville, Texas, thanks to an academic scholarship and tuition help from her grandfather. She earned her bachelor's degree in criminal justice, then a master's in political science from Washington State.

While working on a PhD in criminology at Penn State, Laura grew restless in grad school and curious about the riches she heard were being made in Silicon Valley, so in 1997 she moved west to join the Internet boom. Her first job was as a technical writer, but she gradually honed her programming skills until she became a software engineer.

It was in that first job that she met her husband, Doug, also a programmer. When they married in 2000, they were both working at midsized start-ups, Doug leading the entire software division of one, Laura progressing her way up the ladder of another. "We were working on some really exciting stuff, but the companies weren't doing very well," she says. "We worried every day that we were going to go out of business." Then, in late 2000, Pets.com, one of the darlings of the dotcom era, went under. "When that happened, we thought, *This Internet stuff is never going to work,*" Laura says. "There were Pets.com ads and billboards all over the place, but even *that* wasn't a sure thing."

Laura and Doug reassessed their lives. Both still had jobs, but they decided to make a preemptive move to downscale their lives. As it happened, they had recently bought a house in Truckee, a small town just west of Lake Tahoe. "I thought, *Well, I guess we could move there,*" Laura says. And they did.

But how to earn a living in a town of 16,000? "You need to figure out what a small town needs," Laura says. It was then that she regretted not having chosen medicine, law, dentistry, or another profession that lends daily infrastructure to a community.

Doug got a job in Sacramento as a software engineer, which meant a three-hour round-trip commute. Laura decided to make a go of it building high-end websites for local businesses. But she quickly discovered she had completely misjudged the market. "People move to Truckee to get *out* of the rat race," she says. "They're not looking for someone to build them a $10,000 or $20,000 website." Still, Laura tried everything. She even channeled her six-year-old self and started knocking on doors—with considerably less success. She signed up only two clients.

With time on her hands, Laura took up knitting. She knitted sweaters, then more sweaters, before switching to socks—dozens of pairs of socks. She'd have knitted still more but the closest yarn store was 40 miles away in Reno.

One of Laura's two clients was Lorna Miser, who hand-dyed yarn. They became fast friends, and Lorna persuaded Laura to open her own yarn shop in Truckee. "Doug was keeping us afloat, but I was a little aimless. So I thought, 'I might as well create a job that I'll be happy to go to every day, and if I make $50,000 a year, that would be awesome.'"

Laura and Doug decided to sink their entire savings of $30,000 into opening a 500-square-foot yarn and gourmet coffee store on Truckee's main drag. As it happened, Laura's other client built espresso carts, and the two set up a barter arrangement: Website work in exchange for a deep discount on a cart. Laura and Doug installed the cart inside the little store and named the business Jimmy Beans Wool. ("Jimmy" is Doug's nickname for Laura, after a character in one of their favorite Tom Snider songs; and beans and wool were the shop's signature merchandise.) Two years later, they started a second shop in Reno.

"I didn't have a board of advisers helping me build a brand. Not everyone is lucky enough to have millions in venture capital or a team of experts," Laura says. "But even if you don't have that, it doesn't mean you won't succeed."

The business did well from the start, thanks to a few lucky breaks. First, Lorna, who was closing her own business, sold her inventory of yarn to Laura at a rock-bottom price. Then fashion entered a scarf craze, and demand for yarn skyrocketed. "That was a real boon for us," Laura says.

The next piece to fall into place was online retailing, which was beginning to take off. Because Truckee attracted a lot of out-of-town visitors, "people would come into the shop and spend $100, then go home and spend another $400 online."

Without a dime going to advertising—word simply spread from one happy knitter to the next—within five years Jimmy Beans Wool had reached $1 million in sales. Once that milestone was achieved, Laura and Doug started working on building a brand around their quirky name. As a model, they studied online shoe retailer Zappos.com, with its strong focus on customer service.

Little did Laura suspect when she first opened Jimmy Beans Wool that the Internet, the very thing that had failed to come through for her twice before, would propel the company much further. Knitting can get very complicated very quickly, with difficult patterns to follow, so in 2008, Laura and Doug started making instructional videos and posting them on YouTube. The videos showed customers how to do everything from choosing needles to selecting the right wool for a specific project. Within a few months, sales had increased nearly 70 percent. Since then, the company's revenues have grown to more than $8 million a year. It now has 45 employees, occupies a 20,000-square-foot base of operations, and boasts a following of loyal customers around the world. And JimmyBeansWool.com carries some 2,000 videos, with 1.5 million views.

"This is just the beginning," Laura says. "It's so exciting to see what we have built. We plan to continue growing and growing."

And it's all because of her willingness to pursue a Plan C after Plans A and B failed that Laura Zander landed where she is today.

Luck of the Straw

Dianne Wood, 64

Danville, Virginia

Dianne Wood was always a creative type. When she was a child, friends who'd come over to her house expecting to watch TV or listen to records were quickly presented with a different option. "Let's make something!" Dianne would say, and soon the scissors would be out, or the crayons, or the MixMaster, and they'd be off, baking cupcakes and fashioning pinecones into a holiday decoration for the door. There was hardly a scrap of material or cloth or cardboard that Dianne couldn't turn into something fun and clever.

At least, not until the day she received a notice that her house had been repossessed. That's a hard one, making something from an eviction notice.

That blow, as devastating as it was unexpected, came in 2002, at a point in life when Dianne felt happy and secure. She had a lovely home in Danville, Virginia, her kids were grown, her business was strong. "I felt that I had made it," she says. "My husband and I had worked hard, and we were entering that period of our lives when we expected to reap the rewards of our efforts."

And for Dianne, those entrepreunerial efforts had played out like a string of scenes in a screwball comedy:

In the eighties, it was bunny pillows and ruffled curtains. The pillows were popular at local bazaars, but certainly nothing to live on. The curtains were a huge hit, "but they took me forever to make on my little itty-bitty sewing machine. So we opened a small workshop on my dad's farm and brought in commercial machines and sewers, but after ten years, I was burned out. I felt like I was stuck in home furnishings, and it wasn't where I wanted to be."

Then came women's and children's clothing. "The 'country look' had suddenly become popular, so I made jumpers out of denim and corduroy, and jackets with appliqués." Thanks to her popularity at trade shows, Dianne soon became overwhelmed with orders as Dillard's and other department stores clamored for her clothing line. The business was so successful that her husband, Bill, who had been a manager at a local mill, was pulled in to help. Then, the bad news: "The clothing industry moved to China," she says, "the mills shut down and it got harder to find the material we needed. But it was probably for the best: We'd been at it for 14 years, tastes were changing and we weren't selling as much."

Scrapbooking, Dianne's next hill to take, seemed encouraging. And manufacturers were certainly impressed with the line of die cuts and stickers she created. Only problem was, they never ponied up a check or closed a deal with her. Then the apparel catalog she and Bill had been trying to get off the ground met a similarly fizzled fate. "The fabrics we ordered didn't come through, the designs I created weren't put into production. So there went that idea."

Eventually, the calamities took a crushing financial toll. Dianne and Bill had borrowed $250,000 to underwrite their new ventures, using their house as collateral.

That's when that eviction notice reared its head. "The banker had promised me that he'd never take our home," Dianne says. "He *swore*. Then he did. What's worse, he didn't even tell us that we were being repossessed—I just saw the notice in the newspaper. Our business was worthless and our home was gone. It was the most devastating time of our life."

The Woods' options came down to few and none. "Bill took a job selling cars," Dianne recalls. "It paid terribly, but it put food on the table. It got us by." Their accommodations were equally bleak: the former workshop building on her father's farm. "It had a toilet but no hot water, no kitchen sink. We cleared out space for ourselves, put up a wall just to give us the illusion of rooms, and got a shower, sink, and hot water installed."

But for all the blows she'd taken, Dianne refused to be knocked down. "I wasn't looking for a dream or a success story," she says. "I just needed to make a living so someday we would be able to purchase a home again."

She started slowly. Focusing on gourmet foods, Dianne launched a meal delivery service, cooking the meals herself. That helped with the cash flow and, more important, bought her some time. Then she came up with an idea that felt like a hit: the Cocoa Cone, hot chocolate powder pressed into the shape of a cone that, when dropped into hot water, dissolved into hot chocolate. Another company had invented it, but it wasn't going anywhere. "It was drab and ugly," Dianne says, "so I added sprinkles and chocolate chips, and topped it off with a cheery ribbon. Now it had a wow factor." She priced it at $4.95.

"We decided to test it out at three trade shows coming up in North Carolina," Dianne recalls. "So we made 3,000 cones, figuring that would get us through all three. Well, at the first one, people were grabbing armloads, buying them by the dozens. We sold all 3,000 in one day. When the last one went, a little girl waiting in line just broke down and sobbed."

Dianne knew she had a winner. She immediately signed up sales reps, who rang up orders from department stores and boutiques and gift shops. "At night we would be in bed in that little shed, and we'd hear the fax machine ringing into the wee small hours. The sales reps had come back from selling and were in their hotel rooms filing their orders. I remember Michael's, the craft store chain, bought $260,000 worth for Christmas and placed another big order for Valentine's Day. We eventually did more than $1 million in sales."

It was a solid win, but Dianne missed an even bigger jackpot; she had failed to trademark her product, leaving a larger corporation to swoop in and grab much of the business. But the good news was that after four and a half years in the shed, she and Bill had earned enough to move into a brand-new, bought-and-paid-for home.

Dianne continued to develop products ("though I wasn't sure there ever would be anything like the Cocoa Cone"), and one day she began surfing on Etsy.com. "One of the most interesting things about Etsy is that you can see how many units of a product another business is selling every single day," she says. "And I started to notice that paper straws were selling like crazy. I thought, *I need to get me some straws.*"

But who knew that straws could be such a headache? They were made in China. Supplies were limited. There was a four-month backlog. They came in only three colors (gray, blue, and red). They were poorly made. And some were simply unusable.

Dianne instantly knew she could do better. If two or three colors sold well, what would twelve colors do? Or fifteen? Or maybe even prints and designs? Dianne smelled a hit again. She found an American manufacturer, which at first wasn't interested. There were too many complications. They'd need to stockpile a lot of paper and get FDA approval for inks or dyes. Dianne was undaunted. "If there's one thing I've learned over the years, it's 'Don't take no for an answer.' The plant was saying, 'What if they don't sell?' I said, 'What do you care? I'm paying you to do it. Just tell me what it costs.' Finally they agreed."

On a crisp November afternoon in 2010, Dianne's straws were delivered: fifteen colors arriving on fifteen shipping pallets, 240,000 straws per pallet. "All I had to do was take pictures of them and post them on the website. And people came out of the woodwork, from all over the world. It just exploded." In 2012, Dianne's business, called the Sugar Diva, did more than $1 million in sales. "My mom said, 'I don't get it—they're just paper straws.' And I said, 'Mom, I don't get it either. I'm just so happy I have them.'"

Copycats inevitably sprang up in China, but Dianne remains confident. "You may do something as good as I do it," she says, "but you'll never do it better." She and Bill recently hired an operations manager for the company and brought their granddaughter on board to begin preparing for the day when she takes over from Dianne.

"I have never given up," says Dianne. "You get knocked down, you get stepped on, you get up, you brush yourself off, and you keep going. I've been all the way up and all the way to the very bottom. And look at me now."

The Grandma Graduate

Susan Porter, 56

Ithaca, New York

Have you ever sat cross-legged on concrete with a group of 18-year-olds and had to pretend your knees didn't hurt? It's hard on the body and worse on the ego.

"I was so sore," Susie Porter recalls, "but I didn't dare let on for fear that they'd say, 'Oh my God, she's *really* old!'"

Susie was clearly out of her element. She'd transferred to Cornell University at the ripe age of 54. Going in, she knew she had more than three decades on her classmates, but reality didn't sink in until that first night of orientation in August 2012, when she and a gang of fellow classmates sat on the sidewalk outside the campus dorms.

"We were playing name games, and as I looked out at all these young baby faces, I realized they were looking back at me like, 'Hmmm. We just left our parents. How'd she get in here?'"

Her age notwithstanding, Susie had reason to be proud: She was at Cornell on a full scholarship—pretty amazing, considering that three years earlier she had been working 18-hour days trying to keep her restaurant in a rough Cleveland neighborhood afloat.

"Back then I would have said, 'No way will I ever be going to an Ivy League school!'" But now here she was, the only grandma in the group, biting back the pain in her knees. The whole experience was getting more and more surreal. Just a few days earlier, her youngest daughter, Katy, then 27, and Katy's boyfriend, Pat, had driven her the five hours to Ithaca, New York, in a Subaru station wagon stuffed with clothes, sheets, towels, pots, and pans.

"It was hilarious," says Susie. "They were like my mom and dad driving me up to college, teasing me about how I shouldn't go out partying and really needed to buckle down and do well in school. And I was stunned when Katy actually slipped me 50 bucks at one point. I said, 'What's this for?' She said, 'Well, you never know when you might need it.'"

After they helped her move into her one-bedroom apartment, Katy and Pat dropped Susie off at orientation, and like a good mom and dad headed to Target and a few local thrift shops to pick up some items for her new place.

"It was so sweet," Susie says. "I came home and had new plates, an ironing board, a shower curtain, and food in the cupboard. It was role reversal at its finest."

But when orientation weekend ended and Katy and Pat headed home, Susie's excitement about her academic adventure quickly turned to fear.

"It reminded me of when I dropped the kids off at a new school when we first moved to Ohio, and how scared they were as I drove away," she recalls. "They looked at me like, 'Do we really have to do this?' And there at Cornell, I realized exactly how they felt. I kept thinking, *I'm here all alone. I gotta do this. Can I do this?*"

Susie had spent her entire adult life dodging that question. Right out of high school in North Carolina, she'd started working alongside her dad as a computer consultant. Married by 21 and divorced by 34, with two young girls, she had always longed to go to college.

"That hole in my education always bothered me," she says. "I've always known that I'm very smart, and yet everyone talks about that diploma, and how important it is. So going to college became like a dream to me. But every time I considered actually applying to a school, I'd think, 'Well, I'll have plenty of time when my girls get into junior high.' Then a few years later, that turned into 'I'll have plenty of time when they're in high school.' It was all about 'later'—I kept pushing it down the road."

And it got pushed farther down the road when her father's health began to falter and he needed to be near good hospitals. So in 1998, Susie, her girls, and her parents moved to Cleveland, where her sister lived. With the computer industry struggling, and Susie in need of an income, she had a brainstorm: She'd open a restaurant specializing in southern cuisine.

"Northerners love southern food," she says, "and I'd always been pretty good at making it." So she found a good location, rehabbed a century-old building, and thought of a name she loved: the Town Fryer. And in 2002 she was open for business.

You name it, Susie fried it: chicken, catfish, even Twinkies and Oreos. And at night, she brought in singer-songwriters to entertain the after-work crowd.

"You'd see a cop sitting next to an attorney next to a tow-truck driver next to a guy with a Mohawk and tattoos. And everybody got along. It was a really special place."

The only problem was making money, especially after the recession hit in 2008 and regulars started coming in only one day a week instead of three or four. To add to Susie's stress, in December 2009 her older daughter, Ali, who was 26, single, and had a one-year-old daughter, fell and broke her neck.

"You pick up your baby and you could end up paralyzed," the doctor warned Ali.

So Susie, distraught, took charge of her granddaughter, toting her around on her hip while cooking and taking care of customers. It was physically and emotionally draining—and scary. If her daughter didn't recover, she asked herself, how could she support her and her granddaughter with the little money she was making? And with no health insurance?

"I had no idea where to turn," Susie says.

Enter a longtime customer-turned-friend who'd earned an accounting degree in his thirties and was headed into law school. He and Susie began discussing her predicament—her financial worries and her struggle to carve out a new life.

"Why don't you go to college?" he asked Susie.

No sooner were the words out of his mouth than Susie began tossing off all of the old excuses.

"I can't afford it."

"I don't have time."

"I'm too old."

And on and on.

"Suit yourself," he said flatly. "But beware: Ten years from now, you'll look back on this day and realize it was the perfect time to take the leap. But by then, you'll be ten years older in the same life, rather than ten years into a new one."

Susie didn't argue back—and her friend took that silence as an invitation to continue. Right then and there—in the restaurant booth, with Susie's grandbaby on her lap—he pulled out his laptop and went to the local community college website. The more they cruised around the site, the more excited Susie grew.

"If I'd had any time to think about it," she says, "I probably would have chickened out. And I did balk quite a bit. But he kept saying, 'You can do this, Susie. You can do this.' "

Together they registered Susie for three online classes for spring 2010—Introduction to Jazz, the History of Cleveland, and Microeconomics. "I wasn't thinking about degrees at that point," Susie says. "I just wanted to take some classes and get my feet wet." And she not only completed all of her courses, she aced them.

"That's the moment I realized that my dream wasn't impossible after all," she says. "That's when I thought, *Wow, I can do this.*"

With her daughter making a full recovery, Susie decided to close the Town Fryer to focus on school full-time, funding her education by selling the restaurant kitchen equipment and furniture from her house and taking out grants and loans totaling $17,000.

"I was a woman on an academic mission," she says.

She took more courses over the summer—English Composition, Beginning Algebra, History of Africa—and by the following fall, her 3.8 grade point average earned her a spot in Phi Theta Kappa, the academic honor society for two-year colleges, as well as membership in the scholars program, which centered on social justice.

Susie felt right at home in that program, as it reignited the social conscience she'd had since she was a child. She particularly loved a philosophy class where students pondered open-ended questions: What is justice? Who defines justice—the government or the people? "The class provided an awakening for me—or as I like to call it, an *unfolding.*"

But the best was yet to come. During her fourth semester at community college, Susie received a letter from Cornell University—one of the nation's eight Ivy League colleges—commenting on how impressed they were by her academic success in the scholars program, and inviting her to apply to the ILR

School, founded as the School of Industrial and Labor Relations, with a focus on improving work life for people. Surprised and flattered, Susie decided to visit the campus—and she was wowed.

"The place just enveloped me," she says. "I instinctively knew that I *belonged* there."

Then Susie met with an admissions counselor, and she asked him point-blank if he thought she had what it took to be a Cornell student.

"You wouldn't be here right now if we didn't think you could do the work," he said.

So Susie applied to Cornell, even though she had no idea how she'd pay for the $1,300-per-credit-hour tuition. (Community college had been $100 per hour.) And when she got a call telling her that she'd been accepted—and that she'd had not only earned enough credits to enter as a junior, but that her $60,000-per-year tuition would be covered—she was overwhelmed.

"I just sobbed," she says.

Once in class, Susie demonstrated a kind of real-world authority that only age and experience can provide.

"In my Workers' Rights course, the professor described how women laborers in a small North Carolina town had suffered serious, long-term illnesses from factory work, gluing couch cushions. One student said, 'Why didn't they just find another job? It's a free country.' Well, I found this sort of amusing, because I was actually very familiar with that town! So I explained to the class how poor the area was, and how women didn't have the money or support system to make a change. I also explained how important family can be for working women, and I described how I'd moved to Cleveland so my daughters and I would be closer to our families. I think I helped my younger classmates look at life a little bit differently."

Then again, youth does have its advantages in an academic setting, partic-

ularly when it comes to memory. "The hardest thing for me was retaining information as quickly as I needed to. By the time you reach my age, you can't even remember a grocery list!"

In the fall of 2013, Susie headed for a semester abroad in Ireland, setting her on course to receive her bachelor's degree from Cornell in Industrial and Labor Relations the following spring. She hopes to use that degree to help corporations implement socially responsible practices.

"I want to get this degree so I can get out there and start making a difference," she says.

The Cornell kids no longer look at Susie like she's an alien. On her fifty-fifth birthday, students in one class surprised her by putting up a slide at the start of class that read, "Dearest Susan, Happy Birthday! You are such a wonderful individual and we are so glad to have met someone like you. You continue to be an inspiration every day."

That slide touched Susie's heart.

"Just a few years earlier," she said, "I was the one searching for inspiration. Now I feel like I can do anything. Instead of closing doors in front of me with a long list of excuses, I step through them to see what's on the other side. Maybe that's the best lesson I've learned from going to school."

Perfect Strokes

Layla Fanucci, 56
St. Helena, California

I t was a big, blank space that bugged the hell out of her. And it was smack in the middle of her living room.

Music teacher and choir director Layla Fanucci was standing at the foot of her couch contemplating the empty wall above it. A Monet poster used to hang there, but Layla had taken it down.

"It was nice," she says, "just like some music is nice. But to me, there's a difference between hearing a good CD and hearing a live band that moves you and takes your breath away."

She wanted the wall to take her breath away. And—*boom*—that's when it hit her: live music, live art.

So Layla started scouting out galleries in towns near her Napa Valley home. "I couldn't find *anything*," she says—and, man, the sticker shock! She was not going to spend thousands of dollars on artwork she didn't love.

So she did what any self-respecting DIY-er would do: She decided to paint something herself. There was just one *little* problem. "I had never painted in my life," she says.

But on her maiden voyage, Layla went all out. She bought a six-by-five-foot white board, laid it on the ground, and covered it with an explosion of blue, red, yellow, green, and white paint. As she worked, her hand flew across the canvas with the energy and grace of someone who'd been doing this for years. The design was abstract, but hidden within the paint drippings, Layla had added a clarinet, a Christmas tree, and three figures representing her kids.

"It's big, it's bold, it's got color—we're good to go," she told herself. "End of story."

But, really, it was just the beginning. When friends came over and saw Layla's creation, they were wowed. Over the next year, nine of them paid Layla to produce "real" art for their homes, too: an abstract portrait of children, a postmodern still life.

"I was surprised and delighted, and I had no idea where this was coming from," she says. "One couple painted their whole living room to match the colors in my painting."

Inspired by her friends' reactions, Layla painted, and she painted. She painted between teaching gigs. She painted at lunch. "I just wanted to paint all the time," she says. "I had all of this inside of me, and now it was pouring out."

It also made Layla reflect on her life. "I loved music and loved teaching children," she says, "but I hadn't admitted to myself that after 25 years I was getting tired."

That is, until she discovered her inner artist.

She'd earned a steady salary, money she and her husband, Robert, a tax attorney, counted on to pay their kids' college tuition and to help support their small family wine business.

"But now everybody, including my husband, said, 'Teach part-time and see if the art goes anywhere.' But I knew if I wanted to give art a shot, I had to give it everything I had."

So in 2001, two years after hanging her first painting on the wall, Layla quit teaching cold turkey. "My husband said, 'I feel like we're on the *Titanic* and you just jumped.'"

She'd heard the dismal statistics: Only 5 percent of artists make money. How was she going to become the exception, turning her art into a business? First, she needed to create a body of work. She gave herself a two-year deadline to do so. "If I wasn't able to match my salary, I'd go back to teaching," she says.

Layla put on one of Robert's old white work shirts and started to paint, ten to twelve hours a day. "You know how runners talk about that amazing euphoric feeling they get at the end of a marathon?" she asks. "When I paint, I have that wonderful feeling the entire time."

That joy resulted in a burst of productivity, and within two years, Layla had produced nearly 200 paintings—abstract depictions of flowers, musicians, men and women (she gave them monikers like *Lisou, Madeline,* and *The Martini Lady*). "I was inspired by Matisse's style and colors," she says.

Through word of mouth, Layla was soon selling her paintings and making almost as much money as she had as a teacher.

Encouraged, she sent photos of her work to a top art consultant in New York City and set up a meeting. "I was so nervous riding up in the creaky elevator of this chic French New York hotel to go to the suite of a stranger with a book of photographs of my paintings," she says. "I remember thinking to myself, *What are you doing?*"

The woman (think Meryl Streep in *The Devil Wears Prada*) studied every page carefully, brusquely holding up her hand to silence Layla every time she tried to provide a painting's backstory. When the consultant closed the book, she leveled her verdict:

"It's good—*and we don't care.*"

Then she offered the advice that would change Layla's life: "What does a Layla Fanucci painting look like?" Layla tried to formulate an answer, but the consultant barreled on: "In order to market your work, you have to paint a style nobody else paints"—she got an inch from Layla's face and finished in staccato—"In. The. World."

The art consultant sent Layla home to produce 17 more paintings over the next six months. It was a daunting assignment, but one she welcomed. "I instinctively felt that the process was going to take me where I needed to go."

Over the next two years, they "did a dance," with the consultant critiquing each new batch of work and Layla going back into her studio to experiment some more.

154

Through the process, she developed a one-of-a-kind Layla Fanucci style of cityscapes: She paints layer upon layer of color on linen canvas to communicate the mood of a city—New York, Paris, Venice, Rome. When the paint dries, she takes a brush in black oil and adds architectural details like buildings, bridges, and streets, then gives the painting life with people, motion, and energy before covering it with more color. She may paint three cities on top of the first one, creating depth and texture, so anyone who looks closely can see the other cities and architectural details bleeding through.

"For the first time, I began to recognize the influence of my dad, an architect who died in 1996. I remember from my childhood watching him at work and at home, drafting houses, churches, and buildings," she says. "Emotionally, my art was a tie to my family and my past."

Layla had proven herself as an original to the art consultant, who now introduced her to a prominent gallery in New York City, which offered her a solo show of 16 of her paintings. If they didn't sell, the consultant warned, Layla's big-time art career was done. Nine sold in one month.

Since then, she's had shows in San Francisco and Morocco and has sold her work to collectors all over the world.

Critics also praised her work—and one in particular caught Layla's connection to music, saying, "She captures the rhythm of the great metropolis, the lyrical splendor of its skies and the cacophony of its streets. Looking at these scenes, one understands why people return time after time to these places, like musical phrases we never tire of hearing, always finding something new in them."

In 2006, Layla and Robert merged their boutique winery, Charter Oak, with her art business. She recently sold her largest painting to date, a nine-by-fourteen-foot work called *City of the World Opus II*, for $100,000 when a tourist walked into her on-site gallery and fell in love with it. "In a year, I sold

32 paintings and made as much money as I would have if I had taught for 33 years.

"We all have hidden talents," she continues. "If we find them, we need to work on them every day and let them flourish. I often think of what I would have missed if I had not given up a steady, reliable salary and followed my passion."

PART SIX

Family Ties

"People often ask, 'How do you work with your sister?' Truth is, I couldn't do this with anyone but her."

Her Brother, Peter

Jane Alderman Zeitz, 40
Scarsdale, New York

Liz and Steve Alderman,
Pound Ridge, New York

Late in the summer of 2001, Peter Alderman, age 25, was vacationing with his family. For almost a year, he'd been working at Bloomberg LP, and recently the company had called him to New York. Casually he mentioned that he would soon have his first real assignment in the city, representing the company at a conference in downtown Manhattan the following week.

Ten days after that discussion, Jane Alderman, Peter's sister, was sitting at her desk in the Washington headquarters of Viacom when a colleague ran into her office. "Turn on the TV," she hollered. "A plane just crashed into the World Trade Center."

At that moment, the television news organizations still knew very little, not even what kind of plane was involved; like many people, Jane thought a private plane had somehow gone terribly off course. But she remembered that Peter had said that he was going downtown. She thought maybe she could give him a heads-up, warn him that traffic was likely to be chaotic and he should plan accordingly.

Hey, are you there? she wrote in an email message.

Jane and Peter had always been close. Elated by the birth of a baby brother, Jane had always lavished attention on Peter, and the bond proved enduring. Both Jane and Peter had trundle beds in their bedrooms growing up, and even into their teenage years, they traded off spending the night in each other's bedrooms.

Yes. 106th floor. There's a lot of smoke. I'm scared.

"I couldn't process the message," she recalls. "It never occurred to me that he would actually be in the World Trade Center. I thought he'd be in the neighborhood, have to take a detour."

What building? she typed.

Windows on the World, World Trade, he typed back.

"I freaked out," recalls Jane. "I yelled for my boss. I called my friends. By this time, the second plane had struck."

Can you get out? she typed.

No, we are stuck.

Keep emailing me to let me know that you are OK.

Jane's friends tried to reassure her. "He'll be all right," they said. "He survived the hit. They'll get him out." Then came the shocking report that a third plane had struck the Pentagon. With that, Jane and her colleagues were ordered to immediately evacuate their offices in the Watergate complex. Jane and a group of friends walked to a colleague's apartment in Georgetown, passing army tanks that had taken positions in the street.

"We just waited together," she says. "We didn't turn on the television or anything. I just sat there, waiting for Peter to call and let me know that he had gotten out." Not until later, when Jane and her friends went to a restaurant and saw that the towers had collapsed, did she realize that Peter did not get out. Peter was gone. "I kept checking my phones, but I knew."

Jane and Peter's parents, Liz and Steve, were in France, on "the trip of a lifetime." Peter's boss, Michael Bloomberg, not yet New York's mayor, flew them home on a private plane. The shock was overwhelming, says Liz. "I always felt that if a child of mine was killed, I would never be able to stop screaming. But you can't keep screaming. I realized you only have two choices: You either crawl into bed and never get out, or you put one foot in front of the other."

Though still in the throes of grief, the Aldermans accepted the reality of Peter's death and soon focused on ways to honor his memory. "My dad talked about endowing a chair; my mom talked about setting up a playground," Jane recalls. "But nothing seemed quite right."

Then one night in June 2002, Liz was watching the ABC News program *Nightline*. The show was called "Invisible Wounds," and it focused on Harvard psychologist Richard Mollica's work dealing with traumatized populations. As the program reported, one billion people across the globe—a sixth of the human race—have directly experienced torture, terrorism, and mass violence; at least half and perhaps as much as 70 percent of this group are left suffering such traumatic depression that they can no longer lead functional lives. The vast majority of these people live in places like Cambodia, where psychiatric help is practically nonexistent.

As Liz watched the show, a thought took hold in her imagination. "There wasn't anything we could do to bring Peter back to life," she says, "but if we could help bring these people back to life in Peter's name, what better memorial to him than that?"

Ten days later, Steve and Liz Alderman were in Richard Mollica's office at Harvard. It took almost no time for them to recognize that this was a cause the family wanted to embrace.

"Dr. Mollica talked about a study done in a refugee camp," says Jane. "It showed that there were three things that fought depression among trauma victims. They were work, altruism, and spirituality. Our family recognized that in the midst of our own grief, we were seeking, each in our own way, work, altruism, and spirituality. What we wanted to do for other people, in reality, when we started, was what we were doing for ourselves."

The Aldermans began small, underwriting a master class taught by Dr. Mollica. Approximately thirty doctors from Cambodia, Uganda, and eight other countries came together and were trained in how to treat victims of trauma and terrorism. The Aldermans, too, attended. Once they met the professionals who were confronting these horrors, once they heard their stories, they grasped that what they were doing did not go far enough.

Using money they'd received from the Victims Compensation Fund, they formed the Peter C. Alderman Foundation (PCAF) to help people who have survived terrorism, torture, or mass violence but whose trauma has left them emotionally and mentally fragile, if not broken. Since its inception ten years ago, more than 100,000 victims have been treated by the trained personnel at the foundation and at Peter C. Alderman Mental Health Clinics. Operating on an annual budget of less than one million dollars of donated funds, PCAF has funded eight trauma clinics and sponsored master classes, as well as studies to identify effective therapies.

"Our family suffered one trauma when Peter was killed," says Jane. "Most of the patients we see in our clinics have suffered an average of seven." Among those patients was Esther, a mother in northern Uganda. The Lord's Resistance Army came into her village and murdered her husband with a machete; grabbed her five-year-old son by the ankles and banged him against a tree until he was dead; and trampled to death her two-year-old son. Then they marched her out of the village, raped her for several days, and left her there.

Esther was eventually reunited with her two daughters, who were away at the time of the attack. She showed up at the PCAF's clinic, suicidal. The clinic provided treatment, found a place for Esther to live, and connected her with a church that hosted meetings of women who had similar experiences.

"No one is going to make people like Esther whole," says Jane. "But we have helped her to begin reconnecting to her family and community, and this will help her return to a functional life."

The commitment dramatically changed the lives of Steve, Liz, and Jane. Steve, now 72, closed his oncology practice to work on the PCAF's programming issues. Jane reached the practical conclusion that the PCAF required committed, trained leadership, and she accepted that responsibility. She left her job, enrolled in business school, and earned her MBA. Now 40, she runs the PCAF, managing it in a cost-effective, sustainable way. "My parents were wary," Jane says. "They didn't want me to devote my life to my fallen brother. But I told them no, that I believe in this work."

Liz has focused on communications and marketing. "You never get over the loss of a child," she says. "My grief has not abated one iota. But the foundation has been an effective antidote. It gives me a reason to get out of bed every day; it helps people; and it is a perfect way to memorialize my son, who never had a chance to leave his own mark."

In 2011, President Obama presented the PCAF with the Presidential Citizens Medal at a ceremony at the White House.

"It's almost impossible to admit that anything good came out of Peter's death," says Liz. "But through the foundation we've done some good. I've learned that I'm a lot tougher than I thought I was, that I'm smarter than I

thought I was, and that I can talk to anybody—I went up and introduced my-self to Kofi Annan! And as a result, I've become the face of the PCAF, because I can speak comfortably, knowledgeably, and emotionally."

When the PCAF holds its annual conferences, hundreds of mental health practitioners from around the world come together to learn better ways to relieve suffering. At the foundation's third conference, a Somali imam opened the plenary session.

"Supposedly he was saying a prayer," Liz recalls, "but he was yelling and shaking his fists. We were worried that he was saying 'Death to America!' But after he finished, the translator told us that he had blessed us for coming all the way to Africa, and that he had said a prayer for my child. I started to cry. This is the result that we had wanted—this was the mark we wanted to leave. Here was a Muslim imam from the other side of the world—the side of the world that had brought terror to the World Trade Center that awful day—saying a prayer for my child. That was incredibly uplifting."

Well Versed

Julie Lythcott-Haims, 46
Palo Alto, California

J ulie Lythcott-Haims was nervous. Just what exactly could this young white guy in the audience have to say to the older black woman up on stage?

It was September 2007 and Julie, as Stanford University's dean of freshmen, was in charge of this welcome-to-college event, in which first-year students, assigned three books to read over the summer, listened to the authors speak about their works and then asked them questions. This year, the books had included *Good Woman: Poems and a Memoir, 1969–1980,* by Lucille Clifton.

Ugh, Julie had thought when she'd picked up a copy a few weeks earlier. *I hate poetry.* "I just didn't get it," she says, but her office was hosting the event, so "I read the book because I had to."

Twenty minutes in, she was hooked. "The poems were about race, intimacy, mothering, childbearing, sexuality, sensuality, longing, and struggle— they were about life. I devoured them."

The poet, Lucille Clifton, was an African American woman, so it made sense to Julie—a 39-year-old married, biracial mother of two—that she felt the poems so deeply. But how would this audience of rowdy 17- and 18-year-old college newbies possibly relate?

Then the boy in the balcony raised his hand. "Ms. Clifton," he began, "your poetry speaks to me in ways I can barely understand." And he read aloud the first stanza of one of her poems:

"if i stand in my window
naked in my own house
and press my breasts
against the windowpane
like black birds pushing against glass
because i am somebody
in a New Thing . . ."

There wasn't a single snicker from the 1,700 students assembled—just respectful silence. "In that moment," Julie recalls, "I realized that poetry speaks to people for all kinds of reasons. We make meaning of poetry as a way of interpreting our *own* lives."

Julie had never considered herself a writer; in fact, in her first couple of years at college, she'd been told her writing needed work.

"But Lucille Clifton's poetry loosened a spigot inside of me," Julie says. "I had stories that I had to get out."

Within weeks, Julie started piecing together stories and poems of her own. One was about being a biracial teen, the daughter of a white mother and black father, in the all-white, middle-class suburb of Middleton, Wisconsin. It was the early eighties, and Julie's light brown skin, kinky hair, and wide nose all defined her as black—the only one out of 1,200 students in her high school. With her dad often on the road for work and no black relatives or families nearby, Julie felt no connection to her African American roots.

"I wasn't going to events that black people attended, I wasn't participating in rituals that matter in the black community, I wasn't exposed to black history in America. My racial and ethnic identity was thin, brittle, fragile. It was a label only, and it didn't do much toward helping me understand how to feel about myself or my ancestry."

So she conformed, becoming Middleton's Miss Everything: an academic standout, a choir member, a pom-pom girl, senior class president. "My goal was to be what I perceived white people wanted me to be in order to gain their approval—talking in ways that made me seem familiar to them, behaving in ways that made them feel safe around me."

Even so, there were harsh reminders that she was different. People would ask: *What are you? Why are you so tan?* A friend, thinking she was giving Julie a compliment, said: "I don't think of you as black. I think of you as normal."

"But I *am* black so I wish you *would* think of me that way," Julie countered.

For Julie's seventeenth birthday, her best friend crafted a friendship collage of words and pictures cut out of magazines and hung it on her locker. But by midday, someone had scrawled *Nigger* on it. "I felt like I had been spit on," Julie recalls. "When no one was looking, I took a pair of scissors and cut the word out. I didn't tell anyone, not even my parents. I felt shame. The vandal was telling me what I already knew: I was the nigger of my school and my town. And I didn't want anyone's pity."

In 1985, Julie set out for Stanford, where she was surrounded by other black kids. But she shied away from them, choosing white friends and dating a white guy named Dan.

"Being the daughter of an interracial couple, it was a very familiar construct for me. I never worried about dating someone white. White people were my milieu."

Julie was too intimidated to join a black sorority or hang out in the black community center. "I felt I lacked the cultural savvy to belong. I perceived there was a way to be black—a handshake, a walk, a talk, an attitude. It was like a secret club and I didn't know the password. There was no depth to my blackness. No soul. And I feared that black people could tell instantly, by looking at me, that I was an imposter."

Still, from the moment she stepped on campus, Julie loved Stanford, so much so that, after attending Harvard Law School, marrying Dan, and having a brief career as a corporate lawyer, she returned to the Stanford campus as associate dean of its law school.

"At the law firm, I had been successful and well-regarded, but the job sucked the life out of me one billable hour at a time. At Stanford, my job was to help law students on their path, to be that visible, relevant, credible resource in their life. It clicked in every way possible." Julie moved up to become assistant to Stanford's president and then created a new position: dean of freshmen.

It wasn't long before she became the hugely popular "Dean Julie." Every year on Orientation Day, she'd take the podium and lead the freshmen through a rowdy call-and-response ritual designed to build a sense of belonging to the place.

It was at one such orientation that Lucille Clifton visited Stanford and completely spun Julie's world. She cranked out nearly 80 poems, many sparked by the conflicted emotions buried in her since adolescence about her place among blacks and whites.

She had been actively trying to work through those feelings since two years earlier, when, headed to a Stanford event for African American staff, she felt self-conscious bringing her daughter, who has very light skin and was four at the time.

"That's when I really knew I was screwed up," Julie says. "Of course it was never about her. It was about my own shame at not feeling black enough, and the visible result of having chosen to marry a white guy. My beautiful girl seemed to represent my own ethnic fragility. I knew that for her sake, I needed to figure this out."

By the beginning of 2007, Julie had found a role model in Barack Obama, whose biracial background mirrored her own. But during his first presidential campaign, when she was approached about a position aimed at bringing out the black female vote, she turned it down, saying, "I'm not an authentic voice."

"I had moved from a place of self-loathing toward a more neutral place of acceptance," Julie recalls. "But to be a spokeswoman for the black woman? I knew I still had a long way to go."

That's where her poetry came in. "I realized that writing down my thoughts helped me to heal. It's like a gear was stuck in my psyche; writing was like adding oil to that gear to loosen it up, making the whole psychological me run more smoothly. I felt more whole, more healthy, more self-loving, and when I finally loved myself as a black woman, I found the black community waiting to embrace me; they had been there all along."

Julie had toyed with prose in the past but loved the freedom of poetry. "It was just about the words. I could arrange them on the page however I wanted. I didn't have to worry about punctuation or sentence structure. I could literally fill the page with the essence of my fear, my love, and my thoughts."

In January 2012, after more than a decade at Stanford, Julie had a talk with Dan: What if she went back to school to study poetry?

"After years spent encouraging young people to follow their hearts, I real-

ized that this was my one life and if there were other things I wanted to do, I'd better do 'em," she says.

That winter, Julie applied to the two-year master's in fine arts program at the California College of the Arts in San Francisco, submitting a portfolio of 20 poems. When the acceptance letter came, "I was full of fire," she says.

"After I enrolled, I realized I was older than my classmates by 20 years—the biggest difference was that I didn't have tattoos, body piercings, or hair dyed turquoise. But it doesn't matter. I'm the best student I've ever been. And I've squeezed every drop from it."

And as Julie's poetry has matured, so has her understanding of race. Although she cannot change her own childhood, she knows she can help her kids, now 12 and 14, avoid the pain and confusion she felt. But most important, she has a deeper understanding of who she is. Her first published poem centers on the theme of biracial identity in a culturally white landscape and is told in seven voices.

"I'm no longer somebody who wants to check boxes. I now know I lie at the intersection of boxes. I've come to appreciate that identity is in some small part about how others see us, but mostly it's about how we see ourselves. We can't live our lives worrying about what someone else does or doesn't expect of us."

The Sisters

Kara Gorski, 38
Alexandria, Virginia

Kristin Gembala, 43
Overland Park, Kansas

From the outside, Kara Gorski seemed to have the perfect life. A vice president at an economic consulting firm, she had just landed her dream job giving expert testimony in legal cases. She was a mom to two gorgeous boys, three years and fifteen months old, and was ready to try for another baby. Between her career and her husband's landscaping business, they could now afford to move from their Washington, D.C., neighborhood to an acre-sized property in Virginia.

But on the inside, she felt lost. As she and her husband took a Sunday drive in August 2010 to see the property where they were to build their new home, she made a confession: She was overwhelmed. Stretched too thin. Completely frazzled.

On a typical day, she'd leave the house by seven a.m., work through lunch, and stay at the office until at least seven p.m.; during extrabusy stretches, she was slammed until the early-morning hours. "I loved everything about my career, but it was very high stress," she says. "I was managing clients, managing experts, and managing people underneath me. There were lots of deadlines. And I had these two little boys and a husband. I was getting pulled in so many directions and I never had time to take care of myself. I couldn't keep going like this. Something had to give."

What should she change? What *could* she change? A spiritual person, she had asked the heavens on her thirty-fifth birthday, three days earlier, to send her a sign pointing her in the right direction. Now, returning home from her Sunday drive, she went upstairs to change clothes, pulled off her shirt and sports bra, and her hand brushed a small, hard-as-rock lump on the side of her right breast.

Was this her sign?

Kara flashed back to second grade. She was just seven years old, standing at the side of a hospital bed, staring at the lifeless body of her 39-year-old mother, who has just died of breast cancer. She lightly touched her mom's fingers for a split second—afraid and, at the same time, ashamed of her fear. During all the years since, Kara had tried to push away the pain and confusion of losing her mother when she needed her most.

"After my mom died, my grandmother hugged me and said, 'We'll always be here for you,'" Kara says. "But there was not a lot of conversation to help me understand what had happened and to remember her. So I never really dealt with her death. Honestly, I don't know how you *can* when you're that young."

As an adult, she coped by keeping up such a frenetic pace she didn't have time to worry about getting sick herself. She'd had mammograms but was worried about radiation exposure, so with her doctor's okay had skipped her most recent one. And now, without any warning, a lump. *This is bad, this is so bad* played over and over in her head.

Kara's sister, Kristin Gembala, was having Sunday dinner with her in-laws at her home in Overland Park, Kansas, when the phone rang. She picked up on the distress in Kara's voice right away. Older by five years, Kristin had initially taken on a mothering role after their mom died, leaving just the two of them and their dad. That maternal role still fit: Whereas Kara left home to pursue two Fulbright fellowships and graduate work in Latin America, Kristin married the guy she'd dated since ninth grade, had four babies in ten years, and became a stay-at-home mom and busy school and community volunteer.

Though the sisters had gone down completely different paths and lived halfway across the country from each other, they were close. So as Kara delivered her bad news, Kristin went cold.

"Stay calm," Kristin said, moving out to the deck to pull herself together. "Maybe it's just a cyst. Let's not get out of whack." On the other end, Kara wasn't buying it. She felt condemned, as if she were looking in the mirror and her mother's image was looking back.

After she hung up with Kristin, she lay awake in bed, cuddling into her sleeping boys. "I don't want the same thing that happened to me to happen to you," she softly sobbed. Again, a flashback to second grade: This time, she's back in school and kids are pointing and whispering: *"That's her, the girl who doesn't have a mom anymore."*

Over the coming weeks, the news from Kara's oncologist was mixed: She had Stage 1 breast cancer, but it was a very aggressive type—and one that she had indeed inherited from her mom. Doctors recommended that both her breasts be removed. Once again, she called Kristin.

"Listen, don't worry," said Kristin, still trying to be the reassuring big sister. "I'll go get a double mastectomy, too. We'll do this together." At the

173

time, it was a pledge of support and solidarity. But then Kristin read up on it and learned that she, too, had a 50 percent chance of what she called "this, this *brokenness.*" She went to a genetic counselor, where tests showed she also had the genetic mutation BRCA1, meaning it was nearly 90 percent certain that she, too, would develop breast cancer someday. Having her breasts removed could save her life as well.

"All of the doctors and even my husband said, 'Based on your family history, you don't have a lot of wiggle room here,'" Kristin says. "Deciding to have the surgery was easy for me. I had less attachment to my breasts than most women, because of what happened to my mother."

So here they were, both face-to-face with the disease that had cast a dark shadow over their entire lives. Their worst fear realized. But they also finally knew it wasn't a random act of nature that had taken their mom so young. This cancer was in their DNA.

"There was so much relief in finally having a reason," Kristin says. "All those years of my life, I couldn't understand why my mother died so young. Why, why, why? And now I was learning to deal with life in *whats*. What can I do about this? It was important for me at last to have an answer for *what*."

That fall and winter, more than 900 miles apart, surgeons removed the sisters' breasts. (They had hysterectomies, too, as the BRCA1 gene also greatly increases the risk of ovarian cancer.) Kristin had implants put in right away; Kara had to wait until she was through chemotherapy. For a year, she was infused with drugs that damaged the nerves in her hands so badly that she could no longer get her boys dressed or buckle them into their car seats. Her hair, eyebrows, and eyelashes fell out. Some days she was exhausted; others she couldn't sleep.

Just as she hoped the medications would heal her physically, she knew she needed to heal herself emotionally as well.

She began by poring over her mom's medical file from the Wichita, Kansas, hospital where she'd been treated. She looked through old black-and-white family photos and reread a book that Kristin had put together years earlier, a collection of letters that family, friends, and coworkers had written about their mom after she died.

Kara also tried to coax every detail she could from her grandmother, her dad, her sister, and other relatives about her mother's two-year cancer battle.

"I wanted to try to remember my mother's life and death instead of letting it all be a muddled cloud in my head," she says. "I needed to accept and understand it and let it be a part of me."

Through it all, Kara and Kristin's bond deepened. They were on the phone at least once a day, and sometimes three or four. "We cried—and laughed—more during that fall than anything else," Kristin says.

Kristin (left) and Kara (right)

In one conversation in the summer of 2011, Kristin complained that she couldn't find a bra that fit well anymore. Surgeons had cut out all of her breast tissue and then put in round, flat-as-a-pancake implants. Her breasts no longer filled out regular bra cups; she had two craters where her nipples used to be. Underwire bras looked better but, with no breast tissue providing cushioning, were painful to wear. Another option was a mastectomy bra: to create a more natural-looking breast shape, each cup had a pocket for holding a heavy prosthetic. "I did not have these implants put in to then have to put explants on top of them!" Kristin ranted.

For six months, they tossed around ideas for how to create a comfortable, lightweight, pretty bra that would give them a filled-out look. "We just wanted something we could put on every day, smile, and keep going," Kristin says. They even came up with a name: braGGs, the word "bra," Gs for each of their last names, and S for sisters. "Not only because we're sisters but because of the sisterhood of the breast cancer community," Kristin says. "We also want women to feel like they can brag again." It sounded like a great idea, but taking steps to start their own business was another story. So it simmered.

Until one morning when Kara woke up at four a.m. and thought: *Why can't we just design and market this bra? If we put our minds to it, we can do it.* She got out of bed and shot off an email to Kristin with a to-do list. "Then we started jumping into action," Kristin says.

First, they conducted an online survey with a breast cancer support group, and when the 50 respondents came back with the same complaints they had, the sisters knew they were on the right track.

After a months-long search, they hired a designer who had worked for Jockey and other major undergarment companies and who spent about eight months finding just the right soft, stretchy fabric and creating a prototype.

"To correct those indentations, we made an insert that's built in so there's no prosthetic," Kara says. "It's super comfortable and wire-free."

Then Kara, with her background in intellectual property litigation, applied for a patent. Next, the sisters contracted with a small manufacturer in Pennsylvania, all the while drumming up interest in the bras on their website, braGGsonline.com, and Facebook page and by networking with boutique owners, doctors, and breast cancer survivors.

Still living halfway across the country from each other, they relied on phone calls, emails, texts, Facetime chats, and video conferences. A phone conversation could go from "Which color elastic would be best?" to "You will not believe what happened at school today with the kids."

"People often ask, 'How do you work with your sister?'" Kara says. "Truth is, I couldn't do this with anyone but her."

To date, Kara and Kristin have poured $40,000 of their savings into their creation, plus $10,000 they raised on the crowdfunding website MedStartr. When the first batch of braGGs came off the factory line in the summer of 2013, a D.C.-area boutique had already placed its order and e-customers were awaiting their shipments.

There have been starts and stops along the way, but Kara and Kristin always stick to the M.O. they learned as little girls, the same thing that kept them strong through their mother's death, Kara's cancer, and both of their surgeries: Just put one foot in front of the other.

They work a lot, but not the all-consuming hours of many entrepreneurs. Healthy meals, sleep, and exercise get equal time. "There's no point in working hard if I'm not going to be here," says Kara, who currently has no signs of cancer in her body and who is participating in a clinical trial testing a drug to prevent recurrence. "Most people who knew me before wouldn't recognize me. I have slowed down."

Always on their minds are their testers: women like them, who had their breasts removed and rebuilt, then cried tears of joy after trying on the braGGs bras because they felt "normal" again.

"It's been a wonderful experience coming up with something that helps so many women, including ourselves," Kristin says. "But we have to laugh sometimes. My teenage boys are like, 'Do we have to talk about *bras*?'"

Kara and Kristin always remember the silent partner in their business as well. The one in the 1970s black-and-white photo on the braGGs Facebook page. The one who Kara believes sent her the sign that Sunday afternoon that saved her life.

"Our mom is definitely on this journey with us," Kara says. "It's the three of us."

Rock Star

Kristine Brennen, 63
Duxbury, Massachusetts

If you've ever soldered a circuit board—and most of us haven't—you know that it takes two skills: good hands and a tolerance for boredom. Kristine Brennen had both.

For years, Kristine worked from sunup to sundown in a sterile Massachusetts factory, assembling the electronic components for guidance systems used in space shuttles and missiles. "I was good at my job because I had good hands," she says, "but it killed me being inside all those years, especially working with chemicals, which gave me migraines. I wanted to be outdoors, listening to the birds and seeing all the colors. The outdoors is like a big garden to me. So as I worked in the factory, my mind would often drift back to my grandfather. Every night, he'd come home from work, carrying his tools, covered in dust. I envied that. He'd been outside all day."

Kristine's grandfather, who had come to America from Sweden, worked for New England Cut Stone, shaping limestone and bluestone into libraries and memorials and churches. His work still stands today.

"He lived on the third floor of our house," Kristine recalls, "and I saw him every day until he died, when I was about 20. You could tell by looking at him how satisfying his work was. He just loved the stone."

Life was decidedly different for Kristine. "I had to commute to my job every morning—be there at six and not leave until five. And by then, the day was already gone. I'd look at the setting sun and think, *Oh, no, I missed it again.*"

Despite her longing to do something different, Kristine made a good salary at the company, and she was eventually promoted to a desk job. And that was the dilemma: With more than 20 years' seniority, she had the kind of benefits a woman in her forties couldn't just walk away from.

But then the company was sold. Kristine could have continued under the new management, but when veteran workers were offered a buyout, she jumped at the chance. It wasn't like she had won the lottery, but for the first time in her life, she realized she would have enough money to stop, take a breath, and figure out what she wanted to do with her life.

"It was the best feeling—total freedom," Kristine says. "The buyout gave me the opportunity to take a big step."

Kristine had always dreamed of becoming an artist, but never had enough confidence in her abilities to believe she could make a living at it. So over the years, she had indulged her artistic bent as a hobby, taking up needlepoint and painting. She also enrolled in adult-ed classes at the community college, where weaving and still-life painting classes were a welcome outlet. "But when I took the classes," she says, "I felt like, 'Why am I doing this? Where am I going with this?'" It was frustrating knowing that a richer life might lie outside the factory.

Now, thanks to her $17,000 severance, Kristine had the resources to finally try to connect with her artistic aspirations. So at age 50, she enrolled at a college of art and design, pursuing a degree in architecture ("I figured, I eventually have to make a living," she says), and she was accepted.

"It was like a dream fulfilled," she notes. "I was walking on a cloud every day." In 2006, she was awarded her degree, and her triumph was celebrated by all those who knew her. "My mom lived to see me graduate," she says, "and she was thrilled."

As Kristine surveyed the employment landscape after her graduation, what she couldn't get out of her head was the advice of a favorite professor: "Whatever you do, make sure to have a good time and play."

So play she did. Out in her backyard, Kristine set up large canvases and splattered them with acrylic paint and dirt (yes, dirt), incorporating the soil of the yard into her abstract vision. She loved the results. "In art, you have to find out who you are inside," she says. It might have taken her nearly 40 years, but Kristine felt she was finally making the discovery.

As her artistic spirit emerged, Kristine decided to try her hand at sculpture. While in school, she had taken a part-time job with a landscaper, who taught her how to cut natural stone for patios. She liked visualizing the interplay between shape and texture.

"I began to look at rocks differently," she says. "It's like they were communicating to me. The little round ones I saw as frogs, so I sculpted them that way; the long and thin ones presented whole other opportunities. Rocks have been around forever, and through their shapes, I think they're telling us their stories."

Her yard was the perfect workshop: From the moment she and her husband had begun digging the foundation of their home, they'd unearthed chunks of New England granite. They layered small pieces into garden walls and placed larger ones around the property as decoration.

One of the boulders they had disentombed stood three feet tall and was nearly as wide around; Kristine felt she saw something in the stone and she wanted to bring it out. Using her landscaping tools, she began to carve. Soon the face of a woman emerged—eyes closed, lips pursed, with a contented expression. She looked as if she were sleeping.

"It was my first big sculpture," she says. "I put it out at the end of my driveway, and when the sun came down the street, it would shine on her face. People driving by would actually slow down to take a look. After that, I was hooked. I carved everything I could get my hands on."

Gradually, Kristine accumulated more tools—grinders, chisels, hammers, even an excavator that moved heavier stones. And everywhere she went, she checked out the rocks.

"If I saw something I really liked, and someone was willing to part with it, I'd load it into my pickup truck and bring it home." She turned these raw forms into birdbaths, benches, and fountains, always careful to retain as much of their original shape as possible.

A birdbath, for example, might have a rectangular rock as a base, on which she balanced an elliptical stone whose center she'd hollowed into a bowl. Or an egg-shaped boulder might be converted into a fountain, a hole drilled in the middle with water cascading over the sides.

"It's hard to improve on Mother Nature," Kristine says. "I felt like I was just a tool to put the rocks together. The rocks couldn't do it themselves, so they had me to help."

Kristine began displaying her sculptures around her property and entering them in local art shows. As word of her craftsmanship grew, so, too, did the number of buyers. By this point, the landscaper who'd trained her was working for her occasionally, installing her pieces in customers' yards.

After only a few months of sculpting, Kristine visited a quarry on the Connecticut–Rhode Island border where she spotted a pile of sedimentary rocks jumbled in a heap, half-hidden by dirt and leaves. They took her breath away. Formed beneath a once-rushing river, the rocks were striated with gorgeous horizontal layers of brown and bronze. Kristine hauled them home and worked that entire summer piecing them together into benches. When her hometown art museum paid $4,000 for one of the benches—which Kristine dubbed "Pinnacle," because it represented the high point in her life—she was finally ready to say it out loud: *I am a sculptor!*

"It was as if my whole life had led up to this," she says.

That was six years ago. Since then, Kristine's clientele has grown. Though she sells pieces at local nurseries and via Facebook, her main showroom is still her own yard.

"The garden clubs come here to have their meetings," she says. "And painters bring their students to create pictures of the rocks." A small birdbath might fetch $350, a fountain, $850, and a five-foot sculpture, $2,500. Some clients have a yard full of her works.

"It's all one of a kind," she says. "Nothing mass-produced, that's for sure. That's the beauty of the work I do."

Gone for good is the sense of entrapment that Kristine once felt at the factory. Now she spends most of her days outside, clad in a face mask and earplugs, operating her prized grinder. And when she slices into a boulder, the blade grinding and whining, the dust cloud surrounding her, she thinks of her grandfather and the love of the stone that he passed on to her.

"I'm a different person now," Kristine says. "In the factory, I always felt sick. Now, out in the fresh air, I'm always happy. And things around me seem happier, too. Sometimes, I'll be working on a birdbath, and I can see the little chickadees in the tree just waiting for me to finish. And when I'm done, I'll fill it with water and they'll come zooming in. It's like they're saying, 'Oh, look what she's made for us!'"

Weiss Cater & Son

Mari Ann Weiss Cater, 58
Chicago, Illinois

I n 2008, all five pillars of Mari Ann Weiss Cater's life either cracked or crumbled.

First, her 18-year-old son, Nathaniel, was battling cancer. Then, Mari Ann's husband of 25 years moved out. Three months later, the media advertising company where she had worked for more than two decades closed, leaving her without a job—or health insurance for her and Nathaniel. That fall, her best friend, Janice, died, followed in November by Mari Ann's mother. It was, as they say, her annus horribilis.

"I was devastated beyond belief," Mari Ann says. "I was scared. I really didn't know how anything was going to turn out."

Of course, caring for Nathaniel, her only child, was Mari Ann's first priority. He'd undergone radiation therapy, but then made the risky decision to cut short his follow-up chemotherapy because the treatment had weakened him horribly. The good news was that the cancer, an aggressive form called rhabdomyosarcoma, seemed to be in remission.

"But he'd lost a lot of weight," Mari Ann recalls, "and I had to be strong for him. So I only allowed myself to cry once a day, in the shower. I would melt down in that moment, but breaking down completely wasn't an option."

For the next three years, Mari Ann focused on getting Nathaniel back to college. She also struggled through an ugly divorce that left her vulnerable financially and tried to get a decent-paying job while supporting herself and Nathaniel with money from her 401k.

"Being an older woman, I didn't have an easy time finding a job that matched my skill set and paid enough," says Mari Ann. "I'd been a vice president responsible for selling multimillion-dollar advertising packages and managing 30 radio stations in the Midwest. I sent out dozens of résumés that were never answered, and it was humiliating to now be interviewing with people 20 years my junior who were telling me I wasn't qualified. The few positions that I was offered paid $30,000 a year, not nearly enough. And Nathaniel and I were quickly going through my 401k."

When Mari Ann's friends suggested that she turn a favorite hobby into her new career, she'd just laugh. "You've got to be kidding me!" she'd say. "With the way my life has been, my hobby is *sleeping*."

The closest thing Mari Ann had ever had to a hobby was scouting for furniture and accessories for her home. "I had always loved going to thrift shops," Mari Ann recalls. "I'd buy a beautiful mirror here, a side table there. I was good at spotting little treasures. And I wondered, could I turn *that* into a career?"

Maybe—Mari Ann had a close friend who had recently quit her corporate job in New York City, moved to Virginia Beach, Virginia, and opened a consignment shop selling furniture and home goods. "I visited her and saw what she was doing, and I realized I could do it, too—I just had to learn how."

So Mari Ann went back to Chicago, rolled up her sleeves, and started doing her homework.

"I came across an EPA report that estimated that 8.8 million tons of furniture ended up in landfills in 2005 alone; that convinced me that there would be plenty of people out there with furniture to sell."

She searched online for furniture consignment shops in other cities and called the ones that looked good, asking owners if they'd be willing to share their insights. "I had experienced so much rejection when looking for a job that being hung up on or ignored didn't faze me. When someone was willing to talk, I'd keep it simple and ask for just one or two bits of advice.

"One person taught me about pricing used furniture—the rule of thumb is that it's usually 20 to 50 percent of the original cost, but if a piece is in excellent condition and the manufacturer is still offering it at full price, you can sell it for higher," Mari Ann says.

Several dealers stressed the importance of researching every piece. "If I was selling an item, I had better have the accurate information on the manufacturer and value, or I'd lose credibility." They also warned Mari Ann that working evenings and weekends was part of the job. "If I wasn't willing to put in the time, they said, I should consider another line of work."

But Mari Ann thought it sounded like a perfect second career. She scouted locations and found two side-by-side storefront spaces totaling around 3,800 square feet on Michigan Avenue, Chicago's main shopping street. And they were right in her neighborhood.

"The South Loop, where I live, is mostly residential and had no home furnishing stores," she says. "I knew people here would appreciate having a place to go and browse." Even though the Michigan Avenue address would cost her more in rent, it was on the lobby level of a residential building and had lots of foot traffic.

So Mari Ann took the leap, using most of the money left in her 401k to pay for a one-year lease on the store, which she named Urban Remix, and to buy high-quality, gently used items to stock it with: art, vases, lamps, rugs, small pieces of furniture.

"I got some pieces from estate sales, including chandeliers that helped to create the upscale atmosphere I wanted," she says. She also started going to auctions. "I love them. They're great fun, and very exciting, but you have to be careful. You can get carried away with raising the paddle!"

Because the shop space was austere—unfinished walls and a concrete floor—Mari Ann warmed it up by laying down luxurious used carpets and

hanging up dozens of mirrors and paintings (everything was for sale). Big windows facing the busy street allowed passersby to get a good look inside.

With no budget left for advertising, Mari Ann relied heavily on word of mouth, asking everyone who came into the store for their email addresses so she could invite them to parties she hosted for local artists or trunk shows. "It was risky," she admits. "I would only occasionally put an ad in a free newspaper requesting furniture or announcing a sale." But before long she had compiled more than 1,800 email addresses, and people were regularly sending new customers her way.

Starting the business was unquestionably scary. "I was nervous—and everything was at stake," says Mari Ann. But she always reminded herself that she had weathered worse—*much* worse. When Nathaniel had been diagnosed with cancer as a sophomore in high school, "we were told he might not live that long." But he did, and despite 48 weeks of chemo, he was able to graduate on time three years later.

"Looking back, I realize that the first time he got cancer, I survived by learning to focus on the positive. So when he relapsed and my company was liquidated, I did the same thing: I kept thinking that if I hadn't lost my job, I wouldn't have had as much time to spend with him as he recovered or to be with my friend Janice or my mother in the months before they died."

The emotional support between Nathaniel and Mari Ann is a two-way street. "He has always been my biggest fan," she says. "About two years ago, he wrote me a letter thanking me for making sure he never had to be alone in the hospital, for listening to him when he needed to talk, and for giving him advice without judging. The fact that he was so grateful took my breath away."

Nathaniel has since graduated from college and is back home, having been accepted into a competitive entrepreneur training program at the University of Chicago. He helps Mari Ann out at the store one day a week and is always there for her to bounce ideas off. "He is truly like a business partner to me," she says.

Today, two years after opening, her store is an eclectic mix of items, from something as expensive as a Chagall painting and handmade Asian armoire worth $20,000 to more affordable things like sofas and chairs from stores like Crate & Barrel.

"I love the store," she says. "You know, I took every cent out of my 401k to open this place. I could have used that money just to pay the bills and keep looking for a job that might never have surfaced, but I didn't. I'm glad I decided to use it to invest in myself."

PART SEVEN

Adventurers

"Here I was, holding this amazing creature that had found its way from the ocean to the river to me."

The Wanderluster

Lori-Ann Murphy, 54
Willow Creek, Montana
. . . by way of San Pedro, Belize
. . . by way of Venice Beach, California

Some women are afraid of change. Others thrive on it. And if you have wanderlust like Lori-Ann Murphy, you seek it out.

"I'm a born roamer," she says. "Chalk it up to an abundant amount of curiosity and an extreme fear of boredom."

Lori-Ann was a fourth-generation nurse who had started working in hospitals when she was just 14. To many, nursing is a secure job, but it's also one that fit Lori's restless temperament perfectly. Hospitals everywhere need nurses, so whenever she got the itch to move, she would look for a job in the Southwest desert, or the Rockies, or wherever the Southern California native had never lived.

"The length of time I spent in any one place varied," she says. "On the short side, I'd stay until my curiosity was satisfied; longer stays usually meant

I had something to keep me there: coursework, a nursing contract, a boy-friend (several), or even a husband (two)."

But change was always the most important part of the equation. That is, until one day when she was in her late twenties, and her perception of change . . . *changed*.

Lori-Ann was working at a hospital in Arizona when a doctor friend invited her on a fly-fishing trip to the Deschutes River in Oregon. Tall and athletic, Lori-Ann had always enjoyed the outdoors—skiing, surfing, and playing beach volleyball—but she had never been fly-fishing.

Drifting along the wide river, tucked between the fir-covered cliffs of the eastern Cascades, Lori-Ann was struck by the beauty and serenity of the remote location. But what was truly life-changing about the trip occurred when Lori-Ann caught her first fish. It was a steelhead, a rare sea-run rainbow trout that spends two or three years in the ocean, then returns to fresh water to spawn. In this case, the fish would have left the Pacific, traveled up the Columbia River, then up the Deschutes, before encountering Lori-Ann, who had come all the way from Arizona and had stood hip-deep in the river for four hours before they met.

"Here I was, holding this amazing creature that had found its way hundreds of miles from the ocean to the river to me," says Lori-Ann, "and I was blown away, by both the marvels of nature and the randomness of the world. I felt so present, and had such a deep connection to that fish—and to nature."

Before coming to Oregon, Lori-Ann had been reading *The Power of Myth* by the philosopher Joseph Campbell and had been intrigued by his teaching to "follow your bliss." When she caught that steelhead, Campbell's words echoed in her head:

If you follow your bliss, you put yourself on a kind of track that has been there all the while, waiting for you, and the life that you ought to be living is the one you are living.

Fly-fishing, Lori-Ann discovered, was her bliss, and she began looking for nursing jobs that would allow her to actively pursue it in her free time. She also knew that learning a whole new skill would be somewhat humbling and that she'd have to ask a lot of questions.

"I called myself 'The Queen of the No-Pride Club,'" she recalls. "I decided to learn fly-fishing from the very best. This required finding the right instructors and allowing myself to let go of any need to control—and to *listen*. For an alpha female, that is incredibly challenging. But as I continued to fish, I kept listening, and kept discovering."

As Lori-Ann's fly-fishing proficiency grew, so, too, did her reputation among locals. Eventually, Orvis, the venerable Vermont-based company that is the go-to source for all things outdoors, certified her as its first female guide. The last step before certification is to take a client onto the river; in Lori-Ann's case, her test client was Leigh Perkins, the owner of Orvis.

"I was late picking him up," Lori-Ann recalls, "which left me a wreck until I finally blurted, 'Leigh, it's making me too damn nervous knowing you are the owner of Orvis, so I'm going to pretend you are one of my regular fishing pals and go from there!' He said, 'That's a great idea, Lovely!'—he calls me 'Lovely.' So we fished all day and then sat down to dinner at nine p.m., still wearing our waders."

Lori-Ann's rising reknown as "the fly-fishing nurse" began creating even more opportunities, some completely unexpected. Such was the case when Universal Studios called—out of the blue—and offered her a gig teaching

Meryl Streep and Kevin Bacon how to fly-fish for the movie *The River Wild*. Then Martha Stewart called—she wanted to do a story on fly-fishing in her magazine and needed Lori-Ann's help.

"Talk about amazing," Lori-Ann says. "Seventeen people from the magazine—art directors, photographers, stylists—made this expedition to the Wind River Wilderness, south of Jackson Hole. We hiked 11 miles and fished the creeks and lakes in the area, and we had a blast. There were a lot of bears out that year, and one got into my tent. So I had to move and ended up sleeping next to Martha. There's the makings of a movie in there!"

Though Lori-Ann continued to work as a nurse, which she still considered her "profession," fly-fishing opportunities kept cropping up. "I held an Orvis class for three women," she says, "one from New York, one from Texas, and one from Jackson Hole. They spent two days with me having fun and learning a ton. When it was over, they walked into the Orvis Store in Jackson, Wyoming, and each dropped two grand because they wanted to buy 'everything Lori-Ann had.' Being an astute businessman, Leigh had me start the Women's Schools for Orvis."

The classes were a hit from the very beginning; the first one attracted 27 students. That gave Lori-Ann the idea of offering her own tours specifically geared to women, so in 1994 she and a friend cofounded Reel Women Fly-Fishing Adventures.

With so many stars aligning in her new career, Lori-Ann decided it was finally time to set nursing aside. For the next dozen years, her life was devoted to guiding, trips, schools, trade shows, speaking engagements, and traveling the world to fly-fish. "I had always been looking for that new magic place," she says. "I began to realize it was right where I was!"

Then in 2009, Lori-Ann got an offer she couldn't refuse: She was recruited to interview for the job of director of fishing for El Pescador Lodge in Belize, a tropical outpost along the north-eastern shores of Central America. El Pescador is a beautiful, Orvis-endorsed, saltwater fishing nirvana, where well-moneyed enthusiasts pay $6,000 a week to pursue a grand slam of bonefish, tarpon, and permit fish. The resort interviewed 175 men for the position. "No women applied, not even me. Then a guide friend said, 'Lori-Ann is the one for the job,' and I got it."

But even after they'd made her an offer, she had her doubts. "I wondered whether an outsider like me would be welcomed by the guides, all of whom were men, and a pretty macho bunch at that. But all my friends screamed at me, 'No way are you *not* taking it! This is the job you were *meant* to do!'"

Today, Lori-Ann works at El Pescador eight months a year; the rest of the time she guides trips around the world.

"It's not a profession I ever imagined myself doing," she says. "But it goes to show you: Pay attention to what falls out of the sky. We work and work and work, focused on goals. But sometimes the best opportunities are the ones we don't expect.

"I loved nursing, but even with all the moving around, the job had become predictable. Fly-fishing never is. When you're there wading in the water, there's only one constant: the thrill of catching a fish. Everything else—the people, the day, the fish themselves—is different. And that is the bliss I've been wandering and searching for all of my life."

A Vrooom of Her Own

Mary Petersen, 46

Fremont, Nebraska

"Miss Prim and Proper." That's how Mary Petersen imagined her friends and neighbors saw her—the single mom who raised two kids on her own; the exacting math teacher for whom the most important equation in life is $x^2 + y^2 = 1$; the diligent professional who put in long, hard nights and weekends getting her master's degree. That's Mary Petersen.

Or at least that *was* Mary Petersen. About ten years ago, after nearly two decades of being hardworking and conscientious, she'd had her fill. Her son and daughter were teenagers. "Every day they grew more independent of me," she says, "and eventually it dawned on me that the same thing was happening in reverse: *I* was growing more independent of *them*. And that was a good thing. I began to think that it was time I did something for me."

It didn't take Mary long to figure out what. Ever since childhood, she had been drawn to motorcycles. "I always loved that experience when you'd hear the pipes or an engine rev and it sounded so powerful, and you couldn't help but spin your head around to see it. There was also a sense of freedom I associated with it, the idea that whatever else was going on, you could just get on your bike and ride." When she saw an ad for a motorcycle safety course that was being given nearby, she thought, *I can do this, and I can do it on my own. I don't need a male to do it with me. I can go to the class! I can make it happen!*"

Perhaps to gain a little moral support, Mary showed the ad to a neighbor. "I knew what I was doing," she laughs. "She's what I call an 'encourager.'" Within a couple weeks they were *both* taking lessons.

"They taught us everything," says Mary. "How the engine works, how to make repairs, and lots and lots of safety." Mary proved to be an apt pupil—the instructor even commented that the math teacher was also an excellent student. But her performance in the classroom did not immediately translate into success on the road.

"I was extremely confident during class," she says, "but once it was over, I knew I couldn't just jump on a bike and ride. It wasn't all glory and freedom, but a massive amount of responsibility."

At first Mary struggled with the weight and power of the motorcycle on the road, but bit by bit, she asserted herself and took control. She bought a Honda Rebel 250, a reliable cruiser-style bike with a standard engine but a fairly light weight of 325 pounds.

"I'm a relatively tall woman, so I looked a little awkward on this smallish bike," she says. "My neighbors kidded me, but I didn't mind a bit. I loved coming home from work, getting on the bike, and practicing."

The next big change came when a couple who were also motorcycle enthusiasts asked Mary to accompany them on a jaunt. They also invited a friend named Mark. The two hit it off, but Mary didn't have a lot of time for dating. Mark was persistent: He offered to take her out on his cycle to show her some of the safely paved country roads in the area. She couldn't resist.

"Mark and I were having a fine time," Mary recalls, "but suddenly the paved road turned into gravel, which is always dangerous. Mark slowed the bike to a safe crawl but before we could adjust, a dog charged out of nowhere. Mark stayed cool and executed the most impressive Harley U-turn—on gravel!—with this dog barking and biting our ankles. I was hugely impressed."

Impressed, maybe, but in no rush to start a relationship. Only after a year, when her son was in college and her daughter in high school, did Mary and Mark have their first real date. Four years later, they married.

"I tell you, riding a couple hours through the fields outside of town lowered my blood pressure quicker than lisinopril," Mary says. "And on the way home, I'd make sure to rumble past the skate park, and I'd wave and holler to my students there. They couldn't believe that Ms. Petersen wasn't home grading their quizzes but was wearing leather and wraparound shades and roaring around town."

Now she and Mark go everywhere on a motorcycle—his. "What I had to admit to myself," says Mary, "is that as much as I like riding motorcycles, what I really love is riding *on* motorcycles—sitting on the back, feeling the engine, free to look in every direction and take in the whole view."

Every summer, Mary and Mark take a big excursion. They've been to Yellowstone, Big Horn, the Grand Canyon—all over the West.

But Mary also comes to New York occasionally to visit her son. One recent trip, he surprised her by taking her to a trapeze lesson. "I could see these slender poles going up, up, up, and against the open sky they looked impossibly high. Awaiting my turn, I was trembling with fear, thinking *You've got to be kidding.* So I asked my son what on earth made him think I would do such a thing. He answered, 'Mom, you'll try anything once.'"

Then the former Miss Prim and Proper stepped up and flew through the sky.

Taking Off

Adria Drew, 48

Long Island, New York

dria Drew was not boarding that plane. Not a little puddle jumper with peeling paint and propellers that almost made it look like a toy. She had never seen a prop plane up close, let alone ridden on one. *No way,* she said to herself. *I am not getting on that thing.*

Hysterical, she called her boyfriend, Larry, back in New York to tell him she was terrified of the plane and was going to rent a car and drive from Los Angeles to Palm Springs instead. He failed to calm her down. Less than an hour later, she called him again, this time telling him something so outrageous he hung up on her.

At the time, Adria was in her midtwenties and worked for MCI, a telecommunications company. She began her career there as a secretary, but a colleague who recognized her people skills suggested she go for a job in sales. So she approached the sales manager in Westchester County, New York, where she lived. He refused to hire her on the grounds that she had no track record.

For Adria, the word "no" fell on deaf ears.

"I always say, if anyone tells you that you can't do something, don't listen," Adria says. Rather than retreating to her secretarial desk, she forged ahead and asked the sales manager in New York City, a vastly larger market, to give her a shot.

Bull's-eye!

For the next 11 years, Adria had one goal in mind: Show the cynic in Westchester he'd made a mistake and that she had the right stuff. And she did—successfully convincing many companies, including the New York Times Company, to switch their long-distance service and rising to become one of MCI's top sales representatives. Selling voice and data services to other large companies proved to be lucrative and she won awards, often—and most satisfyingly—presented in front of the manager who wouldn't give her a chance.

Then she won a visit to Palm Springs, the trip that would change her life.

The flight from New York to Los Angeles's LAX was on a large commercial jet, not a white-knuckle affair. At LAX, Adria boarded a bus that took her across the airfield for the short flight to Palm Springs. That's when the panic set in.

"An older man saw how nervous I was," she recalls. "He told me he took the flight all the time and that if I sat behind the pilots, I could see what they were doing and I'd probably feel more comfortable." That lifted Adria's anxiety, and she stepped onto the puddle jumper.

This was in the days before 9/11. The plane, a Beech 1900 twin-engine turbo prop, had no cockpit door, only a curtain separating the pilots from the passengers. The curtain was left open.

"The next thing I know we're going down the runway and taking off," says Adria. "I'm looking out the front window, which is completely different from looking out the side. The sky was gorgeous, with mountains all around us—it was so dramatic. I had never experienced such exhilaration before."

Landing 45 minutes later, she called Larry and told him she was going to learn how to fly. That's when he questioned her sanity and hung up on her.

Months went by, and Adria continued to muse about getting her pilot's license. Then her beloved father was diagnosed with pancreatic cancer. In six weeks, he was dead. He was only 65.

You never know how much time you've got, she thought. *I'm really going to do it—I'm going to learn how to fly.*

Adria was doing well enough at MCI to be able to afford two flight lessons per month. Studying for her certificate and haunting local airports consumed her weekends. Soon she married Larry, quit MCI, and began to work for her husband's hair products business as a sales rep.

Then an old pilot friend pushed her to apply for a job at a major airline. By now she was the mother of two young boys and thought being a pilot for a charter airline would have more flexibility, so she was hired at a charter and took to the skies. Three years later the same pilot friend again urged her to try for a major airline. Her boys were older now and able to cope better with a sometimes-absent mother.

"If you don't ask, you don't even give yourself a chance," she says. "I guess my sales background helped give me the confidence to just go for things."

Adria asked, and two months later was in an intensive eight-week training course in Dallas, working in a simulator and rooming with a 23-year-old candidate.

"I became a commercial airline pilot when I was 44," says Adria. A captain she worked with nicknamed her "Grandma."

When she started flying commercially, it was "an out-of-body experience," she marvels. "I can still remember when I got my first uniform—the stripes on the sleeves, the hat, the whole outfit."

Not much rattles Adria, the sort of temperament one wants in a pilot. A month or so into active training she was the copilot on a flight out of Charlotte, North Carolina, where there were maintenance issues. After a three-hour delay they took off for New York's LaGuardia Airport, where they encountered bad weather and were ordered into a holding pattern. Finally, the pilots had to make a decision about landing at an alternate airport. They radioed air traffic controllers about trying for Kennedy, but that was a no-go, too.

"The captain was phenomenal and let me be part of the decision," Adria says. "We concluded Boston was our best bet, far enough east to beat the bad weather. We made an announcement about the diversion. And all of a sudden, the flight attendant dings us. We had a medical emergency in back."

A passenger, perhaps distressed by the scary weather, couldn't breathe and had to be put on oxygen. To make matters worse, the Boston air traffic controllers informed the pilots they couldn't handle any more incoming flights. Fuel was getting low. Finally, they landed at Bradley International Airport, near Hartford, Connecticut, in the middle of a blizzard. The passengers and crew ended up at a hotel, which soon lost power.

Characteristically, Adria rolled with it. "You can't sit there saying, 'Oh my God.' There's no room for that. You just have to stay focused and do what you have to do to get your job done. That's something that's either in your blood or it isn't."

Adria sees no difference between male and female pilots in this respect, and she's experienced no institutional sexism at the companies she's worked for, reporting that they're well-schooled in protocol and the perils of sexual harassment.

However, not *everyone* has gotten the memo about female pilots. At the Chicago airport, Adria, in full uniform, waited curbside with a group for a hotel van. A woman ran over her foot with her carry-on and then asked her to load it into the trunk, assuming she was the van driver. Another time,

Adria was at an airport shop when she was summoned by a woman alarmed by an unattended bag. She took for granted Adria was security.

Adria laughs off those moments, preferring to focus on the positive. "One time I was standing at the exit door of the plane, saying good-bye to passengers, when a woman in her late sixties asked, 'You're the pilot of this plane?'" Adria acknowledged that she was. "Did you do this flight?" the woman persisted. Adria said she had. "She gave me this huge smile, and said, 'Good for you. It was wonderful.'"

Despite Larry's initial shock when Adria said she wanted to be a pilot, he's been supportive. She can give him two hours' notice that she'll be gone for four days and he's happy to take the boys, now 11 and 15, wherever they need to go and be there when they come home.

Adria recently stopped commercial flying to take a job with the FAA as a safety inspector, but she's still up in the air a lot. She reports that her boys have been exposed to her piloting so frequently, they think nothing of it—until they see their friends' reactions: *Wow! Your mom's an airline pilot?*

"Based on outside feedback," Adria says, "it made them realize their mom is kind of cool."

Without Borders

Patty Merrill, 67
Portland, Oregon

Patty Merrill was in the rut to end all ruts. And the worst part was, just six years earlier, she'd been doing what she loved best: surrounding herself with books.

"I have always been a passionate collector," she says. "I started gathering things when I was just eight years old and found an abandoned teddy bear on the side of the street. But I was especially drawn to books. Just holding a book in your hand can feel remarkable."

That passion had landed her the ideal job at Portland's massive Powell's bookstore.

"Because Powell's is so well-respected," she says, "brilliant authors were always coming in to sign their books. I had the thrill of rubbing elbows with writers like Wallace Stegner and Edward Abbey. It was great to be among creative types."

But in 1996, Patty found herself in that classic business bind: Her aptitude at her job had propelled her through the ranks at Powell's, taking her further and further from the books she loved. She was now a middle manager, overseeing two satellite branches of the store in a different part of town. She spent most of her time managing personalities, schedules, and budgets. It was joyless work.

"I kept trying to adapt to this job, but it never worked," she says. "I thought something was wrong with me, and that led to a lot of anger and depression."

This was not the first time Patty had felt at odds with something in her life. She'd once owned her own bookshop in the small town of Albany, Oregon. "It was the seventies, and it was so exciting when new titles came through the door," she recalls. "Those books weren't just ahead of the curve, they were *setting* the curve."

But as much as Patty had adored that shop, small-town life was too confining for a free-spirited feminist like herself. "Everything was male-dominated," she remembers. "When I went to the bank to borrow money to open the store, the loan officer didn't even look at me. He would only deal with my husband. I tried to make myself small to fit into the life I was living. I always felt unique there, but not in a good way. I kept thinking, *Why can't I water myself down and just be happy?*"

But watering herself down wasn't in Patty's character, and her need for a more progressive culture drove her back to Portland—and the middle-management job at Powell's in which she now found herself stuck. Finally, convinced that she was about to be fired anyway, she took a deep breath and turned in her resignation.

"I spent the next six months in the fetal position," she says, "trying to figure out what to do next. Here I was in my forties; it was a great time for a midlife crisis anyway. Authenticity had always been so important to me, and yet I had spent all these years trying to fit in where I didn't belong. No wonder it had all gone downhill."

Patty was determined to find an occupation that would feel genuine to her, and her mind kept returning to one of the most inspiring periods of her life.

"Just before I married my husband, who was working as an architect in Portland," she says, "he won a traveling fellowship to study monasteries. So right after our wedding, when we were both in our midtwenties, we headed off to Europe and explored all of these wonderful, ancient places."

Given her unquenchable curiosity, the trip was intoxicating to Patty, especially when she visited the Benaki Museum in Athens. The impact it had on her was seismic.

"The museum was simply a collection of folk art, textiles, tiles, and quirky everyday things, objects I had never seen collected before in such depth. It was fascinating." The more Patty flashed back to that experience, the more she believed that it might hold the secret to her future. "Remembering it all made me feel like I had been held hostage in my own life."

Excited and energized, Patty shared her thoughts with a friend, and in just a few days they were hatching a business plan. "We decided we would travel around the world, buy things that no one else had, and sell them wholesale and retail," she says. Using Patty's savings—the severance money she had gotten from Powell's—and some funds that her partner had acquired through a divorce, they got started. First, they rented a space in a warehouse on a busy street in southeast Portland. Their store, they decided, would be called Cargo. Now all they needed were the goods.

Patty describes her first buying trip to Singapore as a "leap of faith." A cousin of hers was a teacher there, so she had a guide, but she had no idea what kinds of products she would find ("I didn't even know what I was looking for!"). But she was excited to get started and to travel to exotic places again.

After arriving in Singapore, Patty first ventured out to big furniture factories where expats were buying sleek, perfectly finished rosewood dining sets. Patty quickly realized that this was definitely not what she had traveled all this way to discover. Instead, she asked her cousin to escort her to the sketchier part of town, where she bought beautiful baskets, old Chinese-style furniture, and Buddhist shrines.

But Patty had her heart set on objects that had even more of a special, even spiritual aura.

The farther she ventured away from the city—toward the rural coastal regions—the more she felt her heart lift. "The towns became quirkier and more chaotic," she explains, "and, all at once, the excitement of Asia took hold of me. I love that feeling of chaos, when you're in a place that's unlike any other you've ever been, and you have to discover its own hidden order."

One morning, wandering on foot, Patty came upon a workshop where a man was making animal figurines out of sticks and paper.

"They were these little mythical creatures that were probably meant to be burned as religious offerings," she says. "They were so beautiful and the craftsman made them slowly and lovingly. He wouldn't let me buy anything, but he did give me one. You had to hold one in your hands to feel how special it was. It was exactly the type of authentic object that I wanted to bring back with me."

As much as the trip to Singapore had been an eye-opener, businesswise it was a bust. "Everything I was interested in was way overpriced," Patty recalls. And her next trip, to Mexico, was likewise a financial flop, thanks to customs agents who tossed fragile items around carelessly, destroying her new investment.

But each misstep taught Patty a valuable lesson: She needed to find cheaper sources and stick to countries where shipping was more reliable. Despite the setbacks, her enthusiasm never waned.

"I was so into this new idea for the future—no doubt because it was my *only* idea for the future—that there was no backing out," she says. Unfortunately, her friend couldn't shoulder the financial losses, so Patty used what was left of her own savings to buy her out.

Now nearly broke, Patty borrowed some money from a family member and prepared to go it alone. At that vulnerable moment, she happened to cross paths with a businessman named John Anderson. An importer who lived in Bali and traveled the world selling jewelry, John took Patty under his wing, inviting her to visit him in Bali to shop for inventory.

"I filled up a container with amazing handmade jewelry, art, textiles, and crafts, which I shipped back to Portland and had much more success selling."

By soaking up John's insights and monitoring sales closely, Patty hit her stride. "In the beginning, I was always interested in the exotic and unusual," she says. "But that doesn't always translate to the buyer. Sometimes I would be too far ahead of the buying curve. So I started to sell useful items that had a more immediate appeal—household textiles, like tablecloths and quilts; and desktop items like stationery, ink pads, and writing journals. I began mixing new products in with the old, a trick I had picked up from Powell's that both raises the perceived value of the older item and gives the new item some context."

Strategies that seem obvious in hindsight took time for her to adopt. "I began to reorder what was selling well instead of always leaping ahead to a new and untested product. I also realized the importance of introducing various price points so that everyone could afford something."

With her husband and daughter, Katy, cheering her on, Patty continued

traveling to far-flung places throughout Asia, Africa, and Europe, taking monthlong trips two or three times a year and bringing back containers full of one-of-a-kind creations. She bought vintage and handmade toys, jewelry of all kinds, paintings and sculptures, pillows and quilts, chairs and tables, shrines and altars—all gorgeous, handcrafted, and hard to find. And of course, there were books—on travel, exotic cultures and cuisines, biographies, and guides to interesting textiles and crafts. In order to accommodate all of Patty's purchases, Cargo had to relocate to a bigger space—and business boomed.

With success, however, came a problem—ironically, the very problem Patty had encountered at Powell's. "The more employees I hired, the more things began to implode from a lack of structure," she says. "But this time, I found a solution: a business partner who is creative and fun, but is also amazing at all the things I'm not. She organizes the staff, works on the online store, and creates displays, leaving me to focus on what I love and do best: traveling and finding fantastic inventory."

Seventeen years after her stomach-churning Powell days, Patty now heads to work feeling relaxed and confident. "I no longer think in terms of whether or not I'm successful at my job," she says, "and that gives me a great sense of freedom. I know how blessed I am to be doing what I love, and I'm grateful for that opportunity every day. I'm 67 years old and I don't see myself slowing down at all. I could be doing this well into my eighties."

Patty continues to travel—seeing the sights, meeting her artisans, and joyously leaping over cultural boundaries with each new adventure.

"It's amazing to have these meaningful connections all over the world," she says. "Thanks to Cargo, I no longer feel like I'm being held hostage. I finally have a life that's big enough for me."

Sails Lady

Ella Vickers, 42
Beaufort, North Carolina

"Almost 15 years ago, I was working as the First Mate on the Columbia, a beauty of a yacht out of Newport that had been the winner of a historic America's Cup race. We were competing in a regatta off the coast of Rhode Island, and there was a great, powerful wind. It wasn't a storm, mind you, just a heavy wind, and it had us keeled over quite a lot.

"But we developed a problem: The head of the mainsail kept coming out of the track. The mainsail is huge—90 feet tall and 68 feet long—and it was taking the force of this wind, really whipping us along; we were rolling up and down with the waves. If it came out of the track completely, we would be disabled, pretty near dead in the water.

"Well, somebody was going to have to do something about this, and since I was First Mate, as well as being the lightest person of the

14-member crew, it was going to have to be me. So I buckled myself into a bosun's chair, which is really just a plank with straps and a harness, and the others hoisted me up in the air, 90 meters, just a yard shy of the length of a football field. My life was in their hands. When I got to the top, I had to wrap my legs around the mast, which kept waving back and forth, and lash the top of the sail to the mast with a heavy line. Then I had to wait patiently in the bosun's chair, swaying in the wind, until the crew hauled me back down again.

"Of course, at night, the mainsail had to come back down, so I would have to go up the mast again. This went on for a week. Up and down, up and down.

"But I was never scared. My love of sailing made me crazy enough to do that."

Sailing is in Ella Vickers's blood. She grew up on the beaches of the Cape Fear River near Wilmington, North Carolina, not far from the coastal town of Beaufort, where she now makes her home. As a child, Ella sailed with her father and her uncle, learning the ways of the sea until she was old enough to earn her keep by crewing on excursions to the Bahamas and back. She raced competitively in college, ran whale-watching catamarans in Hawaii, sailed solo around the Caribbean in her twenties, and raced in the waters off South Africa. And if you saw her today, you'd probably think she could spend a decade at the bottom of a cave and still come out with her skin bronzed and her hair sun-streaked.

But Ella's days racing yachts are behind her. The turning point came a couple of years after that memorable experience on the America's Cup yacht. The *Columbia* was docked in Edgartown on Martha's Vineyard when it was time to replace its sails.

"Racing vessels get new sails every couple of years," Ella explains. "The wear and tear is usually minimal, but after a time the sails stretch out a bit, and when you're racing, you want them to be as taut as possible. After we changed the sails, I realized that the ship's owners were making arrangements to have the sails taken to the town dump."

Ella was appalled—it seemed like such a waste. "It's odd," she says. "I'd been changing sails all my life, but I'd never paid attention to what happened to them next. Once I realized they were going to be tossed, I said, 'I'll take them.'"

Of course, that was not as easy as it sounds. "A mainsail alone weighs 225 pounds, and it's unwieldy," she says. "I didn't really know what I was going to do with the material, but I was sure I'd think of something."

Sailing, as it turns out, wasn't the only thing Ella was good at. As a child, she'd been taught to sew by her great-grandmother and often made clothing and accessories for herself. Ella proved to be such a good seamstress that she was hired by her aunt, who had a marine canvas business that made tarps, biminis, dodgers, and awnings for boats.

Now, after disembarking from the *Columbia*, Ella persuaded some friends to help her haul the salvaged sails back to her apartment, where she sat down in front of her heavy-duty sewing machine and began fooling around to see what she could make with them.

"It was just creative time for me," she says. "Anybody who knows me knows that I can sit down, sew something, rip it up, sew something different— and do that for half the night." She thought the sailcloth might be good for totes or duffel bags. "I played with size, colors, decoration. I figured the bags would come in handy sometime on the boat."

That night Ella created three large carryalls made from the white mainsail cloth, decorating them with brightly colored abstract shapes from smaller Mylar sails. In the morning, she slung them over her arm and was carrying them to the *Columbia* when a voice called out to her from another boat: "Cool bags!"

"Thanks," Ella replied. "I made them last night."

"No way!" said the woman, who came over to get a closer look, joined by her husband. "Can you make some for us?" he asked.

Ella was reluctant; the *Columbia* was about to set sail, and she wasn't sure when she'd have the time to sew more.

"Or can we buy these?" the woman asked.

That was Ella's first sale. "I don't even remember what I charged," she says. "Twenty dollars each? Thirty? Basically I was just charging for my time."

A few nights later, Ella made more bags, and the same thing happened—people bought them off her arm. "I was astonished," she says. "Twice in one week. But that reaction gave me the idea that maybe I could make a living selling these bags."

Ella hadn't been in the market for a career change. She loved crewing on the *Columbia*. "Sometimes, we would take on passengers and go cruising," she says. "There would be three of us on the crew who would handle everything, and it was a great, fun atmosphere. And then sometimes, we would take on more crew, often as many as 14 people, and we would be competing. That was exhilarating; it was a blast to race.

"I wasn't thinking about the long term very much, just kind of assumed that before too many years I would move into something else. The people I knew who crewed professionally, and who did it into their forties—their bodies were hurting. You could see that this career was tough on the body. I was only having the normal aches and pains, but I didn't think I was immune."

More important, Ella was realizing she had ambitions beyond being a member of a crew. "In sailing, you experience a sense of freedom every day," she explains, "but you are also committed to the boat. You travel the world, but you go where the program says you go. You eat on the boat, you sleep on the boat, you don't go home for days at a time. You can't be a professional sailor forever if you want other things in your life, and I did. I wanted a family. I was interested in starting a business. I didn't expect to be making a switch imminently, but here was an interesting opportunity, and I felt I had to act on it."

Within a year of sewing that first bag, Ella quit the boat, but not without misgivings. She missed the opportunity to be First Mate the following year when the *Columbia* sailed to Great Britain for a regatta held in honor of the 150th anniversary of the America's Cup. "I got to go over and crew a little bit, kind of a 'friend of the ship' thing, but the boat did a whole tour down to Sardinia and around the Mediterranean, and I didn't get to go. I was bummin'! But I made a decision, and I have no regrets."

Ella moved back to Wilmington and set up shop. Two years of courses at Cape Fear Community College had taught her business fundamentals.

"I can't say we had that steep a learning curve," she says. "I just got some sewing machines. Reached out to racing friends to tell them about our interest in used sails. Hired some people. My best seamstress, the one who has been with me longest, couldn't even sew when I hired her! It took her a year to sew a straight line. She was just someone who needed a job, and I was someone who needed people."

But one thing Ella was not nonchalant about was her commitment to making the business work. "I put about $60,000 into the business during the first year or two," she says. "I took out loans, maxed out credit cards, and put every penny of profit back into the business. Back then, the principal place we sold the bags was boat shows—we still do that—and every weekend I'd go up and down the coast selling bags. Sometimes when I didn't have enough money for a hotel, I'd park at a friendly yacht club and sleep in my car."

Ella's bags sold well, but rising success brought its own challenges. "You work and work to get boutiques and department stores to open an account and stock your product," she says, "but as soon as someone places an order for $75,000 worth of merchandise, you have to turn around and shell out $37,500 to make them. And then a long time can pass between when you ship the products and when you get paid. The money issues may change, but they don't entirely go away. Eventually, though, like anything else, you figure out how to manage them."

Since it began, Ella's company has had steady growth—through sales at boat shows, small accounts with boutiques and department stores, and larger accounts with retailers like Lands' End and West Marine.

Steady as she goes might also be a good way to describe Ella's managerial style. Early on, a vendor associated with Key West Race Week placed what was then the largest order in the company's history. "It was one of those 'How can we possibly fill this order?' moments," she says. "But everybody got to work—I got on a machine myself—and we just did it."

There was, however, one challenge that almost made Ella want to close the business. Initially, she called her company Nautigear, a pun on the word "naughty."

"We loved that name," she says. "We thought it was catchy, sellable, and cool." But Nautica, the popular sportswear company, thought it sounded too much like its own and sued for trademark violation.

"It was tough, both financially and emotionally," recalls Ella. "Nautica is part of a huge conglomerate, and we were just getting started. So even though we thought the name was different enough and our logo was very different from theirs, we simply didn't have enough money to fight them in court."

Now, she says, it was the best thing that could have happened. "We

changed the name to Ella Vickers, which is something no one can take from us and which also transcends 'nautical' gear. With the Ella Vickers name, we're doing more than selling a bag; we're building a brand."

Today, Ella Vickers does more than $1 million in sales annually. Still led by the venerable Large Zip Tote, with its marine brass grommets and clips and corrosion-resistant zipper, the line has grown to include tennis bags, lacrosse bags, ski bags, snowshoe bags, boot bags, and items for the home like pillows and shower curtains. "We also do a lot of custom work for people who want flight bags or home design products," says Ella. Besides boutiques, department stores, and the retail website, Ella Vickers products can be found at the company's flagship store in Greenwich, Connecticut, not far from the sailboats of Long Island Sound.

After more than a decade in business, Ella has developed a few rules for success. "First, hire the best people you can. Pay a premium if you have to. They will stick around longer and make fewer mistakes, which will more than make up for the difference in wages. Years ago, I let one of my best seamstresses go because she wanted more than I wanted to pay. Instead, I kept some people who weren't as good and who never got better, and I rue the day I did that.

"Second, make a premium product and keep it that way. Don't sell out over cheap materials and overseas labor. Build in America." Ella employs nine people in her design studio and workshop in Wilmington, and has most of her products sewn in a factory in Manhattan. "I was never tempted to make my bags overseas," she says. "Something may look nice, but if it's made by pre-teens in Asia who are running sewing machines for 15 hours per day under substandard conditions, you don't really have a product you can be proud of."

Like climbing that mainsail on the *Columbia* all those years ago, owning her own company has been risky but rewarding. "I am in control of my own destiny," Ella says. "I set my own hours, and I'm spending most of my time designing, which I love."

Ella has built a family, too—she and her husband, Tony, an engineer and fellow sailing enthusiast, have two young children.

When she's not in her workroom, Ella still sails—on her very own fifty-foot cruising boat. "Everyone always says that when you're past forty, you're pretty much through with crewing on sailboats," Ella says. "But I've found a way to keep the sails in my life—and I've got a good wind behind me."

PART EIGHT

To Her Own Drummer

"My inner self was talking—and I listened."

Whiskey Business

Troy Ball, 53

Asheville, North Carolina

I t was as if young Frankenstein met Old MacDonald—with a touch of Austin Powers thrown in for good measure.

Tucked away in a small barn in the Great Smoky Mountains of North Carolina, Troy Ball and her friend John McEntire were like a pair of mad scientists—mixing, boiling, adding ingredients, then taking them out again—trying to achieve just the right formula for their precious concoction. "It was all undercover," says Troy. "But it was also really exciting. I mean, we'd hear somebody pulling up the gravel road, and we'd close the barn doors."

The reason for all the secrecy: Troy and John had built their own little distillery, and what they were doing—making moonshine—was criminal in the minds of some of the neighbors. "I'd come home from John's at night in my Carhartt coveralls, driving my Mercedes," Troy recalls, "smelling like a drunk who had passed out next to a campfire."

Troy's journey from mom to moonshine maker began back in 2003, when

225

she and her husband, Charlie, moved with their three sons to Asheville, North Carolina. Neighbors—usually old men—welcomed the family to the area by bringing over jars of hooch, a homemade, corn-based whiskey. "I would open a jar," she says, "and it would smell so terrible. I'd tell them, 'Yecch! I don't want any more of this bad stuff, so stop bringing it to me!' They'd say, 'Well, you can't get the good stuff, Troy, because people keep that for themselves.'"

Several years went by before an 80-year-old friend named Forrest, perhaps goaded by Troy's teasing about the subpar local liquor, finally brought over a sample of the good stuff. "He said, 'Now, Troy, this is something special. Promise me you'll taste this.'" So she did.

And it wasn't half bad. "It wasn't that burning-hot moonshine," Troy says. "It was surprisingly smooth."

That evening, some of Troy's girlfriends came over. "I said, 'Would y'all like to try some *good* moonshine?' We mixed it with some fruit juice, and they drank every drop."

Inspired by their reaction, Troy decided to do a bit of reconnaissance. "I went to the store and bought every unaged white whiskey available, but they were terrible compared to what Forrest had given me."

That got her thinking about something she'd once heard Ross Perot say: "If you want to be successful, study an industry and figure out what's missing."

"I realized that even though this quality white whiskey was an American tradition, it was unrepresented in the market," Troy says. "People all over the country were drinking Russian vodka when we had our own white spirit right here. It was the hole in the doughnut."

Discovering that hole came at a perfect time in Troy's life. At 48, she was itching to do something new. "I'm a born businessperson, but I got married right after graduating from Vanderbilt, and soon had two special-needs children." Troy and Charlie's first two sons—Marshall, now 27, and Coulton, now 25—were born with a still-undiagnosed genetic disease. "They both came home from the hospital healthy," Troy recalls, "but at four or five months, they stopped thriving." Nonverbal and with limited physical abilities, the boys required round-the-clock care, and still do. "My husband always had a good job, but it wasn't until Marshall was six or seven that we had enough money to hire someone to help out during the day."

When the boys were young, the family lived in Texas, where the droughts, forest fires, and harsh allergy and flu seasons only made their problems worse. So in 2003, Troy and Charlie decided to move with Marshall, Coulton, and their healthy adopted son, Luke, then ten, to Asheville. Just as Troy had hoped, her sons' health began to improve. And by 2008, the family had enough money to expand their home-care staff. "For the first time, we hired a night person and were able to sleep," Troy says. "I was finally at a point where I could consider starting a business."

Troy felt that her vision—to make a high-proof, highly drinkable white whiskey—was the right idea at the right time. But she had no idea how to do it.

"First, I asked Forrest if one of his friends who made moonshine could show me how it's done," she says. "He told me no—these guys don't want anyone knowing who they are. I said that he could blindfold me if he had to, but that I needed to do this."

Forrest eventually did find someone willing to show Troy the ropes. "We drove out to his farm, and around back of the barn he was using a 15-gallon cook pot to boil corn mash with a propane burner. The moonshine wasn't very good, but it was a solid first lesson. Now I needed to talk to someone who was crafting *quality* whiskey." This time, the husband of Troy's best friend came to the rescue. "He found a guy who was using white corn with sugar and wild yeast—this guy knew what he was doing."

Troy couldn't wait to get home to try it herself.

"I walked through the door and told Charlie I needed him to build me a still so I could make my own moonshine. He said, 'That's illegal!' and refused to help, so I bought a five-gallon pressure cooker and started experimenting with that."

Eventually, Charlie gave in and added a condenser to the pressure cooker so Troy could distill the mash. "He came around when he realized that if he wasn't going to help, I'd do it on my own. That tends to be eye-opening for a husband."

Next, Troy needed to find someone who was selling white corn, which is central to the best-tasting moonshine. And that's what led her to her eventual partner in crime, John McEntire.

John's family had been growing corn for seven generations, but when Troy called and said she needed 100 pounds—he was accustomed to selling one or two pounds at a time—John hesitated and asked what she was up to.

"I told him, 'Well, I just have some recipes I'm working on. . . .'

"And he said, 'Are you that lady who wants to make whiskey?'

"And I said, 'Yes, I am.'"

John paused for a second, but then agreed to trade some of his corn for some of her whiskey. "That sounded like a good deal," Troy says, "but when I drove out to his farm and got to looking around, I said, 'My gosh, you've got the corn, you've got these old barns, you've got the grist mills. How about we do some tests for fermentation out here?'

"He said, 'Lady, I do not want to get arrested.'

"I said, 'I don't either. How 'bout this: You let me use your address, and I will file the federal application for a distillery permit.'"

And with that, Troy and John were in the whiskey-making business.

The two started in, working stealthily out of one of John's barns. Day after day, Troy kept meticulous notes, logging every distillation, testing white corn versus yellow, trying different milling techniques, comparing sprouted grains with unsprouted grains, adding sugar or not, and figuring out how best to filter the whiskey. "At one point, I was pouring five-gallon batches of whiskey through a Brita filter!" Troy says, laughing. Eventually they settled on cherry wood charcoal filters.

Through it all, Troy says, "I was willing to do whatever I had to do to achieve my goal, whether that was manning the still in the freezing cold for hours or dragging around five-gallon buckets of mash. And when you roll up your sleeves and work like hell, other people want to jump in and work with you."

Once Troy was satisfied they had something special, she took a sample to a friend, Oscar Wong, owner of Asheville's famed Highland Brewing Company. "Oscar was shocked by the quality," she says. "He invested in the company immediately."

Oscar's involvement couldn't have come at a better time, as Troy had no idea how they could produce enough whiskey to start selling it. "When you distill 50 gallons of mash, after eight hours, you have five gallons of whiskey—if you're lucky," she says. Oscar recommended she think big and order a 2,000-liter German still—and to get the flavor she wanted, Troy decided to age the whiskey in old bourbon barrels.

In 2010, Troy and Sons distillery got its federal license, and in 2011, Charlie quit his job to come work for the company, which moved from John's farm to downtown Asheville, right next to the Highland Brewing Company. Troy, Charlie, John, and Oscar all agreed that the aging process and the higher cost of the heirloom corn they were using were both worth it to create the taste they were after. But they also have something deeper in common. "John has a special-needs daughter, as does Oscar," Troy says. "All of us are parents who have dealt with very difficult situations, and that has brought us together."

Troy and Sons spirits are now available in ten states. And only two years after it started, the company was selected by Disney to join a short list of liquors sold at its resorts across the country. It's their first big-volume account and a major coup in the liquor industry.

"When we made that list, even after people told me it would be impossible, it convinced me we were doing things right," says Troy. The company now produces three barrels a day—not a huge amount, but as Troy says, "our production process is slow and meticulous, a point of pride with us."

Troy's success has filled her with a new sense of accomplishment—and a belief that patience has its own special rewards.

"Because I had special-needs children, I focused all my energy on them instead of on a career. And yet it was the boys who brought us to Asheville, where I have found this wonderful new business. Charlie and I now have enough people to care for the boys full-time, and they have their own interests and passions.

"After many years of caring for Marshall and Coulton, I achieved a certain peace of mind when I realized that the skills I learned raising my boys—to be resourceful, tireless, and adaptable—were the very same skills that would help me be successful in business. And that's a good feeling."

Stand-Up Gal: A Monologue

Robin Fox, 55

Bridgewater, New Jersey

"By age 29, I was a typical suburban housewife, living in New Jersey with a husband and two kids. Now, I love my children, but I was bored out of my mind. A fun night at the Fox house was the kids going to bed and my husband turning on a TV show about the Civil War while simultaneously reading a book about the Holocaust. I wasn't as happy as I thought I should be.

But I was funny. Being funny was my way of fighting back against the boredom and the "mean girl" moms in my community. I was overweight, and these women were so skinny I could have fit them in the crack of my ass, and I didn't care about fashion or who had the nicest house, so they didn't like me.

It was all like being back in junior high: I'd play the clown to win people over. One night some friends and I were playing mah-jongg with the neighborhood bully and queen of mean when she complained that her dog was always eating her underwear. I said, "I hope you take them off first." And everyone laughed. She was livid. I had learned at a young age how to defend myself with humor.

For me, laughter is the opposite of being unhappy. I didn't have the greatest childhood, but I would watch *I Love Lucy* and laugh so hard. Lucy taught me that being funny made you likable. You can't hate someone who just made you laugh. I also loved Totie Fields—she was chubby like me—and Phyllis Diller and Joan Rivers, who also weren't beauty queens. I always wanted to be a comedian like them, but I had no idea how to do it.

Then, when I was in my early forties, a friend signed me up for an audition at an improv group at the Jewish Community Center. She insisted that I try out—so I went and got accepted right away. I was very good at it, and I enjoyed getting the laughs. Phil, one of the men in the group who ran a comedy night at a nearby arts center, started pestering me: "Why don't you come and do ten minutes of stand-up?" I told him, "I don't even know how to write jokes" and didn't follow up.

Then one day I was talking with my daughter, who was considering going to New York University to study art but wasn't sure it was practical. She said, "Mom, I don't know if I'll get a job after I graduate." And I said, "Listen, you've got to follow your dream if you want to get a job you love doing. Do that, and you won't ever feel like you're working. You'll always feel like you're just fulfilling a part of yourself." And she said, in a very PMS-y way, "Like you did with comedy?" I said, "That's different."

Then I thought about it. What was so different about it? So I told Phil, "Put me in the lineup."

I had a month to get material together for a ten-minute show. I wrote and wrote up until the night of the show, and surprisingly it went really well. Two days later, I signed up to take comedy classes in New York City.

As I was walking to my first class, I passed a street fair and a gypsy offered to tell my fortune for five bucks. She pointed at me and shouted, "You. I need to talk to you. You are starting something new today and you are going to be very good at it." I thought, *That's a good sign.*

The class was at the Old Gotham Comedy Club. Back then, it was a small place with pictures of real comics on the walls and little votive candles on the tables. Very nightclubby. Just like on TV. I loved the class. The students were all different ages, all types of people, but they loved comedy the way I did. There was a woman who was an author, a man whose dad owned a deli, a guy who had already taken five classes—he was the least funny out of all of us. We would take turns performing our material and get feedback from each other and the teacher.

Class met on Sundays and Mondays. And the big perk was that you could sit in on any comedy show Sunday through Thursday for free. I became a night owl. Watching the pros night after night was like a master class in comedy. I saw that there were so many styles and ways to be funny. I would also watch the amateurs on the new-talent nights, and I was encouraged by the fact that I was just as funny as they were.

After ten weeks, the class ended, and we had a little graduation show. My improv group and family all came to see me. Afterward, we went to a celebration dinner, and Harrison Ford was sitting at a table near us. I was like *Oh, me and Harrison are both in showbiz now.*

That was 11 years ago, and from that moment on, I've never stopped.

I'd do two or three open mics a night, four nights a week. It was so hard. I'd feed my kids dinner at five, get in the car, drive 50 miles to New York, sit in traffic, get to the first show at six thirty or seven and keep going. I'd get home at one or two in the morning, touch my foot to my husband's in bed to let him know I was there, and then wake up and do it all again the next day.

Some nights I would just cry in my car. I'd be stuck in traffic on the New Jersey Turnpike, I'd have to pee, and I'd be exhausted. I'd think, *This is too hard. I'm insane to be doing this.* But then I'd say to myself: "If you don't quit, tomorrow you'll be that much closer."

I've never been an alcoholic, but there's a 12-step expression I can relate to: Once a cucumber becomes a pickle, it can never be a cucumber again. I couldn't go back to what I had left. I felt reborn. This was the first thing that excited me in a way I had never felt before.

And, really, what were my alternatives after my daughter and son left for college? I didn't want to be a Realtor, or become one of those attendance ladies at the high school—they were like prison guards. I had to make comedy work because the career I had always wanted was *this* career. I was lucky my husband was so supportive. He said to me, "What kind of husband would I be if I didn't encourage you to do what I know is going to make you happy?" Now he's my manager.

During the first two years, people started hiring me to do shows. Early on, I drove two hours to do a show at an Elks Club for $50, and I made everyone laugh. A woman came up to me afterward and said, "Do you do country clubs?" I said, "Sure, I do country clubs." I showed up and they put me on while people were being served food. I performed for 15 minutes and nobody even noticed I was there. I thought to myself, *I don't need this*. But I did. I needed it more than anything, and that's why I kept going. I needed to be good at something. After more shows like that one, I started to become bulletproof.

A comic's next goal after open mics is to get stage time at a real club with a real audience. There are four ways to get stage time. Well, there are five, but no one ever asked me to have sex in exchange for career advancement.

The first is doing a show called a "bringer." You bring five or more people and you get five minutes on stage. You perform for your family and friends and everyone else's—it's more like a recital, not your typical tough New York City crowd. I had few friends and a small family, so I was limited in the number of people I could perform in front of.

The second way is to "bark": You stand in front of a club and hand out flyers, trying to get people to come inside. I would bark for Sal's Comedy Hole in New York in all kinds of weather, from freezing cold winters to roasting hot summers trying to get an audience into the club. Shows started at eight p.m. and I'd usually go on around one a.m., when the only people left in the club were other comics.

Third, you can "intern." I would go to Sal's office once a week and do a little administrative work for him, and he would give me a spot on stage.

The fourth way is by doing "contests," and I did as many as I could. About seven or eight months into my comedy career, I entered the amateur division of the Ladies of Laughter contest and made it through two rounds. There were 1,000 people in the audience, and the wave of laughter I got almost knocked me over. When I entered that same contest in August 2012, competing against 200 comics, I won the grand prize.

Anyway, one night after hours of barking, I saw an ad that a club owner who ran three comedy clubs in Manhattan needed an intern to drive him around. I emailed him right away: "Schlepper mom at your disposal. Seventeen years of dragging my kids all over town. Sure as heck can take you wherever you need to go. I'm punctual, responsible, and promise not to bother you." I got the job that day.

Every Saturday, I picked up "Mr. Big" at his house on Staten Island and drove him to the city. I'd double-park outside clubs for two or three hours. The highlight was when comics would come sit in the car with me for a few minutes. In return, Mr. Big let me go on Wednesday nights at 11:15, one of the last spots of the night, when no one really watched, but it didn't matter. I did that for two years. Finally, he decided that I could drive him in on one or two weeknights and I could perform that night.

By that point, I'd been doing comedy for four and half years and that was my big break. For the next six months, I got to go on during prime time because Mr. Big wanted to move quickly from one club to the next. So he'd say, "Hurry up and get Robin on so she can drive me." I'd go up and hit it out of the park. It was so exciting.

Then I auditioned at a comedy club in Times Square that put on five or more shows a night. I did three or four shows a night, three to five nights a week. I was lucky. I hardly ever got hecklers. But there once was this guy who said, "Let's see your tits," so I threatened to take off my bra and smack him with one of them—without leaving the stage. This was the training ground I had been searching for. Other comics saw me do well and started to ask me to do shows with them. That's when it all started really cooking.

At the clubs, I met a lot of other comedians who were trying to break into the business. You know how a kid goes into the lunchroom and walks around with her tray not knowing where to sit? I felt like that kid my entire life—I mean, from infancy until I started doing comedy. But when I went into comedy, I felt like I was in a cafeteria where everybody was like me. Every seat felt perfect. Yes, other comedians were competitive, but they understood my motives and respected my bravery. We were all on the same ship. That ship might be going down, but we were still on it together.

When new comedians today ask me how to get gigs, I tell them, "The best advice I ever got is to be funny—that they can't deny you."

Today, I'm living my dream. I've had these big show-business moments, like when I appeared on TV on the stand-up comedy series *NickMom Night Out!* I perform all over and I tour doing theater shows with the Ladies of Laughter and other groups. I now perform at a lot of great comedy clubs, like the Gotham, the same club where I took my first and only comedy class. I do shows for fund-raisers, schools, community groups, women's groups, churches, temples, and corporations.

But I also do gigs that other comedians shy away from. I do seventieth birthday parties in people's living rooms with a dog humping my leg. I always feel like my mom is going to jump out of the kitchen and shout, "Sing for grandma!" I'll drive five hours to perform at a club. I flew up to Canada to do a show for 500 women in the middle of nowhere. And when we *got* to nowhere, we drove another two hours! I did a great show and got a standing ovation.

And it's all worth it. Most of my life, I didn't know who I was beyond being my parents' daughter, my husband's wife, my kids' mother. But even when I was five years old watching Totie Fields, I knew who I was *supposed* to be. I always wanted to be able to say, "My name is Robin Fox, and I'm a comedian." And now I can.

Acting Her Age

Lee Gale Gruen, 71
Los Angeles, California

A young doctor is meeting a patient to tell her the results of her tests. She is elderly, frail, and stooped in her chair. The doctor takes a deep breath, holds her hand, and says:

> *"Your cancer is inoperable."*
> *The patient's eyes widen. "What did you say?"*
> *"The cancer has spread. It's inoperable."*
> *"Am I . . . going to die?"*
> *"I'm afraid so."*

With that, the elderly patient loses her stoop, sits up straight, and smiles—and everyone applauds.

Welcome to a scene from the life of Lee Gale Gruen, working actress, whose portrayals have ranged from elderly patient to Puritan midwife to sexy senior to gun-toting granny. She has appeared in commercials, on soaps, in plays—and yes, occasionally, in final exams in med schools, where faculties judge students on their bedside manner.

Not bad for someone who is 71 years old but has been acting for only 11 of them, years she calls the most rewarding of her working life.

"Living in Santa Monica, I've met a lot of actors over the years," Lee Gale says, "and I've always found them so tiresome. They were always talking about jobs, auditions, craft, technique. And now I'm an actress, and guess who's always talking about acting? I can't help myself—I love it!"

Lee Gale's first career was as a probation officer in Los Angeles County. She took the job right out of college and spent the next 37 years visiting prisons, investigating crimes, interviewing convicted criminals, and reporting to judges.

"I found it fascinating," Lee Gale says. "I had a fairly sheltered upbringing and had never known any criminals. Having that job was like getting permission to peek through a keyhole, to see how other people lived their lives."

"But when I turned 60," she says, "I had reached the maximum pension benefit. I knew it was time to move on, I just had no idea what I was going to do."

One day a friend told her about a program of courses for seniors at Santa Monica Community College. Paging through the school's catalog, Lee Gale noticed the Theater Arts section.

Lee Gale wasn't interested in performing; indeed, whenever the probation department had asked her to speak in classrooms and meetings, she always had extreme anxiety. But there was a class called Scene Study that piqued her interest. "I assumed the class read scenes from plays and discussed them," she says. "I like literature. I like the theater. I thought it might be fun."

But Lee Gale quickly figured out that the course wasn't designed to help students dissect literature when a fellow student handed her some pages and asked if she would read with him. She easily agreed, then was shocked to realize that "reading" the pages meant doing so out loud, while standing in front of the class. She had actually signed up for an acting class.

"I briefly thought of bolting," she recalls. "Throughout my career, I had dealt with murderers, robbers, rapists, some of the most dangerous people in society, but I had never conquered my fear of speaking in front of a group. I felt naked and vulnerable." But she stood up and, for the first time, looked at the pages she had been given to read. It was the opening scene of *Death of a Salesman*.

"As I started reading the part of Willy's wife, Linda Loman," Lee Gale recalls, "a totally unexpected thing happened. I became so immersed in the character and the story that I forgot that a roomful of strangers was watching me."

When the scene ended, the class broke into applause. "I'd never felt so uplifted. What a high!"

From that moment, Lee Gale was hooked. And very quickly, she hooked somebody else: her 85-year-old father, Marvin. Her dad had always been the life-of-the-party type, but since the recent death of his wife, Rose, he had grown withdrawn. Lee Gale thought attending the class might help him come out of his sad state. It took some coaxing, but once he succumbed, he became an enthusiastic attendee during the three remaining years of his life.

"He was so joyful about the classes," Lee Gale recalls. "After each one he'd ask me when I was picking him up for the next one." Before long, father and daughter became sort of an act, with Lee Gale writing comic skits for them to perform together, at first just in class, but later at family gatherings. Marvin would play the cranky father and Lee Gale the beleaguered daughter who was taking him somewhere. Here they are on a camping trip:

Dad: Where are we going to sleep?

Daughter (pointing to sleeping bags): There.

Dad: Are you crazy?

Daughter: That's what Native Americans did. That's what Early Man did.

Dad: Well, I'm not a Native American and I'm definitely Late Man.

And on it went: Dad and daughter at the movies, Dad and daughter discuss his new earring.

"During those three magical years, I bonded more with my father than I had in the previous sixty," Lee Gale says.

One day in class a friend exclaimed, "Lee Gale, you are an actress!" And for the first time, she felt confident enough to explore the next steps. She enrolled in a seniors course in commercial acting; and more important, she began acquiring the practical knowledge needed to pursue jobs. A friend helped her write her résumé—there was an alarming amount of white space at first, but with each subsequent job she was gradually able to fill up the page. Another friend helped her line up a photographer to get her first head shots— the eight-by-ten glossy photos used by casting agents. She also learned which newspapers and websites published listings for auditions.

Soon Lee Gale got results: She landed a job in a commercial for a legal services company. Unfortunately, the part called for her to roller-skate, something she hadn't done in half a century.

"During the audition, I managed to stay upright but couldn't get myself to stop," she recalls, "so I had to deliberately roll into things." That was fine at the audition, but when it came time to shoot the ad outdoors, she was forced to confess to the director that she had a "stopping problem." Thankfully, he assigned the on-set makeup artist to catch her.

The commercial paid $400, Lee Gale landed an agent, and she was on her way.

"I've played a trash-talking gangster granny holding a machine gun, I've been a granny rapper, I've played a homeless woman three times—it really is fun," she says.

And in a strange way, the work is connected to her first career. "Being a probation officer taught me a lot about people's vulnerabilities and frailties, and that there is more to a person than meets the eye."

Although Lee Gale's acting income isn't enough to sustain her (for that she relies on her pension), the work has become an essential part of her life.

"Sometimes I have to drop everything to go on an audition in a moment's notice," she says, "but I do it because I adore it. I feel like I've blossomed, like I'm walking in a dream."

Linked In

Paula MacMann, 61

St. Louis, Missouri

When the last of her six kids was, as she says, "off the wallet," through college and out of the house, Paula MacMann embraced her new reality: She no longer had to buy six gallons of milk at a time. She could read a magazine cover to cover in one sitting, with no interruptions. And when she opened the refrigerator the day after going to the grocery, the food was actually still there.

This called for a celebration.

"We were done paying tuition and deserved a reward," Paula recalls. So six months after their youngest got her diploma in June of 2008, Paula and her husband, Bill, frolicked for three weeks in Fiji and New Zealand—hiking over volcanoes, kayaking offshore—a trip they never would have been able to afford while raising the kids.

Life with six children had been nothing short of crazy. When Paula and Bill had said *I do* nearly 30 years earlier, they each brought two kids into the

243

marriage, and then had two more together. To help pay the bills, Paula threw into that hectic mix a demanding career in website development, so when her youngest daughter announced shortly after graduation that she'd landed her first job, Paula felt liberated enough to declare, "I'm done working!"

But she found it hard to wind down. "It took me a year to realize that I didn't have to cook dinner every night since it was just the two of us," she says.

So Paula developed a new schedule. She would wake up at five a.m. to "get a million things done," from a morning fitness class to all of the projects she'd put on the back burner, like cleaning out closets or making a genealogy book for her mother. Then she rode her bike. A lot. Paula had discovered cycling back in 1991 as a way to decompress, and she'd been doing monthly 100-mile rides (called centuries) from April through October ever since.

To call Paula an "avid cyclist" was an understatement: In her first two years of retirement, she logged more than 4,000 miles. But that didn't mean she knew a whole lot about the mechanics of bikes. So in October 2010, when a friend was fixing his bike chain and removed one of the links, it was the first time she'd ever really looked at one close up.

When she picked up the link, a small metal figure eight with a hole on either end, her first thought was: *This looks like an earring!* And when her friend said he was going to throw out the chain, Paula asked if she could keep it. "Sure," he said, wondering what in God's name she was going to do with it.

With the help of her sister, who made jewelry as a hobby, Paula attached an earring back to each link and put them on. "It made perfect sense to me to wear an earring that was part of a bike chain," she laughs.

To give the earrings more pizzazz, her sister suggested adding "jump rings," which are used to connect beads in jewelry and come in dozens of colors. Mixing and matching the rings with the four pieces of a bike chain—the outer link, inner link, roller, and pin—Paula was able to come up with a wide variety of looks.

Which got her to thinking: Could she sell them? She loved them, but would other people wear pieces of bike chains on their ears, too?

To find out, Paula brought a sampling to her morning fitness class, where three of her friends asked, "Can I buy that?" Her husband got the same reaction when he showed some of Paula's jewelry to his friends at work.

Not long afterward, a local hospital honored Paula as Healthy Woman of the Year; her friends had quietly nominated her because she was such an inspiration, motivating them to be fit by taking them along on bike rides. Being celebrated in front of the crowd of 1,000 people made the wheels in Paula's brain turn. *What if she sold jewelry made out of bike chains to inspire others to get up and move, the way she had inspired her own friends?* "My inner self was talking—and I listened."

So Paula, using colorful used bike chains she got for free from local bike shops, began experimenting with even more designs, including bracelets and necklaces. And wherever Paula wore her creations—at the mall, in the grocery store, on a group bike ride—people loved them.

"I thought, gosh, if people who don't *have* to say 'This is cool' say 'This is cool,' maybe it *is* cool!"

She and Bill put up $5,000 as seed money, converted one of the kids' bedrooms into an office, and Paula started working 40 to 50 hours a week to get her business off the ground. Having never been an entrepreneur, she understood that she was faced with three different types of challenges: "There was what I *knew*, what I didn't know, and what I *didn't know* I didn't know!"

First, she took on the nitty-gritty: talking with bank officers and credit card companies to figure out the best way to process charges, researching shipping options so customers could receive automated emails with track-

ing information, and investigating how to handle sales taxes that varied from state to state. She felt like she'd just taken a business course. And she had.

Then, the fun stuff: teaming with her brother, an amateur photographer, to take product shots for her website and designing pretty petal-shape packages containing fun, inspirational fitness quotes.

It was exciting to take this new turn in her life, and Paula was grateful she and Bill had the resources to make it happen. So they decided it was time to give back: If the company made it, they'd donate 10 percent of the proceeds to two nonprofit organizations. They chose the YMCA and Trailnet, a nonprofit that develops bike and pedestrian trails.

In 2011, Paula's Web business, under the name "Chainspirations," was launched. To get the word out, she contacted the TV reporter who had presented her the Healthy Woman of the Year award, who then featured Paula on a local morning show; she set up a display table at the YMCA; and Trailnet handed out brochures at the bike rides they sponsored. Then the owner of a local outdoors store asked to carry her jewelry at all three of its locations. They were in business.

Next, Paula signed up to be a vendor at the Tour de Grove, a local bike race, and logged in a lot of face time with customers. That experience proved so valuable that she signed up for more; and by the end of the summer, Paula took a giant step and decided to sell her jewelry at a bike race ten hours away: The Hotter 'N Hell Hundred in Wichita Falls, Texas.

Paula understood this was a risky investment—she'd have to pay $400 for the booth, plus spring for a hotel room for herself and Bill—but she also knew that the attendance would be high, with 12,000 riders. And the gamble paid off: Visitors loved the idea that she could make a custom piece for them in ten minutes. She sold $2,000 worth of jewelry during the three-day show. Since then, Paula, with Bill as her trusty wingman, has traveled to bike rides all over the country, from New York and Arkansas to Washington and California.

In addition to seeing her business thrive, Paula discovered a hidden bonus in the work: "Bill and I found out that we're a really good pair working together," she says. "It's given our relationship a whole different dimension."

Since the business launched three years ago, sales have been comfortably consistent, totaling around 2,000 pieces of jewelry a year, including four styles of earrings, two bracelets, eight necklaces, and 23 decorative zipper-pulls.

"I have no idea where this creativity is coming from," Paula marvels. "I've always considered myself a left-brained person, big into numbers and computers, but I love sitting there and creating."

Paula's goal now is just to break even, so when she turns a profit, she puts it back into the company. She also offers deep discounts to individuals and teams who use her jewelry to raise money for their causes. And once a year, she drops off a check in person at the YMCA and Trailnet.

"If I were doing this just to make a profit, I don't think I'd have the same passion for it," Paula says. "Being able to give back is what I truly love."

Lumberjane

Judy Peres, 67
Chicago, Illinois

For most of the quarter-century that Judy Peres's byline was a regular fixture on the front page of the *Chicago Tribune*, it's fair to say she seldom thought about a second career—and it's a sure bet that on those rare occasions when such a notion *did* flit through her mind, she did not envision herself driving a forklift for a living.

But today Judy is the CEO of Old Globe Reclaimed Wood Company, a Wisconsin outfit with aspirations far bigger than its shoestring staff. Which means there are days when Judy has to pull herself away from her financial statements and climb in behind the wheel. "Everyone should try it. It's a blast."

Judy had been a classic casualty of the Internet, which had all but eclipsed the newspaper and magazine business. She had come to the *Trib* in 1980 after a 12-year stint at the *Jerusalem Post*, working first as an editor, then as a *Tribune* feature reporter.

"I loved my job," she says. "It was interesting and exciting. There were years when the *Trib* paid me to do nothing but follow things that caught my eye."

But as the twentieth century wound down, and the Internet geared up, newspaper managers had to reduce their budgets, cutting even star writers like Judy.

"I felt like I had a bull's-eye on my back," she says. "I could see the end coming, and I didn't know who I would be the day I stopped being a journalist."

While all this was happening, Judy's partner, a former investment banker named David Hozza, made an interesting discovery: There was an enormous granary called the Globe Elevator Company eight hours away in Superior, Wisconsin, made entirely of rare old-growth pine, and it was slated for demolition. He wanted to save it and salvage the lumber. So he bought it.

David took Judy to see the granary. From the outside, 15 stories high, it resembled a Jenga tower before anyone has removed a piece. But inside the grain bins, the wood was *gorgeous*. The flow of tons of grain pouring in and out of the bins over the years had worn the most beautiful patterns into the wood. A forest's worth of exquisite and irreplaceable wood was destined for a landfill.

At first, Judy was happy merely to support David in his pet project. "I was still working at the paper so I made an initial small investment," she says. But with money at stake and her journalistic curiosity piqued, Judy began to research the project, and it soon became clear that David had underestimated the challenge of recovering the wood.

"We planned to have the first of the three granary buildings down in a year, and the others would follow," says Judy. "But the recovery was much more difficult than we'd imagined. Stacking the lumber turned out to be a very complicated process; and there was a lot of trial and error until we brought in heavy machinery. We had raised $250,000 for the operating budget—which came from Dave, me, and several other investors—and went through all of it without getting a single board onto the ground. We had to figure out what we were doing wrong, and at the same time master other facets of the business, like marketing and finance strategies." And of course, learning how to drive a forklift.

As life at the newspaper became more untenable, Judy became increas-

ingly immersed in the Old Globe project. Eventually the threads all came together. She took a buyout from the *Tribune* and became Old Globe's CEO.

"Why not? Our kids were grown and we could afford to do something wonderful, risky, and challenging. And once I made the decision, I realized that all that time I'd spent worrying about leaving the paper had been a complete waste. I don't miss the paper at all. I've been too challenged to miss it. And here's the bonus: I'm stronger, leaner, healthier, and calmer than when I worked at the paper. I look, and feel, ten years younger."

Unfortunately, at first their lumber company wasn't as fit as she was. The recession and the housing glut dealt blows to their prospects. "Recycled, aged wood is actually more expensive than cutting new growth," Judy explains. "Our wood is for high-end consumers who are looking for something special in their home, office, restaurant—whatever they're doing. We thought those people would have deep enough pockets to keep us going throughout the recession, but they didn't and we had to shut down for a while."

But things eventually picked up. The company salvaged about 18 percent of the lumber in the complex, and the high-end buyers began to return. Customers included an oil company executive who used the timbers in his home in Colorado, a lakefront hotel in Wisconsin that features reception desks constructed out of the bin walls, and an upscale Chicago restaurant whose entire floor was handcrafted from two-by-eight planks from the granary.

And most surprising of all, Old Globe's team was featured on episodes of the History Channel's program *Ax Men*. Not bad for a group of people trying to take a building down.

"It's been a great adventure and very gratifying," Judy says. "Every time we see our beautiful boards in a new building we say to each other, 'We saved those babies!'"

Editor's note: Before this story went to press, the bank foreclosed on Old Globe—but for Judy, it was all worth it. "I don't regret a minute of it," she says. "The stress was significant at times, but I learned a great deal. I count my blessings."

PART NINE

Mothers of Invention

"Taking a chance led me toward a more fulfilling life, the kind of life I want to show my children it's possible to lead."

Getting a Grip

Sari Davidson, 40

Bellevue, Washington

"Oh, dammit!"

Sari Davidson's one-year-old son, Jake, had just downloaded his sippy cup onto the kitchen floor. In recent weeks, Jake had elevated his cup-chucking to a minor art form:

He dropped it from his high chair.

He upended it into his car seat, where the slow dribble would soak his clothes.

He let it slip quietly over the side of his stroller, where its absence would go unnoticed until Sari was five blocks away.

When Sari reacted with exasperation, it just made Jake laugh. "Oh, you booginhead!" she'd say, booginhead being the family term for someone who does something he or she shouldn't do, just to get a reaction out of mom.

But one day Sari reached her limit—she *had* to find a tether for that sippy cup. So she looked in stores. She looked in catalogs. She questioned her friends.

255

"Nope, never heard of such a thing, but let us know if you find something," they told her. Flying sippy cups were driving *them* crazy, too.

As it turned out, Sari never did find a sippy cup leash. But she did find her niche.

From the time she was little, Sari had wanted to be in business. In grade school, she'd sometimes join her father when he had to work on Saturdays, taking the train from their home in Smithtown, New York, to his office at Wells Fargo Bank in Manhattan.

"I'd pretend to carry a briefcase and sit at a desk and type," she recalls. "I always saw myself as a businesswoman."

As a teen, she watched her mother open a bookstore in a local strip mall. "The store sold new and used books, especially collectibles," Sari recalls. "Mom worked seven days a week, getting up early to hit yard sales and flea markets to find interesting titles. Within a year, she'd driven the other bookstore in her mall out of business and opened a second shop."

At the University of Arizona, Sari studied business. "If they'd offered a program in entrepreneurship, I would have studied that," she says, "but they didn't. So I majored in human resources."

After college, she put that degree to good use, working in H.R. at, among others, New Line Cinema and Microsoft. But Sari felt something was missing—she still wanted to run her own show.

But it wasn't until that day in 2005, when Jake sent his sippy cup skittering across the kitchen floor once too often, that Sari Davidson, inventor and entrepreneur, was born.

Using dog leashes and an $80 sewing machine that she had set up in the corner of her living room, Sari fashioned a number of straps that would attach to a cup to keep it from going airborne.

"It was like a crafts project," she says. "I would work something up, then take it down to the park to see what other parents thought. One of them suggested we use suction material to attach the strap to the bottle or cup. That's how I came up with the name SippiGrip."

In early 2007, finally happy with her invention, Sari formed BooginHead LLC and began the task of learning how to make and sell her invention.

Her first big break had already happened: She worked for Microsoft. "They gave me a completely flexible schedule. As long as I achieved the results they'd set for me, they were supportive of me having interests outside the office."

Her second break came when she demonstrated the SippiGrip at a children's products trade show in Las Vegas. Target took a look and was impressed enough to offer Sari a spot in its Parent-Invented Product Program.

"It was like getting an MBA," she says. The program taught Sari about finance, manufacturing, and marketing, prepping her for many of the challenges BooginHead would face before it could become a sustainable business.

"One of the first issues we had was getting enough capital to manufacture it," she says. "In the beginning, the entire business was financed out of my own personal bank account, but that wasn't going to be enough. We still needed about $10,000 to start manufacturing. So my husband and I took out a second mortgage on our house. Within a year, I was able to open a business line of credit and pay myself back the initial investment."

The actual manufacturing was also difficult. Sari hoped to find a factory in the United States, but couldn't locate one that would make such small quantities, so she turned to China. "Communicating with people who live far away and speak a different language created lots of unexpected issues," she recalls.

But when the first batch rolled off the assembly line, she says, "It was all worth it. To see a product that I had first stitched together in my living room being mass-produced—with packaging, a brand, and a logo—it was thrilling."

Now all she had to do was get her product into stores. "Working in the Target program I learned a lot about how stores think. From the beginning, my ultimate goal was to get the product into Babies R Us, and Target taught me to time my pitch to exactly when they were looking at new products. I was also able to show Babies R Us that I'd already learned the ropes of dealing with a large retailer."

Now the SippiGrip is available not only through Babies R Us but also at Walmart, Amazon, and boutiques from Los Angeles to New York.

But Sari says it's one thing to get onto store shelves, quite another to stay there. "There's always competition, from both upstarts and giant companies." What she has learned is that the best defense is a good offense: The smartest way to protect a spot on the shelf is to enlarge that spot by adding products. In recent years, SippiGrip has been joined by BooginHead's PaciGrip (a pacifier attachment), PaciPouch (a small bag that can be attached to a stroller to hold pacifiers), SplatMat (easy-to-clean mats for under high chairs), and Squeez'Ems (reusable food pouches for puréed food)—all Sari's inventions.

"We're always trying to be innovative and give parents what they need," Sari says. "For example, after reading reviews online about the PaciGrip, I realized it needed to work with all types of pacifiers. So I changed the design— and it's now my bestselling product."

It's also the product that taught Sari a couple of important lessons.

Number one: Don't scrimp on legal counsel. "The original name of the PaciGrip was BinkiGrip," she explains. "To save money, I just checked to see if that name was in use, which it wasn't. But had I hired an attorney to do a full trademark search, I would have learned that Playtex already had a trademark on the word 'Binky.'"

The second lesson? "Don't give up." Sari already had thousands of Binki-Grips on shelves and 20,000 more ready to be distributed. "We were facing an enormously expensive withdrawal, then a redesign, a repackaging, and a relaunch. So much wasted money! I wanted to give up." But Sari didn't, and Playtex gave BooginHead a reasonable amount of time to sell the BinkiGrips already on the shelves before replacing them with PaciGrips.

In 2010, BooginHead passed $1 million in sales, so Sari decided to cut her remaining ties to Microsoft and devote herself to BooginHead full-time. The company now has nine employees, and Sari's sales are up to $3 million.

The best part, though, is that Sari is now what she always wanted to be: an entrepreneur and her own boss.

"Taking a chance on BooginHead led me toward a more fulfilling life," she says, "the kind of life I want to show my children it's possible to lead. With some structure, a good support system, and the right entrepreneurial spirit, any dream is possible."

Finding the Different Road

Julie Azuma, 62
New York, New York

What Julie Azuma remembers most from her baby's first year is a sense of bewilderment and despair. A successful designer in the apparel industry, Julie was past 40 when she and her husband adopted an infant from Korea. And things weren't going well. Baby Miranda would scream and scream, and she couldn't be soothed. She wasn't reaching her developmental milestones on time either—didn't sit up on her own, didn't walk well, didn't talk at all.

"I was extremely patient and just waited for these issues to go away," says Julie, now 62. "We couldn't figure out what was wrong. And it hurt when a lot of people in my family felt that Miranda's delays were due to my lack of parenting skills."

When it became clear that the issues were ongoing, Julie took Miranda to a series of pediatricians, neurologists, psychiatrists, and speech-and-language pathologists, all in search of answers that didn't come. "They said she had speech and developmental delays; they said it was because of the adoption;

they said a lot of different things," Julie says with a sigh. "They never said she had autism."

Miranda didn't demonstrate autism's defining symptom, which is failure to make eye contact. By the time she was six years old and still not talking, however, it was clear to everyone that something was very wrong. Julie and her husband had adopted a second child, Sophie, who was developing just fine. But even at a special-education preschool, Miranda was not progressing.

"Miranda was six and a half before she was diagnosed, and by that time, sadly, it was tough to change her trajectory," says Julie. Today we know that early, intense therapy can make a tremendous difference in how an autistic child develops, but for Miranda the opportunity seemed lost.

"Twenty years ago, autism was a death knell," Julie says. "Autistic children were thought of as kids without language and academic skills. They were often institutionalized."

Not about to give up on her daughter, Julie started her research, which was a lot harder in the days before Google. "But I found a book called *Let Me Hear Your Voice,* which led me to a parent movement that advocated using Applied Behavior Analysis." Now a standard therapy, ABA was then a largely unknown method for teaching language and social skills to children with autism. "This ABA method was the one thing that gave us parents hope."

Armed with that hope, Julie now had to put ABA theory into practice for Miranda. That meant finding the very specific developmental products that were crucial to the therapy's success—like wooden blocks, but without letters or numbers (which can be frustrating for children who don't recognize them). And flash cards that showed emotions, actions, household items, and food, but used actual photographs (not illustrations, which may be difficult for children with autism to interpret).

"These products were so hard to find!" exclaims Julie. "I would spend weeks tracking down what I needed. I was a desperate woman; I went from place to place to place." At one point she even asked a friend who was traveling to London to call a British company while she was there, to get her a product that wasn't available in the United States.

Amazingly, though, the new therapy worked. "Within six weeks of starting ABA, Miranda spoke. She was able to say, 'I want orange juice.' It was a revelation," says Julie, who by that time had left her fashion-industry job to stay home with Miranda and Sophie. As tough as the product search had been for Julie, she realized it would be impossible for a working mom. So she began to think about starting her own company to help other families.

Almost 30 years in the apparel industry had taught Julie how to buy and sell, how to merchandise, and how to make a profit, but they hadn't prepared her to become an entrepreneur. Eager to learn, she took a once-a-week night course on starting a business.

"I knew I couldn't afford a real store," says Julie. "I didn't have a lot of start-up money. Then a woman in my class said, 'Why don't you go on the Internet?' It seemed like a great deal: You could have a store for five or six hundred dollars a year, as opposed to paying New York City rents."

Though it made financial sense, this was 1994, when most people didn't even have an email address and e-commerce barely existed. To make things worse, Julie says, she was at the time "completely computer illiterate." Determined to create her store, she found someone to design a website and she set to work learning how to use a computer—even though she didn't have a lot of confidence in herself.

"I was scared to do it on my own," she recalls. "I tried to find partners for the business, and they all turned me down. They told me they didn't think it was a good business model. But I was really thinking of this as support for other parents. I couldn't give up."

In 1995, Julie launched Different Roads to Learning, an online store at DiffLearn.com. ("There was a limit then on how long your URL could be.") The site initially offered about 30 products, but the problem was getting parents to find it. Word of mouth in this close-knit community, along with a simple black-and-white paper catalog, created traction.

"Parents would tell other parents," Julie recalls, "or take the catalog to their schools. We all had a lot of sympathy for each other. It was cathartic to make these meaningful, intimate connections, especially back then, when parents of autistic kids were isolated and just working with their own home programs."

Julie was careful to keep her costs low, and she never needed a bank loan. She estimates that her start-up cost was $40,000 total.

Different Roads to Learning grew slowly. "I was still taking all the packages to the post office myself when I got orders—that's how small we were. But then one day my accountant said, 'Congratulations! You're profitable!' I said, 'That's impossible. I thought we were still in the hole.' That's when I realized, *Wow, this could actually be a good business.*"

Julie doesn't carry orders to the post office anymore. Today, Different Roads to Learning has four full-time employees, carries more than 600 products, and earns $2.5 million in annual sales. The company has also added a book division and four apps—something Julie could never have imagined back in 1995.

"We're still a smallish company," says Julie. "But we've come so far, and so have the kids. Because of early intervention and enough ABA work, they're so much more skilled now. A lot of these kids can be mainstreamed by the time they're five, in kindergarten. That just wasn't happening before. And because we sell to a lot of schools, I like to think that we've been a part of bringing about that change. Sometimes I look back and I'm amazed."

Miranda is still developing language at 25, and lives in a small group home that provides care, support, and vocational training. It's not the way

Julie hoped things would turn out, but she's glad her older daughter is happy and healthy. Her younger child, Sophie, recently graduated from NYU with a degree in psychology, which Julie thinks was inspired by her sister's struggles.

Julie becomes reflective when she talks about her own struggles and the emotional obstacles she had to overcome in order to start her business.

"I'm Japanese American; my entire family went to an internment camp during World War II," she says. "I grew up always having a little bit of fear of being not quite American enough. And a lot of my life was spent feeling like I needed to be apologetic, to not stand out. I've always been very timid. I wish I'd had the courage to do this earlier. I wish I'd had the courage to have confidence in myself at an earlier age, and the courage to take a risk."

As for those partners who turned her down when she was afraid to launch a business alone? Julie has a new perspective on that, too.

"At the time I was so disappointed, but now I'm happy because they would have driven me crazy. I know today that my success is about me, not anyone else. Whenever anybody asks me if they should start a business, I tell them if you have the passion, you've got to go for it. I believe in letting go and not being afraid."

Veggie Mama

Veronica Bosgraaf, 43
Holland, Michigan

Veronica Bosgraaf had a big idea. And it was hatched on a typical night around the dinner table after an atypical question from her six-year-old daughter, Anna: "What are we eating?"

It was lemon chicken. Stay-at-home mom Veronica had made it many times before for her husband and three kids, and always without a question. But on this night, Anna was giving her plate the evil eye.

"Chicken?" she said. "What do you mean, *chicken*?"

That morning, Veronica had chaperoned Anna's first-grade class on a field trip to a farm near their hometown of Holland, Michigan, where she watched her daughter play with baby chicks and hold a beautiful orange hen in her arms. "I could see what was happening in her little brain," Veronica says. "She was putting it all together, what was on her plate with the experience she'd had at the farm."

Trained as a scientist—she was a former high school biology teacher—

Veronica had never been a "Santa Claus kind of mom" ("I've always been completely honest with my kids: I would tell them that Santa is not real and then explain the legends behind him"). So she gently told Anna that people eat animals. Anna persisted: "So when they get old and die, *then* we eat them?" Not exactly. "I told her that people raise animals, then slaughter, sell, and process them and that's the meat we eat. Anna was horrified."

A few days later, Anna officially declared herself a vegetarian. "I don't want to be a part of killing animals." Veronica wanted to honor her feelings but worried how she'd get her to eat foods she wasn't used to, like lentils, beans, and other vegetables, to make sure she would have a nutritionally balanced diet.

So Veronica began looking online for meatless recipes, reading ingredient labels and visiting health food stores. "It was one of the many times I've realized that you can learn a lot from your kids. They have this simple, innocent wisdom that we often lose as we grow up."

What Veronica discovered from her research was that the simpler the meal, the more her kids (she also had a preschooler and toddler) liked it. Breakfast might be oatmeal with sliced fruit and dinner some baby spinach, rice, hummus, and crackers.

"I remember one night our friends came over, saw my kids having dinner and were like, 'Your kids will eat that? We just left our kids with a plate of mac and cheese and hot dogs.' It made me realize that even though I wasn't creating gourmet meals for my kids, they were leaps ahead of where a lot of kids were in terms of nutrition."

While mealtimes sailed relatively smoothly, packing Anna's school lunch every day proved trickier, as the traditional bologna or tuna sandwiches were now clearly off-limits. "And there was only so much peanut butter and jelly she could eat," Veronica says. At that time, it was difficult to find packaged foods in her local grocery that tasted good, gave Anna all the nutrients she needed, and were easy to toss in a lunch box.

Veronica's solution came through experimentation. One evening while she was trying out a new dessert recipe—a piecrust made of dates, almonds, and a little bit of salt and cinnamon—she decided to mix in some cocoa powder, too. "It tasted like a brownie," she says—and her kids gave it a thumbs-up.

"So I began to think like a sneaky mom," Veronica says. "What else could I hide in this newfound 'brownie' that would be good for my kids' lunch boxes? I thought about Anna's needs as a vegetarian, so I substituted walnuts for some of the almonds to get in the omega 3 fats and added brown rice protein." Then Veronica took a reindeer cookie cutter, reshaped it into a rectangle, punched out bars from the rolled-out dough, wrapped each one in waxed paper, and stored them in the freezer. The next morning, she put one in Anna's lunch box, knowing that by the time the school lunch hour came, the defrosted bar would be soft and chewy.

"That did the trick!" Veronica says. "It ended up being my sandwich replacement, and Anna loved it. It was filling but better than a sandwich because it was nutritious and had everything I wanted to put into my kids."

Buoyed by her success, Veronica started trying out different variations on her invention, adding high-antioxidant fruits like dried cherries and cranberries. "I would pulverize everything in the food processor so my kids couldn't see chunks of stuff," she says. "You know how kids are, they tend to pick out things that are bigger than a fingernail. I threw a lot away until I got the texture and taste down to where I wanted them."

Then Veronica started widening her consumer base. When she was the "snack mom" at school, she'd bring in a batch of the food bars, or take them along to parties. "Everybody seemed to love them. They said the cocoa ones

tasted exactly like brownies. They couldn't believe they weren't baked in a pan with eggs and sugar."

As Veronica continued to get raves over the next year, she started to wonder: Wouldn't other moms want these healthy snacks for *their* kids? In the back of her mind, she could hear her dad's voice: "That's a million-dollar idea!" A physician with an entrepreneur's mind, her father was always coming up with revolutionary ideas and taught Veronica how to think outside the box. "Because of Dad, I was always coming up with ideas for what I thought would be innovative products, and I thought this one might just work."

So she did it. In 2005, Veronica brought a sample to a friend of a friend who owned a nearby bakery and had turned part of it into a manufacturing plant for Kellogg's. He looked at one of Veronica's bars, opened it, tasted it, then leaned over his desk and looked her in the eye:

"I would never tell anybody in a million years to get into the food business, but I think you have something here."

Those words were just what Veronica wanted to hear, even though she knew the odds were stacked against her.

"It's a cutthroat business," she says. "And I had heard that 99 percent of new food products fail. But the fact that he was encouraging was huge to me."

"So what do I do next?" Veronica asked her new mentor; and, on the spot, he gave her a crash course in how to proceed: Send a bar away to an expert to get its nutritional breakdown; connect with an ingredient broker to save money by buying in bulk; and, most important, find a company to manufacture the bars.

Easier said than done. Despite her efforts to engage an eager manufacturer, no one was interested—unless she wanted to produce at least 50,000 bars. Still, she made call after call, hoping to talk some factory owner into working with her, even promising to give them her business if she grew.

"I wanted to make this happen so badly. So I decided I would do a little something every day to try to push it forward. The way I figured it, if I didn't do this now, I'd always wonder what could have been. I had to at least try."

Nine months later, while chatting with a salesman from a California farm where she had bought her dates, she was introduced to a small, family-owned and -operated food manufacturer in Oregon that was interested in giving her bars a try.

By now, Veronica had dubbed her company "Pure" ("That word really described what I was trying to do: create something pure and wholesome for my family"); and with $10,000 from savings and a $50,000 bank line of credit to get started, she watched the first 4,500 bars—chocolate, cherry cashew, and apple cinnamon—come down the conveyor belt. "I could have stood there all day," she says, "it was so exciting."

Stuffing as many bars as she could into her suitcase, Veronica flew home to wait for a truck to deliver the rest to her tiny office. Her brother-in-law called her crazy: "You made 5,000 bars and you don't have a single customer?" But Veronica wasn't worried. "The customers will come," she said.

To make sure of that, Veronica went door-to-door. Hitting the streets in her SUV—with boxes of Pure bars packed all around the kids' cars seats—she delivered samples to every natural food store, coffee shop, and juice bar within an hour of her home. "At every single store," she says, "they took one bite and said, 'We'll take a case.'" And one month later, she got the break she'd been dreaming about: The CEO of the Meijer grocery store chain read an article about Pure bars in the local paper and wanted to stock them in all 200 of his stores.

"I called my manufacturer and said the four most exciting words of my life: 'I need more bars!'"

For the first time since spooning that experimental dollop of cocoa into her home recipe, Veronica now knew this thing was for real. With her older two children in school, she started sending her little one to day care two days a week so she'd have the time—from eight a.m. to three p.m.—to contact distributors who stock food-store shelves. She also worked during the kids' nap times, after they went to bed at night, and, of course, on weekends.

"I was a still a full-time mom," Veronica says. "I was really adamant about being present with my kids as much as possible."

Trade shows took Veronica's business to the next level. She'd pay a friend a couple hundred dollars to come along and they'd set up a table where the floor space was cheapest—in the back corner near the restrooms. Although the spot was less than glamorous, Veronica knew that everyone has to go to the bathroom. "And as they came by I'd have my chance at them. By nature, I'm not outgoing, but I would grab people, smile, and stick a sample in their face. It was nuts."

But the effort paid off. "A lot of those buyers were looking for the next cool thing," she says. "My bars were minimally processed, organic, and had never been heated," at a time when "raw foods" were becoming a big thing.

A little more than four years after making her first batch of bars in her kitchen, Veronica had placed her product in thousands of natural food stores across the country, including the very important Whole Foods chain.

"By 2008, my sales were about three-quarters of a million dollars," she says.

But Veronica was still a one-woman show, handling the finances, inventory, marketing, and even hand-delivering shipments to local customers.

"It was exhausting," she recalls. "I needed capital, people, and experience. I had very little knowledge of how things worked in the grocery world or what my next steps needed to be."

So when Promax Nutrition, a California maker of high-protein energy bars, offered to partner with her in 2008, it was a deal she couldn't refuse. "They had a sales team, accountants, operations managers, order takers—all the jobs I was doing alone," she says. "It freed me up to concentrate on marketing the brand and growing the company."

Veronica agreed to a deal that was incentive-driven: The bigger and more successful her company got, the more she would earn. "I had people say, 'You should just get the big check right now,'" she says. "But I had so much confidence and faith in my company that I wasn't afraid to take this deal—and I was right."

Today, Veronica maintains a share of the company, sits on the board, and okays every major decision that has to do with Pure.

"We have grown the company by over 50 percent a year since Promax came on board," she says.

Pure is now also sold at Trader Joe's, comes in nine flavors, and has expanded to include a new line of ancient grains bars and fruit and veggie strips. The best part of her job, she says, is hearing from customers. She gets daily emails saying, "These are a lifesaver!" or "My kid will eat two!"

"Even if all of this ended tomorrow," Veronica says, "knowing that Pure helps people eat better and feel better means the world to me. It's fun, rewarding, and a huge blessing to grow a business that enriches people's lives and gives back to the community in a meaningful way."

Picking Up the Pieces

Laura Treloar, 42
Vancouver, British Columbia, Canada

In college, Laura Treloar was the artsy, tattooed girl who vowed that she would spend her life as an artist, making art every day. But that's not quite the way it worked out.

"The day I got out of art school, I slipped into a panic, asking myself, 'Oh my God, what am I *really* going to do?'" So she enrolled at the University of British Columbia to get a teaching degree.

There, at a pub near campus, she met a six-foot, four-inch, dark-haired, blue-eyed lifeguard, also studying to be a teacher. His name was Dave. It took a year for their first date to happen, but ten months later the two were a solid couple, and they bought a small, dilapidated heritage house in Vancouver and began restoring it to its original condition.

Shortly after their dream cottage was complete, the punk-rock-girl-turned-high-school-art-teacher and the high-school-gym-teacher-and-basketball-coach married. For five years they worked, adopted rescue dogs (three) and cats (two), and tended multiple fish tanks. During all that time they had exactly one fight. "It was so stupid," Laura recalls. "It was about which restaurant to go to, and at one point Dave just picked me up and held me upside down over the sidewalk until we both started laughing."

Then one day Laura, who'd never thought she wanted children, was on her way to pick up a third cat and had an epiphany. "I realized that it wasn't really a cat I wanted. I wanted a baby." She went home to tell Dave. "He literally started jumping up and down with joy. 'I *knew* you'd change your mind!'"

After struggling to conceive, Laura had three miscarriages, but finally Austin arrived. "We called him the lucky swimmer," she says, laughing. Six months later, lucky swimmer number two, Michaelie, was conceived—and suddenly the couple who had given homes to cats and dogs and now kids was in need of a bigger place.

Their second fixer-upper was a 100-year-old, apocalyptic mess. "Rats. Bedbugs. Everything you can imagine was wrong with it," says Laura. "People would walk in and say *What have you done?!* And we'd laugh and say, 'You gotta have the *vision!*'"

Their common work ethic and Dave's "Failure is not an option" motto kicked in. Dave lived and worked in the house for months until it was habitable enough for Laura, Austin, and Michaelie to move in for good. The family soldiered on and, room by room, the restoration began to take shape.

Less than a year later, baby Aiden came along. Feeling the financial pinch of raising three children on two teachers' salaries, Laura also started tutoring to bring in extra cash, but it was too stressful. So Dave suggested she try something creative instead and urged her to do her jewelry-making on the side.

A few years earlier, Laura's school had asked her to add a jewelry-making class to her art curriculum, and she jumped at the chance. She had always fantasized about taking up jewelry-making so she eagerly checked out some books on the subject from the local library to keep one step ahead of her students.

Now Laura bought some basic tools and set up shop on their dining room table. From the start, Dave was her biggest fan. "Everything I made, he would be like, 'Wow, this is the best thing you've ever done! What are you going to sell that for?' And then he would tell me to charge more."

Selling her jewelry on Etsy, the super-popular e-commerce site where craftspeople market their wares, Laura was able to pay for the family's groceries. "Whenever they featured one of my pieces, Dave was the first one I'd show and he'd go crazy texting all his friends."

During spring break of 2011, Dave asked his mom to watch the kids for the weekend so he and Laura could spend some time together. "Between the kids and work, it was just really tough for us to have any time alone," Laura says. But that Saturday morning, their romantic weekend turned into a shattering nightmare.

"Dave was sleeping next to me in bed and I couldn't wake him. I called 911 and while I waited for the ambulance, the operator took me through how to try to resuscitate him. As I tried, I could hear the deafening sound of the ambulance; then I watched the paramedics work on him for 20 minutes until they told me there was nothing they could do." At 38, Dave was gone.

"I remember sitting in the living room with my sister, looking out my window as the kids came home," says Laura of the moment she had to tell the three boys that their dad had died. "I watched them walking up the path to our house and they were all laughing and giggling, and I remember thinking *That's the last time those kids are going to feel truly happy for a long time. Their life is changing the second they walk through that door.*" Austin was six; Michaelie, five; and Aiden, three.

At first, they couldn't take in what their mom was trying to tell them. "Once they sort of realized, they started to cry and almost immediately Austin said, 'You're going to die, too! When are you going to die?'"

Their terror was so strong, the kids wouldn't let Laura out of their sight. "I'd be taking a shower and I would suddenly turn and look through the shower door and all three of them would just be standing there. It was heartbreaking.

"Our world crashed and then stopped. I spent those first days immobilized, trying to make this horrific thing sink in. I felt as though someone was following me around, sucker punching me in the back of my head."

Haunted by images of Dave, Laura couldn't sleep in their room, so every night she'd crawl into bed with one of the kids. If she heard a siren, she'd start hyperventilating and go into a panic. One night about a week after Dave's death, when the kids were asleep, she sat in the living room with her dad and several of her siblings and voiced her fears.

"Dave and I could barely take care of these kids together when he was alive. I can't possibly do this by myself." Her dad leaned back and said flatly, "Well, then, I guess you're going to have to put them in foster care."

Laura became enraged. "I was just hysterical. I screamed, 'How can you say that?' and stormed up to my room. But then I got to thinking about my dad—how once when I was a little kid, a piece of hot plastic landed on my arm and I ended up with a third-degree burn. I was screaming and crying, and my dad just looked at me and said, 'Stop crying' and picked it out of my arm—and I immediately stopped.

"Now he'd done the same thing to me 30 years later, kind of like a big slap in the head. He made me see the situation more clearly. I thought, 'If I just curl up in a ball and am unable to deal with any of this, what's going to happen to my kids? They're little, they didn't deserve this, and they'll be ruined if I screw this up.' So I wiped away my tears, came downstairs, and said,

'Dad, you're right. I've got to pull it together,' and the next day I did. I got up. I packed their lunches. And I drove my kids to school."

A few months later, Laura started working again part-time as a teacher, but on many days she had trouble getting from the parking lot to the classroom. "I would sit in the car crying. I had been at my school 13 years and I'd built a reputation as the smiling, positive art teacher. It was exhausting to try to still be that person when I wasn't feeling that way." It was then that Laura's principal suggested she try getting back to her jewelry-making.

It was hard. "Metalsmithing takes tons of concentration, and if you're a fraction of a millimeter off, you've screwed up your piece," she says. But she had Etsy orders she was behind on, and as she sat back down at her workbench, something happened: that once-familiar feeling of her working hands returned. She felt something else coming back as well.

"I've always thought of myself as a super-strong, really in-control person. Workwise—you have to be in control of yourself every second you're in front of a classroom of kids. Losing Dave was a situation out of my control, and it had made me anxious.

"So getting back in my studio—and being able to make something that I could send to someone, knowing they'd be overjoyed with it—calmed my brain down and got me into a rhythm," she says. "When I'm on my workbench, everything melts away. It's the only thing I've tried that has really helped with my anxiety. I can control what I'm making, my finances, and my time."

Laura's business took off. Etsy began including her pieces in its promotions and late in 2011 the site contacted her to say that she was going to be promoted as a featured seller. "That means they choose you and your shop as being exemplary and they give you a feature on their front page with an interview and pictures of you in your studio for three days," she says. "You cannot pay for advertising like that."

After that, things got over-the-top busy for Laura. She does some occasional business from her home studio through local word-of-mouth, but Etsy is her true marketplace and she has had no trouble cracking her monthly goal of $10,000; in a good month, she can now make $20,000.

"I'm grateful every day that I don't have to worry now about how we're going to buy groceries or pay property taxes," she says. "I could never stop

teaching fully, because I'm so invested in my students. But my teaching job basically pays for child care. My jewelry business is what sustains us.

"For me, this is all about stability for my children. Our home is everything to us. It's filled with all the things that my husband fixed, repaired, or replaced. I am so proud that I can keep the home Dave and I put together. I have even established college funds for my kids. It's very cathartic and empowering."

The kids have also gotten in on the act. "Like one night," Laura says, "I was sketching some new ring designs and my little guy, Aiden, came over and sat beside me and said, 'I want to draw rings, too.' Within five minutes all three of the kids had paper and pencil and were coming up with ring designs, too. One of them said, 'When we get married, Mom, are you going to make our wedding rings for free, or are we going to have to pay you?'"

The joy of Laura's success goes way beyond her family and their living room. Most of her one-of-a-kind pieces are for engagements and weddings, or are mementoes in someone's life. "I've had men contact me because their wife is having their first baby and they want something to present to her on the day the baby is born. And I get pictures from guys who do all these crazy surprise engagements, like one guy who had the waiter make my ring a part of the dessert."

And then there was the woman who said she planned to pass Laura's piece down to her daughter. "Jewelry is such a special heirloom in many families, and it's kind of cool to think something I've made is going to become one of those pieces," she says. "It's very fulfilling to be attached to a joyful point in someone else's life."

Laura's own life is gaining joy, too, though it's been only a few years since the loss of Dave. She feels him everywhere, and his love and enthusiasm are a big part of her creativity. "I've finally become the artist I always wanted to be, making my own designs and supporting my family. I'm really proud. And I know Dave would be, too."

The Date Keeper

Amy Knapp, 48
Kalamazoo, Michigan

my Knapp had it all under control. That's because Amy Knapp was super-organized.

She had to be. As the young mother of two, she was the owner of her own specialty advertising company, which produced custom pens, folders, and other promotional items—and she did it all: ran meetings, scheduled conference calls, managed sales incentive programs, juggled deadlines. It all came naturally to her; it was a talent she'd nurtured back in high school, when she was president of the student council and in charge of planning the senior prom. Years later, her former classmates even counted on her to organize their first reunion.

So imagine Amy's surprise when she could barely manage her own household.

It started in 1995, when her two-month-old daughter, Natalie, was hospitalized for meningitis. The baby recovered, but several months later it became obvious that the infection had left its mark. Natalie would have lifelong disabilities from the illness, doctors told Amy, and would require intense therapy to overcome them.

With an active toddler son and now a disabled infant, Amy decided to sell her business and dig in as a full-time mother and care manager. Who better to oversee the dizzying schedule of medical appointments for Natalie than the ultimate planning pro?

"I thought, *I have this in the bag*," recalls Amy. "I'm used to multitasking." But she soon discovered that running a busy household for a family with special needs was different from running a business: Natalie had appointments with occupational therapists, speech therapists, and physical therapists; she had to see a neurologist in addition to her regular pediatrician; she needed to travel to the Mayo Clinic for specialized testing. Three-year-old Kyle, by the way, had needs, too—the never-ending preschooler kind. And on top of managing all that, Amy was supposed to do the grocery shopping and get dinner on the table every night.

She was in a tailspin.

Within six months, Amy realized she needed to do something to get her life under control. "That's when my managerial side kicked in," she says. "I was desperate. I had run a very tight ship at the office, and I wanted things to be just as structured and organized at home."

So she went to her local Barnes & Noble to pick up a day-by-day planner or calendar—any kind, she figured—just to help her get organized. There were certainly a lot to choose from: some offered daily, weekly, or monthly layouts; others had spaces for phone numbers, or pages for to-do lists. Many of them had pretty covers, cute cartoons, or inspiring quotes.

Amy wound up spending $17.99 on a calendar with a beautiful Monet painting on the cover. She took it home and began filling in her schedule.

But then she ran out of room.

"Within three months, the entire painting was covered with sticky notes," Amy says. "I tried really hard to write small and squeeze the words together on the Post-its, because I couldn't fit them into the calendar. The more I looked at them, the more I realized that these notes were not appointments, but rather all the other parts of being a stay-at-home mom—or any kind of mom, really—things you absolutely need to keep track of."

Among these notes were Amy's grocery list, what she planned to make for dinner, and reminders of personal calls she needed to make—a blizzard of jotted reminders that make up *life*.

Amy thought, *This is ridiculous. I'll make a planning calendar for myself.*

"I knew what I needed," she says. "First, I needed to see everything I planned to do in a full week—starting on Monday, not Sunday. You don't want to be flipping back and forth, with the calendar in one place and the grocery list on the back page, and your to-do list somewhere else. You needed it all in a format that can lie open on your counter, where you can see all of your responsibilities in one glance. And you definitely needed to see the weekend as one unit—not divided up with this Sunday at the beginning of the week, and next Saturday at the other end of it."

In a flash of inspiration, Amy grabbed a spiral notebook and a Sharpie and sketched out her own system—one that chronicled her crammed schedule across a two-page spread.

"It became my lifeline," says Amy, who then hauled her spiral notebook everywhere she went, its ratty cover and curled-up corners a testament to its indispensability.

Amy's design wasn't as simple as it appeared—it was actually rather ingenious. In addition to her one-glance, seven-day spread, there was a separate area for to-do notes and reminders. Down the far right column of the right-hand page, there was a space for her to list her dinner menus for the week. The grocery items she'd need to make those dinners went on the outside of the left-hand page—on a perforated column she could tear off and take to the grocery store with her. Since this week's shopping list appeared on the front of last week's menu, the tear-off left her current weekly view completely intact.

"I could go right from my menu to my grocery list, without turning the page," she says, "so it was very convenient. People would see me carrying it in the grocery store and ask, 'What is that?' and I'd say, 'This is how I organize my time.' Invariably they'd say, 'Wow, that's a really good setup. Let me see how you did that. I'd like to make one.' After hearing that a couple of times, I put my sales and marketing cap on and thought, 'Boy, there are a lot of people out there who need something like this.'"

Amy's makeshift spiral organizer served her well for a few years; and once Kyle and Natalie were both in school, she decided to turn her brainstorm into a business. She began by showing her idea to the owner of her local copy store; together they sat down with one of his designers to translate the hand-written book into a digital format.

"As we perfected the design," Amy explains, "it became obvious that we were not creating a business planner that people would just add their personal chores to," she says. "It was created specifically for a family, by a family. And that made all the difference."

Amy placed an order for a print run, producing 50 simple versions of her planner. Holding that first one in her hands, she was simultaneously proud and nervous.

"I was probably more scared than anything," she says, "because I knew the print bill was coming right around the corner! But I said to myself, 'Okay, you made it, now you've got to go out there and sell it.'"

But what if they didn't sell? she wondered. "I remember telling my husband, 'If no one buys them, we'll just hide them up in the attic, and someday our grandkids will find them and say, "Oh, look, another one of grandma's harebrained ideas."'"

Amy decided to give away most of that first batch of planners in order to get feedback. "It was like an expensive focus group," she says, "but it paid off big, because the original design evolved and improved." Then, once she decided the planner was finally ready for prime time, she took a breath and followed her old marketing instincts, calling the head buyer for calendars at Barnes & Noble in New York.

"It was a cold call!" she says. "They transferred me about five times, but I finally got through to him. I later discovered that he never took those types of calls. I still don't know why he took mine."

But he did take the call—and he was intrigued.

"He asked me for a real prototype, which would cost real money, and I said sure. I hung up and thought, *Yikes!* I called my husband and asked him if we should invest the money—a couple thousand dollars. He said—and I'll never forget this, because it was probably the nicest thing he's ever said to me—'I will put my money on you every time.' Boy, he did not realize what he was getting into!"

The buyer recommended some changes to the prototype, and after Amy made the tweaks he agreed to carry the calendar at Barnes & Noble, sold under the name Amy Knapp's Family Organizer.

Amy was ecstatic. "It was incredible to see that my idea had become a reality," she says, "but it was also scary. On one hand you have this great success, but on the other hand you suddenly have these huge pallets of organizers being delivered to your house."

But Amy was jazzed—and when those first three pallets landed in her driveway, groaning under 40-pound boxes of planners, "I turned our living room into a shipping warehouse. In that first year, I repackaged planners for every Barnes & Noble across the country. I put six planners each into individual boxes, printed shipping labels, then hauled them out to my garage to get picked up. My neighbors thought I was insane."

Then she started doing business with local retailers, and launched a website—TheFamilyOrganizer.com—to begin direct sales. And in 2004, she struck gold, traveling to Arkansas for a meeting with a buyer for Walmart, who agreed to carry Amy Knapp's Family Organizers in its stores. In a single year, the business she had created with a Sharpie and a spiral notebook sold $1.2 million worth of calendars.

But then things took a downturn.

"The recession struck," Amy says, "and Walmart eliminated many of its smaller vendors, including me. That was a big shock for me. No one plans for the day that half your business disappears."

To make matters worse, a number of her smaller retailers went under because of the bad economy. But Amy doubled down and fought her way back. Although it took another full year for her to adjust her sales strategy, today her business, though small, continues to thrive.

"Our yearly sales are around $328,000," she says, "and that's okay. We've gone from tiny to huge, then smaller, then back to making some money. But you know what? I don't have to make a ton of money. If I was working on the company all the time, I would miss being with my family—and my family was the reason all of this began."

So Amy the organizer is organized once more. She divides her time between tending to business and keeping up on all the family activities, including going to Natalie's softball games (now 18, Natalie plays in a league for children with disabilities).

"Would I have liked to maintain Walmart?" asks Amy. "Absolutely. There's a little bit of mourning for things that won't happen. But you have to accept that and make the best possible opportunity for yourself that you can. I tell my kids, 'Eighty percent of life is made up of things you do not sign up for. But you can take that 80 percent and turn it into a blessing.'

"I didn't sign up to be a parent of a child with disabilities," she continues, "but I am so thankful for Natalie. And it's the same with my business. I didn't sign up for what happened after the recession, but, had my business not changed the way it did, I would have missed out on so much time with my family."

What also gives Amy great pleasure is connecting with the families who use her calendars and share with her how invaluable they are.

"Many people tell me they save them as a record of their family's activities over the years," Amy says. "That makes me feel like they've invited me into their home to be a part of their family."

And for the ultimate family organizer, that just might be the ultimate success.

PART TEN

The Spirit Moved Her

"I was a woman on a mission, and nothing could stop me."

The Celebrator

Lois Heckman, 63
Saylorsburg, Pennsylvania

That's it? That's my wedding?

Lois Heckman couldn't believe she was walking out of the mayor's office with a ring on her finger and a new husband at her side only two minutes after she'd walked in. "It felt like two seconds," she says.

To Lois, the brief, sterile ceremony was a poor reflection of the relationship she had built with Kent. "One of the reasons I fell in love with Kent," Lois says, "is the way he folded my son and me into his life so readily."

Twenty-four years later, the disappointment of that ceremony still stung.

In 2003, Lois and Kent were listening to NPR on their car radio when a story came on about a gay wedding. "The reporter kept referring to the 'celebrant' who had performed the ceremony," says Lois. "I thought, *What is that?*" It was clear that he wasn't a priest, a preacher, a minister, or a rabbi—but he wasn't just a city clerk either. Instead, he was a professional officiant who delivered a meaningful, loving, secular wedding service for a couple in love.

Someone like this, Lois thought, *would have been the perfect fit for Kent and me back in 1979.*

And it felt like the perfect job for her now. It spoke to all of her interests: performing (she and Kent had supported themselves for two decades playing in a band); advocating for social change (Lois was currently working at a center for victims of rape and domestic violence); and spirituality (Lois had been a religion major in college).

Kent laughed, and Lois knew he was thinking what she was: "It's me!"

But how, exactly, did someone become a celebrant? As soon as Lois got home, she went online to find out. She learned that the ordination involved months of serious study and training to learn how to perform not only weddings but also funerals and other "life ceremonies" for anyone who wanted to bypass traditional religious institutions. It was a new and growing field, but one that CNN and *Money* magazine had named the third best job for people over 50, in part for its flexible hours, meaningfulness, and good pay—as much as $80,000 a year.

The more Lois learned about celebrants, the more she was drawn to the job. While a celebrant-led service could incorporate religious rituals like the breaking of the glass or sharing of the wine, it also offered a more personalized experience than a traditional worship service. "The heart and soul of any celebrant wedding is crafting words about the couple," Lois says. A celebrant might spend hours interviewing two people about their history in order to weave parts of their story into a ceremony.

The same was true for funerals, an idea that greatly appealed to Lois, who had felt a sense of intimacy missing from many of the funerals she'd attended over the years. She flashed back to a memorial for a friend's mother, where the pastor clearly knew nothing about this woman over whom the entire room was grieving.

"He was reading a bunch of prayers, and it had nothing to do with her life," she says. "Sitting there, I was angry. I thought, *This is not the way it should be.*"

A few weeks after hearing the NPR story on the radio, Lois enrolled long distance at the Celebrant Foundation and Institute in Montclair, New Jersey, where she could pursue her study at night and on weekends.

The training was rigorous: Lois was assigned to read about cross-cultural customs, history, and anthropology, from *The Power of Myth* by Joseph Campbell to *On Death and Dying*, by Elisabeth Kübler-Ross. She attended a variety of religious ceremonies—Presbyterian, Roman Catholic, Jewish. Perhaps most important, Lois wrote her own sample ceremonies. "I learned to recognize not just the big stuff, but the little details that make a ceremony personal and genuine, and that touch the hearts of those who are present."

The years she had spent working with victims of abuse came in handy. "If I learned anything working at the women's center, it was how to listen," she says. "A celebrant's first job is to learn about your clients. After all, the day is about them."

Lois's years of experience performing on stage as a musician also helped. "When you marry a couple, you're not just reading a script," she says. "Colloquially, we say we *perform* a wedding. A good officiant—whether a minister, priest, rabbi, or celebrant—is able to move people emotionally."

In 2004, a year after she first heard the word "celebrant" on the radio, Lois graduated and was ready to officiate. "I felt like everything I had done in my life led me to this," she says.

Now Lois had to build the business. She bought ad space on wedding websites, left her business cards at wedding venues, and created her own website that reflected the kinds of ceremonies she could provide.

"Instead of using generic, flowery words or images of roses and doves, I spoke about myself and my background in a more direct and authentic way. I felt that was the best way to connect with people who were looking for someone to officiate their important day," she says.

Within a month of her graduation, Lois performed her first wedding, and by the end of the year she had married 24 couples. After many painful years of working with abuse victims, Lois found this work healing. "I was meeting people who talked about how much they respected and supported their partners," she says.

When a couple hires her for their wedding, Lois interviews them for more than an hour, then has them fill out a questionnaire: How did they meet and fall in love? What are their hopes and dreams? What parts of their religious and cultural backgrounds do they want to share with their guests? They can make the ceremony, typically a half hour, as traditional or as creative as they want it to be.

A huge portion of Lois's clientele are interfaith couples, lapsed churchgoers, or people who consider themselves spiritual but not religious. "They do believe, but they don't feel right having a church wedding," she says. "Or they say, 'We really don't believe, but our parents do.' Then the big question is, 'How do we honor your parents and make them feel respected without selling out your own beliefs?'"

Lois might ask the parents to stand, thanking mom for carting the bride to dance class, or telling dad how much those fishing trips meant to the groom, before asking them, "Do you support your child in marriage today?" and waiting for a parental "I do."

"One of the challenges in creating the ceremony is to make sure nobody feels dishonest about who they are or what they believe," says Lois. After one wedding ceremony, in which Lois incorporated several Catholic symbols, like the sharing of the sign of peace and the Holy Eucharist, the bride's mother came up to her and said, "In the beginning, I was disappointed that she wasn't getting married in the church, but this was wonderful."

Whether or not her ceremonies reference prayer or religious rituals, Lois always takes care to delve into a couple's story. "I want the guests to feel the journey the couple took to get to this point. It's a great compliment when people say afterward, 'How did you know all that? You must be a friend of the couple's.'"

With time, Lois's business grew to include not just weddings, but also ceremonies to mark other life events. "With some couples, I've married them, performed welcoming ceremonies for their babies, buried their parents," says Lois. "That is the role of clergy, but if you don't have a minister, priest, or rabbi, you want to have someone you trust and feel comfortable with during these life-changing events."

In 2012, Lois held a funeral for a woman she had married in the same spot only one year earlier. "Her husband called me and asked to have the funeral there, too. He said, 'This place meant so much to us.'

"Even though I don't consider myself religious, it's during times like these that I feel my work is a calling. Not every ceremony is joyful and uplifting—sometimes it's hard and emotional—but it's always meaningful."

Makana

Romely Levezow, 40
Mission Viejo, California

Romely Levezow was *absolutely, positively* going to start an exercise routine. Tomorrow. Or maybe next week.

And she was *determined* to eat healthier! If only her law firm's free cafeteria didn't serve those fresh Krispy Kreme doughnuts daily. . . .

And she was going to *stop* falling asleep on the couch at night in front of the TV.

But as much as Romely wanted to get her act together, her work life kept getting in the way.

"I was constantly multitasking to meet deadlines," she recalls of her job as a legal assistant at one of the country's biggest law firms, with all-star clients like Google and eBay. "Late nights were common, and all-nighters and weekends were fair game, too."

And whenever she felt burned out, Romely would dream of her fantasy careers. *Interior designer. Wedding planner. Event coordinator.*

"Martha Stewart was my idol," says Romely. "I'd watch her show and just be inspired. I loved to make jewelry out of wooden beads and wreaths out of dried flowers and give them as gifts to friends." But whenever Romely thought about having a creative career, she'd hear her mother's voice in her head: *"You need a financially stable job."*

Romely's mom had died of cancer a few years earlier, but the work ethic she'd instilled in her daughter remained potent. "Mom brought me here from the Philippines when I was very young," Romely explains, "and she worked hard as a single mother, as a chemist, and a high school teacher. That left a lasting impression."

Still, Romely nurtured her creativity wherever she could. In her cubicle, she hung pictures of Hawaii, where she visited her family—it helped her feel connected to her mom. "There's a warmth in that culture that's all about giving," she says, "and the spirit of aloha called out to me. Aloha means hello and good-bye, respect, and unconditional love."

Romely even tried to bring some of that aloha spirit to her office, coordinating events like AIDS walks and the American Cancer Society's Daffodil Day. And she sought aloha after-hours, too, with hula dancing classes once a week, something she'd done as a kid.

"The minute I set foot in the dance studio, I felt like I was home," she says. And to bring a feeling of warmth into the house she shared with her husband, Josh, Romely filled the rooms with flickering candles. "The ritual of lighting a candle every evening brought me peace, serenity."

Then in January 2008, Romely received a phone call that put her positive spirit to the test. Three weeks earlier she had gone in for a checkup, and one of the test results revealed that her blood platelet counts were elevated. It could be nothing, said her doctor, but she advised Romely to get retested and referred her to an oncologist.

At the word "oncologist," Romely began to panic. *Cancer. Just like Mom.*

The doctor, however, urged her not to worry: This was just a routine follow-up.

A few days later, Romely sat in the oncologist's waiting room, trying to remain calm.

"I remembered my doctor saying, 'It will be okay.'" But after running a blood test, the oncologist asked Romely to step into his office. The news wasn't good: Romely had a blood disorder called essential thrombocythemia. Among other complications, he said, it put Romely at an increased risk for leukemia.

Romely was stunned, and she wished Josh were there with her. Dizzy with fear, she tried to pay attention as the oncologist detailed a preventative plan of action: For the next month, she would undergo mild chemotherapy in the form of a daily prescription pill. Her doctor hoped the chemo would lower her platelet levels, which he said would help keep the cancer at bay.

Tears streamed down Romely's cheeks as she left the doctor's office. All she could think about was her mom. Eight years earlier, her mother had gone to the doctor with what she thought was the flu, but blood tests revealed high levels of disease-fighting white blood cells. Her mom's doctor couldn't figure out what was behind it, so he admitted her to the hospital for more testing. Two weeks later, Romely's mom fell into a coma. She never woke up.

"When I got there in the morning, she was gone," Romely says. "Losing her felt like a bad dream, and I was just waiting to wake up." A few days after her mother's death, an autopsy finally revealed the cause of her symptoms: stomach cancer.

"I sat in the parking lot of the oncologist's office, clutching my prescription. I was paralyzed. My mom didn't get a chance to fight. Part of me thought, *I've got to do this for her.*"

Driving home, Romely sped straight past the pharmacy—she couldn't bring herself to fill the prescription. "I put it on the refrigerator with a magnet. I didn't even want to touch it."

The next day at the real estate investment firm where she now worked as a paralegal, Romely tried to keep a lid on her emotions. "Things were just as busy as always, and all I could think about was that prescription on my fridge," she says. *I'm working so hard in a job that I don't even like, and for what?* Overwhelmed, she broke down in tears at her desk. "I felt like I was in a tailspin." After work, Romely called a friend who worked at the hospital: *Should she start the chemo?* The friend said Romely needed a second opinion and offered to arrange an appointment with another oncologist.

This time, Romely had Josh in tow for moral support. A new blood test revealed that her platelets were still high, but lower than the previous tests had shown. *Chemotherapy isn't what you need,* this oncologist told her. Still, he explained that essential thrombocythemia can also cause blood clotting, which increases the risk of heart attack and stroke. He prescribed aspirin to help prevent clots and advised her to maintain a healthy immune system by eating well, exercising, and reducing stress. The doctor also told Romely that he would need to continue to monitor her platelet count. Filled with relief, Romely made an appointment for another blood draw the following month.

That night, Romely lit a few candles to try to relax. Determined to get a handle on the healthier lifestyle her doctor had recommended, she began googling. But online, Romely was inundated by sober warnings: chemicals in cleaning and beauty products, processed foods, pesticides, a sedentary lifestyle—it seemed like everything was linked to cancer. "Now that the initial shock had worn off, I realized I had to be my own advocate." It was time to make some serious changes: no more Krispy Kremes, no more falling asleep in front of the TV, no more excuses.

Together with her husband, Romely began exercising daily. She replaced her household cleaners, soaps, and shampoos with chemical-free products. She excavated her kitchen and threw out the TV dinners, sugary cereals, and snack foods. "I was like a madwoman," she says. For the first time in her life, she filled her grocery cart with organic produce and green, leafy vegetables.

Romely also continued to research ways to reduce her cancer risk. One night she stumbled upon a report about a parrot owner who always lit a candle near the bird's cage. After the parrot died, an autopsy found traces of chemicals emitted by the burning candle. Jarred, Romely immediately gathered up every last candle in her home and tossed them in a garbage bag. Afterward, though, she missed the ambience and serenity of the twinkling lights. So she began looking into safer alternatives.

"I knew the candles weren't going to kill me, so I may have been going a little overboard," says Romely, "but I was a woman on a mission, and nothing could stop me."

So she ordered a kit to make nontoxic candles herself. Soon she was spending weekends experimenting with waxes, wicks, and fragrances. After a lot of trial and error, Romely began crafting tea lights to share with family and friends. To help raise money for a charity benefit, she made 50 vanilla-scented soy candles in simple tins—each adorned with the word *"makana,"* a Hawaiian term meaning "giving a gift."

And then something amazing happened: Even before the event was over, every candle had sold and Romely had requests for more. So she did what any entrepreneurial businesswoman would do when the demand suddenly surged: She ramped up her production. She made candle after candle, incorporating new and delicious scents inspired by the fresh leis she wore while performing hula.

At first, she and Josh sold the candles at local craft fairs; then in January 2009, she took the plunge and started an Etsy account, using the name Makana Studios. Within a few months, Romely was inundated with orders.

Suddenly, what had once been a small kitchen operation—melting wax, curing candles, packing shipments—had spread over the entire house. By May, she and Josh decided to rent a small manufacturing space near their home. Soon after, Romely attended two big trade shows in Los Angeles and San Francisco, and sales reps began contacting her about distributing her products nationally.

Today, Makana Studios' candles are sold in 500 boutiques, luxury resorts, and organic markets throughout the United States, Canada, and the Caribbean. The business grew so fast that at the end of 2011, Romely's husband left his job as a university professor to devote himself to Makana Studios full-time. And after much deliberation about letting go of that predictable salary, Romely has decided to quit the legal field, too.

"Ironically, it is my mom who is giving me the strength to leave," she says. "Looking back, I realized how brave she was to come to this country, alone, as a single mother. I took her courage with me."

Romely also makes regular visits to her doctor to monitor her platelet levels. Although her counts continue to fluctuate, they've never become excessively high. Romely still gets a little anxious before each blood draw, but she mostly feels empowered.

"At first, the diagnosis immobilized me," she says. "But now I just think, *I've got this*. I've not only taken control of my health, I've found my way out of a stressful job and into one that's fulfilling. Now I see that the diagnosis was a gift that completely changed my life. A *makana*."

After Hunter

Jennifer Otter Bickerdike, 42
London, England

I t took a funeral for Jennifer Otter Bickerdike to start living.

In truth, she thought she already was. Having risen from an internship to become the West Coast marketing director for Interscope Geffen A&M—the biggest record label in the world—"I got to do things I had only dreamed about, like going to birthday parties at Gwen Stefani's house with Sting and Bono and driving in limos with Eminem," she says.

She had access—to artists, to concerts, to parties, and to awards ceremonies. "I was constantly being told how lucky I was to have my position, how glamorous it was, how anyone would kill for it," she says.

The job was all consuming, but Jennifer didn't mind. Almost every night of the week, she was out entertaining—at VIP parties with band members listening to new records, at concerts with clients. She was a bona fide insider, and she liked it. It was a stark contrast to her childhood years in the small California beach town of Santa Cruz. "The job said to me that I had made it," she says.

Then, as Jennifer was approaching her ten-year anniversary in the music industry, her best friend from high school called with horrifying news. A former classmate named Hunter had been mugged and fatally shot while walking home with his girlfriend in San Francisco, just five minutes from where Jennifer now lived. Jennifer hadn't seen Hunter in years, but his name brought back warm memories of her high school years, playing water polo and being "just Jen." She decided to go back home to attend his memorial service.

Walking into the massive church, filled to the rafters with more than 300 mourners, "I was surrounded by people who knew me before I was Jennifer Otter from Interscope, before I had this whole persona of *music executive,*" she says. Without the mantle of her job to hide behind, Jennifer's confidence faltered. She wasn't sure anymore why, or if, people liked her outside of what she could do for them.

"I felt like I did not exist unless I was glued to my corporate black AmEx card and had a backstage pass around my neck," she says. Suddenly she was embarrassed to be seen at a memorial service for someone she didn't know well—so embarrassed that she couldn't even bring herself to say hello to anyone from her past. She'd been back to her hometown many times, but (except for the best friend who accompanied her) this was her first time seeing all of these people she had known back in high school.

Sitting in the church, listening to Hunter's family and friends tell loving stories about him, Jennifer felt incredibly sad. Sad for his close-knit family. Sad that the world had lost this young, handsome guy who "really seemed to know what was important in life—enjoying every moment of everything and letting all of the people who were important to him know how much he loved them." ("He was the most caring, loving, likable, humble, God-loving person one could ever meet," his family later said in a statement after the gunman was convicted.) Hearing their words, Jennifer also came to see Hunter as someone who was tenacious, who took chances with his life. They described how "Hunter would always shoot beyond what he thought he could accomplish, and just go, go, go for it," says Jennifer. One friend recalled him saying: "If you're going after Moby-Dick, make sure you bring the tartar sauce."

Jennifer couldn't help comparing Hunter's optimistic, fearless life to her own. After college, she had entered the music business full of hope, determined to make a difference in a business that often seemed to value money above artistry. But "people told me early on that I was just too idealistic and naive, that I needed to accept things as they were and relish the perks," she says. So she did, losing herself in the process. "The values I had at the outset of my career had been pushed down," she says. And she had ignored her own dreams outside the music industry, like going back to grad school.

When the service ended, just before dark, Jennifer exited quietly and made her way with her friend to dinner at the beach, where they sat watching the waves roll in and out. The funeral had made her realize "I was alive, and I had a choice that Hunter had been robbed of, an opportunity to breathe and dream and act, to pursue even the most seemingly outrageous, against-all-odds ideas," she says. "I had been so busy trying to 're-create' myself, that when I was confronted with my past, I realized I was just fine from the start. I could see what was really important."

Jennifer awoke the next day like it was the first day of the rest of her life. On the drive back to San Francisco, she called her off-again, on-again boyfriend, a guy who couldn't choose between her and another woman. She broke up with him, for good.

In her apartment, she hung Hunter's picture from the funeral program on the wall. "Every day when I looked at that picture, it was a reminder to keep moving forward," she says. "My goal was to find a new way to be happy with *me*."

She applied for a master's program in humanities at San Francisco State University, which she began that fall, scheduling night classes around her job. "Humanities encompasses so many different mediums that had such a powerful influence on me—writing, literature, art, film, music," she says. "I wanted to learn more." Halfway through the school year, she knew it was time to cut the connection to the job that had kept her from being who she really was. So she quit.

"Afterward, I had so many friends who disappeared overnight," she says. "When I called a band I had traveled the country with—I'd even been there when their kids were born—to tell them that I was quitting, I thought they would say, 'Don't leave us!' But all that mattered to them was who was going to help them now. It gutted me. It illustrated how replaceable I was, and how I now had to do what was right for *me*."

She'd always dreamed of one day earning her PhD and becoming "Dr. Otter," but after being rejected from six elite graduate programs (Harvard, Stanford, Brown . . .), she hit rock bottom.

"After I got my last rejection letter, I drank an entire bottle of Jack Daniel's and got a bad tattoo," she says. "The next day I applied for a job at Banana Republic and they told me I wasn't Banana Republic material. I couldn't even get a job in retail!"

To figure out her future, Jennifer looked to the past: Ever since she was little, she had been "totally obsessed with all things British." She fell in love with Jane Austen as a child and later devoured Charlotte Brontë. Her parents would let her stay up to watch PBS period dramas. ("It seemed so exotic," she remembers.) And she especially loved music from the UK: The Smiths, Morrissey, Joy Division.

And then Jennifer thought about Hunter.

"He really seemed to know what was important in life."

"He would always shoot beyond what he thought he could accomplish."

"And he would just go, go, go for it."

So Jennifer decided to go for it. She would combine her two dreams, move to London and get her PhD.

She applied to two British doctoral programs and got accepted into the prestigious Center for Cultural Studies at London's Goldsmiths University.

At 37, Jennifer sold almost everything she owned and prepared to move across the ocean to start her new life. She thought of bringing Hunter's picture to England to hang on her wall there, but instead stashed it away in an album. She didn't need it anymore. She was finally being true to herself.

"Hunter helped me get to the next chapter," she says.

Today, Dr. Otter teaches arts and cultural management at the University of East London, where she was named Best Lecturer of the Year out of 300 professors. "I'm getting paid to talk and write about the things I've been passionate about my whole life," she says. And speaking of passion: She found love at age 40, marrying an Englishman.

"Leaving behind everyone and everything from my old life was hard, but it has also been the most liberating experience I could ever have asked for," she says. "Now nothing scares me. Nothing is beyond my grasp. You only get one shot at this life, so I try to rock every opportunity.

"I'm no longer hiding behind a business card. I am just me. "

Breathing Again

Diane Dennis, 62
Aurora, Oregon

Diane Dennis felt like there was an elephant sitting on her chest. Her second marriage was ending, and she couldn't breathe. "Before the separation, I was hiding our problems from the rest of the world, trying to patch it together and keep it going," she says. But now a different kind of heaviness had taken hold. "I went from feeling safe and secure to not knowing how I was going to pay for gas," she says. "I was in terror." And though she had always been told she *looked* 10 years younger, at 50 she felt "washed up, middle-aged, menopausal—discarded."

Over and over, Diane asked herself: "How did this happen? Why have both of my marriages ended up in this place?" Oh, and the guilt. It had been only five years since she'd uprooted her kids, asking them to move in with a new stepdad, go to a new school, and make new friends. Her daughter was now off at college, but Diane's 13-year-old son, Max, had suffered from living in a dysfunctional home. "He was good at covering it up, but he was emotionally frozen," she says.

When her husband moved out, Diane had bills to pay, but she couldn't just snap her fingers and get a job. During her marriage, she had let her nursing license expire and, for fun, began writing a family column for a community newspaper and hosting a local radio show based on it, but neither job brought in much money. So to pay for groceries (and attorney bills), she took out a line of credit on the house.

"I knew I was dipping into the equity that would be part of my settlement, but I had no choice."

Depressed, Diane stopped exercising, subsisting on a "divorce diet" of three small meals a day and losing ten pounds off her already small frame.

"My appetite was gone," she says. "Eating wasn't on my mind."

She cried all the time. "I called my girlfriend every day, and she would just sit on the other end even if I didn't have anything to say. It was a comfort just having the phone up to my ear, knowing there was someone else there."

For months, Diane felt like she was suffocating. But she didn't realize it until one day when she was crossing the Willamette River on the way to her mom's house—a route she had taken "thousands of times" over the years.

"I looked down at the water and suddenly I could breathe again."

When the same thing happened two more times, Diane says, she "followed the feeling" and turned down the road that ran alongside the river. It was sprinkled with houses, some dilapidated, some newer, some cheek by jowl, others sitting on wide parcels of land.

If I could just live near this water, she thought, *everything would be okay.*

Diane spent a year thinking about living there, wondering how it could happen, *if* it could happen. "I figured I could take some cash from the settlement for a down payment, then sock the rest of it away in a savings account to use for the mortgage and other living expenses. Then I'd set up a strict budget and shop only at discount stores. I was determined to carve out a new kind of life for me and my son."

Diane had her heart set on one particular three-bedroom house that was for sale. It wasn't large but it seemed perfect for them, with wide windows overlooking the river and a dock.

"The sellers had built the house themselves and had such an emotional attachment to the river, they cried when I met them," she says. "I told them that I was also living a dream, and that I would love their property the way they had."

After Diane moved in, she felt a transformation. Where once family life had been crowded with turmoil and unhappiness, now there was room to breathe.

And her love of the river was always a part of it. When she heard people say it wasn't as clean as it used to be, she and Max would go down to the dock and pour Epsom salts into the river to cleanse it. They'd stand there in silence looking out over the stillness.

"We were healing the water; we were healing us."

And on the weekends, the river came alive—boaters blasting music, children tubing and squealing with joy. Diane's relatives and her kids' friends descended on their new home and its "backyard" playground. "It was a juicy life."

When a relative offered Diane a good deal on a small, used boat, she decided to buy it, dreaming of sitting on its deck on quiet mornings, drinking coffee and writing. But one morning she saw other boats zipping by, pulling strong-looking guys on wakeboards who would go airborne as they jumped the wakes. It was beautiful to watch. *I want to do that!* she thought.

So what if she was in her fifties? Diane knew nothing about the sport, so she found an instructional video and watched it over and over until she felt she knew the basics. She taught her son how to drive the boat—"before he even had his driver's license"—and waded in.

Max called it "Driving Miss Crazy." But when Diane was "in the zone," the boat speeding along at 30 miles per hour with the wind whipping through her long blond ponytail, it was a pure rush.

"I felt free, like I was flying."

Each time Diane "caught air" was another opportunity to get lost in the moment, feeling the elements—the air, sun, water—and catching glimpses of blue herons, bald eagles, and hawks. And her son at the wheel.

"There was so much to be thankful for," she says. "There was also a lot of crash and burn." She got sore muscles, bruises, whiplash. One time she face-planted so hard, she wondered, *Is the left side of my face still there?*

But the more she was out there, the more she built muscle. "I felt strong, empowered."

Diane wasn't just getting stronger physically; she was gaining strength

mentally, too. She began to examine the dynamic of her second marriage: How had she ended up feeling so disempowered? When she'd worked as a nursing manager, she'd felt like she could do anything. But after her second husband swept her off her feet, "I unintentionally became totally dependent. I realized that there had always been a little girl inside me looking for a rescuer. I began to see that the rescuer was only a myth, a fantasy. *I had to rescue me.*"

Diane decided she wanted to turn the writing she loved so much into a paying career. She got a loan to go back to school to study communications, then in 2005 launched a new career as a publicist and writer, even starting a new radio show that focused on life transitions, interviewing guests about how to overcome adversity. Her grit was put to the test four years later, when the economy tanked.

"I lost savings, I lost equity, I lost clients, I almost lost my house. But I still had my life," she says. "And I still had the river." It took her two years, but she finally dug herself out.

Now that Diane is in her sixties, people sometimes ask if she is *still* wakeboarding. It makes her wonder: *Am I supposed to stop this at some point?* She got her answer recently: While flipping through a magazine, she saw a photo of an 82-year-old woman, face weathered, waterskiing. By Diane's calculations, that gives her 20 more years to rock a bikini.

"Wakeboarding is a metaphor for my identity," she says. "It reminds me that I have the strength, the wisdom, and the power to know I can overcome anything."

Gotta Dance!

Ofelia de La Valette, 56
Atlanta, Georgia

What is given to us can be lost. But what we create is forever ours.

It was a lesson that had been imprinted on Ofelia de La Valette as a little girl, a lesson unwittingly taught to her by her father.

The grandson of a wealthy tobacco farmer in Cuba, Ofelia's dad spent his youth living the good life—no worries, no responsibilities. Though he became captain of Cuba's international equestrian team, he never finished college or got a job. There was no reason to—he had all the money he needed. So he married and started a family.

But in 1960, with Fidel Castro rising to power, he fled the country with his wife, three-year-old Ofelia, and her older brother. They arrived in New York City with only a few suitcases and no access to the family money back home. Within a year, at age 33, he was broke.

"Our lifestyle plummeted from the lap of luxury to abject poverty," Ofelia recalls. "It was a very hard fall, and although I was only a child, I felt it. The memory has never left me." Her father had never learned how to hold a job, and after being fired from several office positions, he relied on the only thing he knew: teaching horseback riding, moving the family around New York and New Jersey to be near stables.

Thirty years later, as a young woman and single mom, Ofelia took a job selling insurance for its flexible hours, doing so well that she opened her own Atlanta insurance company, de La Valette & Associates, in 1990. The firm took off and by age 34, Ofelia had a successful business, a beautiful house, and a flexible schedule that most days allowed her to be home to spend time with her family.

Then her world did a little spin on its axis.

One day, about a year after her second child was born, Ofelia was on the treadmill at the gym, determined to lose 25 pounds of stubborn pregnancy weight. As she was grinding her way through the workout, some funky music called to her like the Pied Piper. She followed the pounding bass to the next room, where she stood in the doorway watching a gaggle of sweaty men and women swinging their hips and pumping their arms to the beat. At the front, a guy wearing black-and-white-striped leggings, a skintight turtleneck, and jazz shoes was calling out the moves. Everyone looked like they were having a blast.

What am I doing on a machine? Ofelia thought. *Why am I not in here?*

Dancing was something she had loved as a child. "When Latin families and friends get together for happy occasions, there's always music and dancing," she says. "Anchored in me is that connection between joy and dance."

Ofelia had fantasized about becoming a professional dancer someday, but her parents couldn't afford classes so she taught herself. In high school she joined various dance troupes, and later put herself through flamenco school.

Then she married, had kids, and started her company; there was no longer time for a little girl's silly dreams.

Still, this cardio-funk class at the gym looked like too much fun to pass up. But walking in, she froze: In front of her was a wall of mirrors that reflected her frumpy figure and a sea of incredibly fit people around her. Ofelia wanted to sink through the floor.

At first, she tried hiding out in the back of the room. But as the playlist of oldies and modern music—remixed with dance club beats—heated up, Ofelia let go and really started moving. Breathing hard, she struggled to keep up, but she was also smiling and laughing. "I felt invigorated," she says. "I felt happy. It made me feel like I was a kid again."

After class, Ofelia went up to thank the instructor. "I want you to know, I'm going to be your best student," she told him.

Soon she'd found a dance studio and signed up for nearly every dance class it had to offer, taking as many as twelve a week. But they were far above her level, geared toward professionals, not beginners like her. "I couldn't touch my toes or complete a turn properly or remember choreography, but I was determined to learn to dance despite my embarrassment."

With hard work, her great rhythm and natural talent kicked in. One of her instructors pulled her aside after class one day. "You missed your calling," he told her. "Had you started training younger, you would have become a successful dancer." His words inspired her to keep going.

"Something magical would happen to me when I danced," she says. "Something therapeutic and healing. And the better I got at it, the stronger those feelings became. My self-image soared. My body changed, becoming flexible and lean and graceful. I felt beautiful when I danced. And I wanted to feel this way for the rest of my life."

So she kept at it, taking modern dance, jazz, hip-hop, and ballet. "I rearranged my office schedule so nothing could interfere with those classes," she says.

In 2002, at age 44, after eight years of intensive training, she started teaching adult beginner dance classes part-time at Emory University. After one class, five students told her how much they loved her teaching style and urged her to start a studio that specialized in beginning dance classes for adults, which didn't exist in Atlanta at the time.

It was tempting but scary. Ofelia didn't know the first thing about running a dance studio and she'd have to close the insurance agency to create a business model, run the studio, and teach full-time. She'd be risking everything she'd worked for her entire career. "My family was mortified," she says. "My life was stable and secure. Why would I throw all of that away to start over, especially in a field I knew nothing about—at 46 years old?"

But once the idea was planted in her mind, it germinated. "I understood how therapeutic dance could be and wanted to share it with the world. I wanted to make my life count by contributing to others'."

In 2004, Ofelia opened Dance 101, a studio just for adults. The curriculum was modeled after her own journey: She offered "discover" classes for newbies and higher-level classes for those who wanted bigger challenges.

She had only 35 students at first and little support from the local dance community. She couldn't even find teachers willing to work for her and was logging 14-hour days. "I affectionately refer to that period of my life as 'two Advil and a Redbull,' because that is how I got through it," Ofelia recalls. "But I was determined." And through word of mouth, new clients started streaming through the doors. Within a year, she had to relocate to a 10,000-square-foot space.

Today Ofelia has more than 20,000 registered students and 40 instructors (that first cardio-funk teacher now works for her) teaching more than 100 different classes, from ballet and jazz to salsa, samba, tap, musical theater, and belly dancing. Her students are all different body shapes, ages, ethnicities, and cultures. You might see a high-powered attorney dancing alongside a neurosurgeon dancing alongside a seamstress. "Dance is like the great equalizer," Ofelia says. "Everyone shares a passion to move their bodies."

In her office, Ofelia keeps a box full of cards and letters from her students who, like her, have been transformed by dancing. "I hear stories of people who've recovered from illness, grief, breakups, and divorces because they were able to spend a few hours a week in one of our dance classes. In my own small way, I'm going to leave this world a little bit better than I found it. The studio has given my life renewed meaning."

It has also taught her a new lesson. "When I embarked on this journey, I was intimidated and filled with fear and self-doubt. But I have learned to embrace these emotions as necessary components of success. When you truly believe in yourself and in your dream, every obstacle you face is simply another stepping-stone on your journey—not a reason to quit."

PART ELEVEN

Biz Wiz

"We were naive when it came to big business—we learned the hard way."

Mary's Gone Crackers

Mary Waldner, 62
Gridley, California

Mary Waldner woke up on a January 1 morning resolved to make a change in her life—and her New Year's resolution was a doozy. She wanted to scrap her successful 26-year career in clinical psychology and, at age 48, start selling crackers. Seriously.

And all because of a decades-long tummy ache. For most of her life, Mary had severe digestive pain, depression, and fatigue. "Ever since I was a child, I had been to so many doctors," she says. "But no one could ever figure out what was wrong."

Finally, at age 43, Mary got the diagnosis that would change her life: She had celiac disease, an immune reaction to eating gluten, a substance found in grains like wheat, barley, and rye. Such gluten sensitivities are common knowledge today, but when Mary was diagnosed, celiac disease was virtually unknown. "I had never even heard of gluten," Mary says. "Nobody had."

Immediately, Mary cut gluten-rich foods like bread, pasta, and cereal from her diet ("I joked that I could cut out bread but I couldn't live without my aunt Enid's brownies") and she finally felt healthy—really healthy—for the first time in her life.

But what to eat instead? It was almost impossible to find gluten-free foods in supermarkets or even health food stores. "Anytime I *could* find anything that was gluten-free, it tasted terrible."

So Mary decided to concoct her own gluten-free recipes. Ever since her childhood, when she'd go to her grandmother's house to make cakes and cookies, Mary had loved to bake. Now, using gluten-free flour, she put those baking skills to work creating muffins, bagels, and desserts.

"I think of myself as a jazz musician in the kitchen," Mary says. "I'm always improvising." One of her improvisations was a thin but dense cracker made from brown rice, quinoa, flax, and sesame seeds. They were delicious.

"Whenever there was any kind of gathering, I would bake a few things and bring them with me so I'd have something to eat. My friends liked most everything I made, but the crackers were the big hit. Not like, 'These are good,' but, 'Oh my God, these are fabulous! Where'd you get them?'"

So she made bigger and bigger batches—and wondered, *Could I actually turn these crackers into a business?*

To find out, Mary brought a bag of the crackers to a local health food store, where the owner put out samples for customers to nibble on. "As I was going up and down the aisles, I overheard all of this fabulous reaction," Mary recalls. "Then the owner came up to me and said, 'I think you're going to have to bring me more.'" Mary had found her first distribution outlet. "I'd bring in ten bags of crackers and they'd quickly sell out, so then I'd have to make another batch."

She began taking her treats to other health food locations, and the response was always the same. "Everyone went crackers for my crackers," she says. "And I knew I had to get them out there for other people with a gluten intolerance." When she asked friends for suggestions for a business name, one jokingly proposed Mary's Cracking Up. Close. Another friend quickly came up with Mary's Gone Crackers.

With local demand rising, Mary was spending all of her spare hours in her kitchen, while still maintaining her full-time psychology practice. "I was doing two things with my life: working as a therapist and making crackers. Don't think everyone didn't make a joke about that."

Mary bought a new, larger oven to keep up with the demand, but she was still making the crackers by hand, and couldn't churn out more than 240 at a time. Not only was the hot, sticky dough difficult to work with, but she had to hand scoop and form each individual cracker on a tray. It took her five hours to make each batch.

Then came her New Year's epiphany: If this side project was going to grow into a sustainable, efficient business, the process needed to be automated. And if she was going to shift from cracker baker to cracker manufacturer, she needed to scale back her psychology practice.

"I had thought that somehow I would always be a therapist," she says, "but it became clear that unless there were two or three of me, that wasn't going to happen."

Once Mary was in, she was in. "I tend to be someone who doesn't have a lot of regrets. I do what I do and I don't look back. And in those decisive moments, that's me at my best."

Mary didn't know a thing about manufacturing, so she started doing research. "I cold-called companies that made gluten-free products and asked about packaging materials, equipment, ingredient suppliers, distribution, food brokers, and even graphic designers. I went to food shows; people in the natural food business are very helpful. There's a lot of passion and love in this industry, if you look for it."

Convinced that Mary had a winning idea, her husband, Dale, quit his general contracting job to help her write a business plan and join her full-time. With family and friends investing in the new venture, they raised $750,000. "It was incredible that so many people, some who knew us well and some who didn't, would invest their money in us," she recalls. "It was a big reason that failure was not an option. We were always very aware that these people had entrusted their money to us, and we were not about to lose a penny of it."

Mary's initial idea was to sign on a comanufacturer, but finding a company with both gluten-free production space and the special equipment needed to handle the sticky dough proved difficult. So she rummaged through her cupboards, collecting the names on the labels of the gluten-free companies. Then she began making calls. As it turned out, only one company had both the equipment and experience. In 2004, Mary's Gone Crackers was incorporated.

The next year, Mary closed her psychology practice, and she and Dale went full-time into the cracker business. Then a stroke of luck: Because awareness of gluten sensitivities had been building in the media, gluten-free products began moving into mainstream grocery aisles; as a result, annual sales for Mary's Gone Crackers soared to $1.5 million. Soon Mary and Dale moved the company into their own manufacturing facility in Gridley, California, and expanded the product line to include new cracker flavors, pretzels, and cookies.

That doesn't mean there weren't bumps along the way. "It was a steep learning curve, and we were naive when it came to big business—we learned the hard way." When a venture capital firm approached the couple with an investment substantial enough to cover their escalating operating expenses, they were flattered. "These guys were the godfathers of the organic food industry and they wanted to invest in our company!" she recalls. But after just a few months, it was clear the investors' plan was to keep swallowing equity until Mary and Dale would lose majority ownership and be ousted. No longer naive, Mary and Dale took the battle to court and, along with their original investors, retained control of the company.

Fifteen years after that New Year's resolution, Mary's Gone Crackers is a powerhouse in the natural foods industry, growing more than 40 percent a year since it started.

In 2013, Mary and Dale sold a large stake of the company to Kameda USA, but this time, they were smarter at cutting a deal and they remain in charge.

"Every step of the way, whenever we wanted to do something, people told us, 'That's impossible.' What I've learned is: You have to hold on to what seems like the most outrageous dream you have because often it's really not that outrageous."

Glisten Up

Cinnamon Bowser, 43
Alexandria, Virginia

Cinnamon Bowser could think of ten good reasons to start her business. Twenty, if you count *both* fingers and toes.

It was 2002, and Cinnamon's good friend Wanda was nine months pregnant with her third child. Feeling huge and uncomfortable, Wanda craved one tiny pleasure: to get a pedicure in her own home. Could Cinnamon help?

"I called around from salon to salon, searched the Internet, and couldn't find anyone," Cinnamon recalls. "I said, 'I know this is not New York, where they have everything, but Washington, D.C., is a major market. We should have this service!'"

So she created it herself.

A public relations expert who was then working with the Alexandria public school system, Cinnamon had always itched to have her own business. "In P.R., things work in a cycle: The same stories come up every season, over and over. I loved all my P.R. jobs, but to be honest, at about the two-year mark, I'd always start to get restless to move on."

Cinnamon was always dreaming up small-business ideas. She even kept a little notebook where she'd jot them down. "My husband, Steve, was usually not terribly excited when I'd mention one of my brainstorms, but when I told him about my mobile manicure plan, he said, 'Honey, that's a great idea!' I thought, *Maybe I really need to look into this one.*"

Of course, Steve was a guy—he thought that buffers and shellacs were things you found at car washes and that Opi was the name of the little boy on *Andy Griffith*. So Cinnamon asked her women friends. "They loved the idea, too. One said, 'My sister got married last year and we could have really used someone to come to the hotel and give us manicures.' Another one told me, 'My grandmother is stuck at home, and it would be so nice if someone could drop in and help her with her nails.'"

Cinnamon knew nothing about the mani-pedi business—other than getting her own nails done—so she got to work researching nail schools, certification credentials, industry standards, and website design. "I'm so thankful I had an office with a door because otherwise I would have been fired!" she recalls. "I remember so clearly sitting in my office with a girlfriend one whole afternoon brainstorming names for the company. We'd come up with one and then I'd go to the domain name site and it was already taken. Then she said, 'What about Nail Taxi?' I loved it—and it was available. I bought it on the spot."

Cinnamon also took night and weekend classes in entrepreneurship. "I learned about everything from finance to human resources to the legal aspects of owning a business," she recalls. "The classes also taught me how to write a detailed business plan, which I needed in order to get Nail Taxi off the ground."

Now all she had to do was find the customers, but without an actual salon to attract walk-in business, how could she do it?

The answer came when Cinnamon heard about an upcoming women's conference in nearby Falls Church, Virginia. "In addition to the speakers, they were going to have vendors offering chair massages and mini-makeovers. I thought Nail Taxi should participate—the *next* year. So I sent an email to introduce my company and got an email back ten minutes later saying, 'We want you to come *this* year.' I panicked. I thought, 'I'm not ready to do this!' But even though I wanted to say no, I said yes."

She's glad she did. Cinnamon's two nail technicians were booked the entire day at the conference, giving mini-manicures. And at the end of the day, Cinnamon kept the sign-up sheet and used it as the beginning of Nail Taxi's client list. "Afterward, those women at the conference called to schedule more appointments. Most important, they told other women in the area about us. That one event is really what got Nail Taxi out of the gate."

Within five months, Nail Taxi had so much business that Cinnamon decided to quit her school job. "It was bananas. It got so crazy that I was spending a lot of my time at work answering emails and calls from Nail Taxi clients. But the business was giving me such fulfillment, I thought, *I have to roll out of here.*"

Cinnamon also realized she needed to go to nail school and actually learn how to do mani-pedis herself. "I figured that if I was ever in a crunch, I could be that extra pair of hands," she says. So she enrolled at a nearby school operated by two Vietnamese men in the back of a nail salon. "It was a challenge. I could read and retain what they were teaching, but it definitely took some time to learn how to use my hands. Even buffing takes practice. And it took me awhile to get comfortable touching people who weren't family members or friends. I was not what you'd call a natural."

What Cinnamon *was* really good at was marketing her business. That first year, she'd send out a press release every six weeks about Nail Taxi, emphasizing the mobility of its services: Technicians would go to homes, hospitals, senior centers, parties, weddings—wherever.

"Those releases got an incredible response," she says, "which led to media coverage, which led to more business. It helped that this was a feel-good story. In between articles about budget cuts or schools underperforming, here was a story about a service for women and men who cannot get out and have their nails done. Even though it's a small thing, a manicure can change a person's outlook on her day."

And media feeds off media. So within a year, Nail Taxi was featured on many local stations in D.C., and got coverage in several national magazines. "That's how I got the first inquiry about opening Nail Taxi in another city. A woman saw our name in the press and wanted to open one in Richmond. It's also why corporate clients started calling."

Today, besides the D.C. area, which Cinnamon oversees herself, Nail Taxi has licensing agreements in ten other major U.S. cities, Canada, and the Bahamas. "My goal is that someday, women and men will go to their hotel wherever they are and tell the concierge, 'Schedule me an appointment with Nail Taxi, please.'"

Nail Taxi has done in-store events or promotions for companies like Neiman Marcus, Stride Rite, and Guess. It has worked with designers to prep models for Mercedes-Benz Fashion Week in New York. CoverGirl even hired the company for a two-day "NailGating" event at Baltimore's Inner Harbor before the Ravens' 2013 season opener. The "fan-icures," done by a team of ten technicians, featured the Ravens' team colors—purple, black, and gold—in a variety of designs. The day's only bad news: The Ravens were shellacked by the Broncos, 49–27.

That kind of promotional work has been a delightful surprise to Cinnamon. "When I started out, I thought most of my clients would be women in

the hospital, on bed rest, pregnant women, seniors. I was not thinking Fashion Week and the NFL!"

Nine years after starting her business, Cinnamon's restless days are behind her. "I love running Nail Taxi. No two days are the same, I get to work with creative people, and the hours are flexible. So if I want to go on a field trip with one of my three kids, I don't have to ask someone—I can just go and enjoy it.

"Best of all, clients are always happy to see us. Nail polish has replaced lipstick as the go-to cosmetic for women. It's recession-proof; no matter what's going on with the economy, women will still get their nails done. It doesn't cost a lot and, as I say all the time, 'It's not a tattoo, it's just polish.'"

Recipes for Success

Deana Gunn, 44
Encinitas, California

Wona Miniati, 45
San Francisco, California

There's made-from-scratch, and then there's made-from-*almost*-scratch.

Deana Gunn was a specialist in the latter. She had to be: A pioneering PhD rocket scientist who developed technology for an optics start-up company, she woke up early for conference calls with European partners before handing off her two kids to a full-time nanny so she could head to the office—then at the end of a frenetic workday ran in the door at six o'clock to cook dinner. "It was quite a juggle," she says.

To make it all work, Deana had to become a genius in fast-track meal prep. The truth was, she had a sneaky little secret: She was always amazing dinner guests and delighting her kids with fancy concoctions like bruschetta-stuffed bread, black bean soup, or corn bread layered casserole. But all of that time-consuming prep work for her meals? It was being done by the pros at Trader Joe's, the nationwide gourmet supermarket that specializes in already-prepared ingredients, like sauces, doughs, cooked shredded meats, or cut-up veggies. "I could buy little pouches of brown rice from the freezer section and something that usually takes 45 minutes to cook was ready in three minutes," she says.

Deana had never been shy about sharing the tricks of her trade with friends, but it took a visit to her favorite grocery store (yes, Trader Joe's) to inspire her to share the wealth with other customers. During one of her twice-weekly shopping runs, she noticed a stranger staring glassy-eyed at a box of quinoa. "I heard Oprah say it's good for you, but what do you do with it?" the woman asked. Deana rattled off three recipes, wished her happy cooking, and continued shopping.

Walking down the next aisle, she noticed a man puzzling over a jar of curry, putting it in his cart, then studying it again before returning it to the shelf. "Why don't you stir it into some veggies, add yogurt to make it creamy, and serve it over rice?" Deana suggested. Bingo.

"As I drove home, I thought, *Why isn't there a Trader Joe's cookbook?*" she says.

It wasn't a rhetorical question. Deana had been tossing around "exit strategies" from her job for a while. She missed little daily moments with her young kids ("Whenever I squeezed in time for a mommy-and-me class, I always felt stressed that I had to get back to work," she says). And after seven years pursuing her PhD and investing another ten in her field, she was ready for something new.

When Deana told her husband about her idea to write a cookbook using ingredients from Trader Joe's, he thought it was a home run (and this from a usually skeptical engineer who had given the thumbs down to all of her previous brainstorms, like marketing a baby food warmer). Only one problem: He, too, was thinking of starting a new company—his was in biotech—which might mean going without a salary for a while.

"We wondered if it was wise for both of us to make such drastic career changes with two small kids and a mortgage," she says. Over a sushi lunch at a Japanese restaurant, they both decided to go for it.

First, Deana needed a partner in crime. So she called Wona Miniati, an old pal from MIT and fellow foodie who struggled with balancing her high-tech marketing job and being a mom of two. "When she called, it was like a lightbulb went off in my head," says Wona. The answer was yes.

The long-distance friends—Deana lives in Encinitas, Wona in San Francisco—didn't waste any time: "With millions of Trader Joe's followers, we were positive someone else had this idea, too, and we wanted to be the first to market," says Wona.

After long hours at their day jobs, dinnertime became R&D time. Deana and Wona would whip up as many as five main dishes each night, along with sides and desserts, holding off kids and husbands until they'd meticulously photographed each plate. Only then could the family dig in. One Saturday morning, Deana was helping her five-year-old son, Mason, make pancakes. "When I told him it was time to eat, he said, 'Wait, Mom!' and ran out of the room. He came back in with a toy camera, snapped a picture of his plate, and then said, 'Okay, *now* I can eat.' That made us all laugh."

The women made as many as four Trader Joe's runs in a single day and often worked well past midnight, paring down the recipes, photographing the dishes, and writing the stories behind their inventions. Their concoctions were global and varied, influenced by their ethnic backgrounds. Deana's heritage is Middle Eastern. Wona is Korean but grew up in Venezuela. "We're comfortable fusing all kinds of foods together—bringing together an Italian dish and Indian flavors and making a Saag Paneer lasagna, for example—or making really approachable versions of food we grew up with." Dishes like Chicken Pot Pie, California Fish Tacos, and Apricot Baked Brie made the cut.

Within five months, their already-full plates were now overflowing, and they both quit their six-figure jobs. "Our friends thought we were joking," says Deana, "asking us why we thought we could change course like this at our age. But to me, it was like that great *Winnie the Pooh* line: It's today, my favorite day."

But they needed time to learn the ins and outs of publishing, marketing, and distribution. Eager to get the books out by the holiday season and wanting to expedite the process and control the final product, they chose to self-publish. "There were things that were super important to us, like color photos and a hard cover, and we didn't want to compromise," says Deana.

One obstacle they didn't count on: When they called Trader Joe's to arrange for the cookbook to be distributed in its stores, the company said no—it had a strict policy against carrying books. Wona turned to some old Stanford business school colleagues for help and they advised her to close up shop and move on. But Deana and Wona had already quit their jobs, and they *knew* they had a hot product. "It forced us to make lemonade out of lemons," Wona says.

So they launched Plan B. (Always have a Plan B.)

On a rainy afternoon in November 2007,

Deana (left) and Wona (right)

Deana maneuvered a rented forklift to unload a pallet of 10,000 *Cooking with All Things Trader Joe's* cookbooks (their favorite 125 recipes, plus suggested wine pairings and nutritional info) from a semi-truck into her garage. Then she and Wona set up a website (now called www.cookTJ.com) and an 800 number and, through word of mouth, orders started trickling in. Wona couldn't help answering the 800 number at all hours of the night—even at four a.m. when an early riser on the East Coast called. "One by one, we started selling every one of those 10,000 books out of my garage," says Deana.

Though the November release date meant they missed a lot of holiday "best cookbook" lists, the women forged ahead, reaching out to food editors across the country. When the *Sacramento Bee* ran a rave review but failed to include the website for ordering, the women were disappointed—that is, until individual bookstores getting requests from customers looking for the book started placing orders. Soon, Borders and Barnes & Noble came calling, too, taking distribution to a whole new level. "That was the silver lining," says Deana.

Trader Joe's still doesn't carry cookbooks, but no matter. Deana and Wona now have nine titles in the Cooking with Trader Joe's series. They also have vegetarian and gluten-free editions and a portable version to fit into readers' purses or back pockets and be taken into Trader Joe's with them.

"Who knew when I was leading PhD research teams that in a few years I would be walking by Barnes and Noble to see my cookbooks displayed in the window?" says Deana.

What's more, they've created a flexible work schedule that allows them to chaperone their kids' field trips or volunteer at school—even if it means staying up until two a.m. to work on new books or blog entries for their website, which now has a database of more than 800 recipes and product reviews.

"We *love* what we do—it's fun, not a chore," says Wona. "I never would have expected, coming out of MIT with an electrical engineering degree, to eventually end up authoring cookbooks and writing recipes. No one should feel trapped by their formal training or what their past experience points them toward. We need to give ourselves the open space to think beyond what our career path looks like."

Hoops and Dreams

Susan Walvius, 48
Michelle Marciniak, 39

Columbia, South Carolina

It was a sweltering August afternoon, and coaches Susan Walvius and Michelle Marciniak had just finished running a day of basketball camp at the University of South Carolina. Hot, sweaty, and exhausted, Susan tugged at the high-tech athletic jersey she was wearing and said, "This stuff is so soft and silky. I would *love* to have bedsheets made out of it." And then Michelle, without missing a beat, responded with a comment that they'd both retell hundreds of times over the next few years: "Why don't we make them ourselves?"

The more they talked about the idea, the more convinced they became that this could be a business. Athletes loved this material—it breathes and wicks away moisture.

Both hoped they could make such a business happen—they needed a break from the stress. Like all head coaches, says Michelle, "On any given day, Susan was either the savior or the scapegoat, depending on how the team was doing." Michelle, a former WNBA player who had been Susan's assistant coach for five

333

years, was also ready to move on. "Coaching meant a life of never-ending ups and downs, and I didn't have the same passion for it that I had for playing."

But was this a viable business idea? "I called up the dean of international business at South Carolina, told him my idea, and asked if his classes ever built and vetted business plans," says Susan. "He said, 'Yes, we do,' and put his students to work on our idea for two semesters."

That fall, Susan and Michelle came up with the name SHEEX (inspired by the success of SPANX), and Michelle even created the brand's Under Armour–esque logo while sitting at her kitchen table over Christmas break. Then the business students came back with their plan, which projected mind-blowing profits for SHEEX. Susan and Michelle were ecstatic.

"The students had worked out a top-down plan," Michelle says, "how and why the business would work, who the sheets would appeal to, even how we could get it off the ground. It seemed like a sure thing. Once we said, 'We're doing this,' we locked in and it was game on."

Both women resigned from their coaching positions in April 2008. Now that Susan and Michelle were going to be partners, their relationship quickly changed.

"Michelle told me, 'I don't work for you anymore,' " recalls Susan. " 'You have to learn to make decisions with me.' And I respected that. Michelle has a skill set that I don't. I'm levelheaded and strategic. She walks into a room and brings energy and emotion. Would I have tried to start this business without her? Maybe. Would I be successful? Probably not."

Step one of their plan was to raise start-up money, and they were able to collect $500,000 in surprisingly little time. "Most of the money," says Susan, "came from successful women who were part of a mentoring program I had developed to connect the girls I coached with professional women in the community—doctors, lawyers, and high-level business executives."

When Susan and Michelle pitched SHEEX to these women, a few handed over as much as $100,000. They culled additional money from friends and relatives and even rented out their houses to save cash.

"It was clear that we were going to be on the road constantly, visiting factories and meeting with people," says Michelle. "We figured we'd stay with friends or sleep in motels."

So the two ex-coaches hit the road, pursuing meetings with every top business executive they could. "I had read a bunch of books on how to start a business, and one lesson I never forgot was that you should ask successful people for their advice," says Susan. "That rang true to me—you don't win games with freshmen, you win games with talent and experience, and Michelle and I were freshmen. We had a lot to learn."

Their athletic background came in handy. The two towering blondes (Susan is six feet two inches and Michelle is five feet ten inches) project killer confidence. "We're both extremely driven," says Michelle, "and as teammates, we know how to zig when the other one zags."

And their ability to talk sports gave them an instant advantage. "There's absolutely no question about it, men love to connect through athletics," says Susan. "We'd often sit down with mostly male senior management, and spend as much time talking about sports as we did business. It helped us build relationships."

Among those relationships was one they formed with Bob Damon, head of Korn Ferry, the largest executive search firm in the country. "It took forever to get 15 minutes with him, but once we got there, we ended up talking for two hours," says Susan. "He said he had grown up in a tough neighborhood and on two occasions he was headed down the wrong path when a coach helped set him straight." He clearly had a soft spot for coaches.

When Bob asked how much capital they had raised, they told him $500,000. "That's all?" he said, laughing. Then he proceeded to connect them with investors who were willing to put up larger sums of money.

Michelle (left) and Susan (right)

While Susan and Michelle maintained their game faces in meetings, behind the scenes, it was chaos. They slept on couches and floors, took red-eye flights to avoid shelling out for hotels, and camped out in Starbucks making phone calls, sending emails, and learning how to use Quickbooks.

"Laughing at ourselves made rough times easier," says Michelle. "I remember one night we were catching the midnight bus out of New York City's Port Authority back to Allentown, Pennsylvania, where we were staying with my parents. I was so tired, I had fallen asleep while waiting and Susan had snapped a picture of me passed out on the bus station floor. When we finally got on, the driver told us there were no more seats. It was the last bus of the night, and our only option was the aisle. We were still dressed in suits and heels from a business dinner, but we just looked at each other and cracked up. Then we sat down back-to-back on the floor and opened our laptops. Chivalry, by the way, is dead."

336

About six months after meeting with Bob, they had secured enough financing to start production. Then they hit a major snag. "We had talked to bedding manufacturers all over the country and no one could make the fabric we wanted on their machinery," says Susan. "We tried to source it from Asia, but none of the fabrics were right. It was a dig-deeper moment."

Susan and Michelle called the manufacturers that worked with athletic apparel companies but, wary of breaking confidentiality agreements, none would get back to them. Finally they connected with the president of the company that makes the yarn used in Under Armour products. "He introduced us to a designer who helped us figure out a manufacturing process that would create our ideal product," says Susan. "The economy had bottomed out that year, and there was so little business, factories were willing to alter their machinery to fit our needs."

They started out selling directly to consumers online and promoted SHEEX at athletic events like the U.S. Women's Open. "It was really interesting to listen to what customers had to say," says Susan. "Guys talked about the cool technology. Women liked that they were breathable." Now it was time to get SHEEX on store shelves. "Our big break came," says Susan, "when we landed a unique partnership with Bed Bath & Beyond," which introduced SHEEX in almost 1,000 stores.

Since then, Susan and Michelle have expanded the brand to include pillows, mattress toppers, comforters, duvet covers, and sleepwear.

Although many people see Susan and Michelle as crackerjack businesswomen, they trace their winning skills back to the basketball court. "You're always anticipating how your opponent will play the game," says Susan. "Even though you don't have an opponent in business, you need to anticipate every possible setback—that you may not get paid on time, that a delivery may not come through—and be ready to execute an alternate strategy."

Their ultimate game plan now? "To become a billion-dollar brand," says Michelle. "That would be like SHEEX winning a national championship."

Something to Chew On

Robin Béquet, 54
Bozeman, Montana

The summer of 2001 was a train wreck, and Robin Béquet had a front-row seat.

She was an officer at the high-tech firm ILX Lightwave, and sales of its newest telecommunications equipment had been booming. Then, three weeks before ILX was to go public, the tech bubble burst, and six months later the company began laying off thousands of workers. After 20 years in technology sales and management—where she had earned the highest reviews—41-year-old Robin was let go.

"I tried to take the news as professionally as I could," Robin recalls, "but after the meeting, I stood up and my legs gave out from under me. That's how devastated I was."

For the next two months, Robin spent time with her daughters—Rachel, eight, and Hannah, nine—while trying to figure out her next move. Unfortunately, there weren't a lot of options in the small town of Bozeman, Montana,

338

where she and her husband had relocated four years earlier for his job. She tried to stay positive, telling herself, *A new chapter in my life is about to start, and I get to decide what to write on that page.*

Still, "it was very scary. I knew I needed to choose wisely, because I didn't know how many more chapters I would have left."

That summer, Robin kept coming back to an interview she had read with business expert Tom Peters (the bestselling author of *In Search of Excellence*), who was asked, "If you were going to encourage someone to start a business, what industry would it be in?" Robin never forgot Peters's answer.

"He said, 'It doesn't matter. Drive down Main Street in any town, and you'll see all sorts of successful businesses on your left and on your right. What matters is finding an unserved or underserved niche. Do something no one else is doing and do it well.' I found those words so striking," Robin says.

They were also humbling. What *could* she do well that no one else was doing? Starting her own high-tech company was out—it would take too much money and carry a lot of risk. Still, "I didn't want to work in a sector that I didn't fully understand," she says. "I wanted to be a master at what I did."

She knew that left only one thing: making caramel.

It was a talent she had picked up accidentally a couple of years earlier. A candy lover and experimental cook, Robin had set out to make toffee at first. "A coworker mentioned how much she liked great toffee, so I thought, *I wonder how hard that is?*" Robin says. "I bought a candy thermometer and followed a recipe I found in a cookbook. But it was a disaster—completely inedible!"

However, fate sometimes intervenes in fortuitous ways: On the cookbook's facing page was a recipe for caramel. Refusing to end her candy-making experiment on a failed note, Robin made a test batch—with delicious results.

"I always liked caramel, but I had no idea how much better it was when made fresh with real ingredients," she says. She brought a plateful into work, then watched and waited. "People went crazy for it."

From that point on, Robin and her coworkers were hooked. When she'd cook a batch at home, the leftovers came with her to the office the next day. She once made a gallon-sized bag as a going-away gift for a friend who was leaving the company, and afterward she passed out copies of the recipe. "I became known as the Caramel Lady," she says.

From techie to the kitchen. Not a logical step. But she knew that what she had done in the tech world she'd have to do in the candy world—be the best. "I knew that was the only way I could be excited about it."

So Robin decided to find out if what she was making *was* the best. She started asking friends and family to take part in blind taste tests using samples of her caramels alongside other brands that sold for $15 to $20 a pound. The results: "Seventeen out of 18 adults chose my caramel over the others," she says. "That was the moment I knew: I'm on to something here!"

Robin decided she wanted to use her family name, Béquet, for the business, so she sent caramel samples to her seventy-six-year-old dad on Long Island to get his permission. Her father, Ray, had been in the U.S. Merchant Marine during World War II and was now retired from his job as a cargo superintendent for a New York steamship company. After Robin's mom died of cancer when she was 11, he became a stalwart supporter of his three kids.

"I remember my dad sitting me on his knee and saying, 'You can be anything you want to be in this world. If you want to be president of the United States, you will be president of the United States.' I'm not sure every little girl heard that growing up."

Robin's dad not only gave her permission to use the family name for her caramels, but announced that he was coming out to Bozeman to help her start her business.

"It was just Dad being Dad," Robin says, "but it meant so much to me. He knew I was going to be working long hours trying to get it all done by myself. Plus, he wanted to be closer to his granddaughters."

Nearly every weekday morning that January, there they were: Robin and her dad, in the kitchen stirring up five-pound batches of caramel.

"It turned out my dad was great at it," Robin says. "We did everything by hand: cutting the caramel into identical squares, weighing and wrapping each piece. At this point, I knew what professional looked like!"

Next, Robin called around to box makers, found one that had leftover boxes in just the dimensions she needed, and bought them for 14 cents each. "I found a way to launch the whole business for under a thousand dollars," she says.

In the afternoons, Ray would pick up his granddaughters from school, always bringing candy for them and their friends. Robin, in the meantime, began driving to candy shops, espresso bars, and gourmet markets with a cooler packed with caramels in her car trunk. "I'd walk up to a clerk who didn't look too busy, explain that I made high-end caramels and ask if they'd like to try one."

And they always did. "Then, while they were eating, I would ask to speak to whoever makes decisions on purchasing new candies. I sold many orders that way."

Before long, the stores began calling to reorder more caramels. Robin took a deep breath—she knew it was time to make a real investment that would take her business to the next level. That winter, she and her husband took out a second mortgage on their house and rented a former photo repair shop in a strip mall, transforming the space into a new kitchen. In all, they spent nearly $40,000, with the biggest chunk going toward a $27,000 candy-wrapping machine.

"By then I had wrapped more than 10,000 pieces of caramel by hand," recalls Robin, "so this purchase was my favorite!"

Soon, caramel making became a family affair. After school, Hannah and Rachel would do their homework and then pitch in, pulling on plastic gloves to transfer squares from the cooling table to cookie sheets. When the cooking was done for the day, Grandpa Ray would offer up the long-handled spatula that he used to stir the caramel and ask, "Who wants to lick the stick?"

"A lot of family bonding happened at the shop," Robin says. "We had fun."

The first year, however, sales were just $35,000—less than Robin had expected, and not enough to pay herself a salary. "It wasn't clear whether we were going to make it," she says. "I remember sitting in the office, feeling my throat tighten with this horrible sense of 'What *have* I done?' "

So to supplement her income, Robin decided to take on a second job, working 40 hours a week as a technology manager for a government-funded company at Montana State University. Using part of her salary, Robin hired someone to help her dad make the caramel during the day—then she spent another 20 hours a week at the shop on nights and weekends.

"It was exhausting," she admits. "I remember taking the kids to piano lessons and nearly falling asleep in my chair while they were pounding away on the other side of the room."

With the help of her new income, Robin also financed a trip to New York for the Fancy Food Show, where 25,000 buyers could sample her wares. That gambit paid off. "People would take a sample, walk five steps, bite into it, and then retrace their steps back to our booth." Food show judges deemed Robin's caramels one of the top 17 products at the show.

"It was amazing," she says. "Here I was competing against Ghirardelli, Godiva, Jelly Belly—every big name in the gourmet-food industry—and they picked me as a winner!" Because of her selection as a top product, *Gourmet*

Retailer magazine did a full-page story on her business. "That really helped get us on the map, since we couldn't afford advertising," she says.

As sales picked up, Robin quit her job at the university to devote herself full-time to caramels again. By the time the business had reached its five-year anniversary, she was able to pay herself a modest salary for the first time: $2,000—or about a dollar an hour.

Now Robin was on a roll. She began hiring more employees—though her daughters, who worked at the shop during the summer and on Sundays leading up to Christmas, were always on call. "When the girls were in high school, if we were having trouble with the machines and it was time for the other employees to go home for the day, I'd call and say, 'I don't know where you are, but we need you,'" Robin says. "And they'd coming running, because they knew that meant 'all hands on deck!'"

Today, Robin operates Béquet Confections out of an 8,300-square-foot facility, and she is making plans to double its size. Her caramels can be found in some Whole Foods stores and 900 gourmet markets and natural foods stores across the country, and Robin says annual sales are well over $1 million. "Right now it's the off-season and we're making 25,000 caramels a day," Robin says. "Last year during the holidays we were making more than a ton of caramel a day."

To fulfill all those orders, Robin employs 24 year-round workers (her dad is now 87 and in an assisted-living facility, and her girls are off at college). "One of my goals was to create jobs here in Bozeman," she says. "Making a living in Montana is not easy. My proudest day was when we added health insurance coverage for our employees.

"Every now and then, I think back to that day the tech bubble burst and took my job with it. Out of the lowest point in my life came something that is truly my own. Like Tom Peters advised, I found that underserved niche that very few were doing and I'm doing it well."

PART TWELVE

Giving Back

"To find your passion, you have to show up. You have to look around and see what needs doing, and just do it."

Spreading Warmth

Nancy Sanford Hughes, 71
Eugene, Oregon

The request sounded reasonable enough: "Could you please delay dinner?" The 120 doctors, nurses, and support staff assembled in the dining hall looked up, curious to hear what the young Guatemalan woman with the striking dark eyes had to say. She began to speak.

"My name is Irma, and at the age of two, I fell into an open fire and burned my hands shut," she began, a translator changing her native Kechiquel words into English. For 16 years, she said, she hadn't been able to gather wood or cook, leaving her with little hope of ever attracting a husband. Now one of the team's plastic surgeons had repaired her hands, separating her fused fingers. For the first time ever, she could make tortillas. She could marry. She could start a family. "Thank you," she said. "You are my miracle."

No one spoke. "We were all weeping," says Nancy Sanford Hughes, a volunteer who was cooking dinner for the medical team. "It was so profound. She had suffered for so long."

On her three mission trips to the Central American country, including this one in 2004, Nancy had witnessed the medical team do so much good—restoring a 14-year-old boy's eyesight, excising a man's grapefruit-sized tumor, removing the ruptured appendix of a woman whose brother had carried her, strapped to a chair, for four days in order to reach the clinic. But this team had only ten days in the country, and when it was time for the doctors to go back to the United States, there were still a thousand people waiting in line. Sometimes at the end of a mission trip, another volunteer medical corps was on its way, sometimes not. "It's appalling," Nancy says. "There's basically no medical care for the indigenous people, and there's a desperate need."

But Irma's story moved Nancy on a whole different level. The most dangerous activity for a woman in that part of the developing world was cooking for her family, often with a baby strapped to her back, leaning over an open campfire in a tiny, unventilated home. She had watched mothers and children come into the clinic with chronic coughs, debilitating burns, and hernias caused by having to lug heavy bundles of wood. "There were medical teams who couldn't insert tubes down babies' throats because they were so choked with creosote," she says. There must be something she could do for these families, she thought.

Helping others had been a big part of the very full life she had led back home in Oregon. She and her husband, George, known to everyone as Duffy, had three kids—a son and two daughters. But you'd never know it from looking around their dinner table most nights. You might see an exchange student from China or Finland (Nancy has hosted more than 50 in all), a couple of neighbors, Duffy's brother and his four kids, or maybe a few of their son's rowing buddies, fresh from a workout in the basement, where they'd set up their team training room. "I was always cooking for a mob," she says. "Our house was a busy place, and that's putting it mildly."

Nancy welcomed the chaos. She'd always been the type who couldn't sit still for long. While Duffy was building his family medicine practice, she volunteered for everything under the sun—"the library, the symphony, the theater, my kids' schools," she says. "You name it, I did it."

Then, in 1993, a shock: Duffy was diagnosed with breast cancer at age 51. "I'd get mad when I saw those pink ribbons and say, 'Men get this disease, too, you know!'" Nancy says. But she tried to stay upbeat. "Lots of people get breast cancer and lots of people do fine afterward," she told herself. Duffy was less optimistic. "From the very beginning, he looked at me and said, 'I always knew something odd would kill me.'" His doctors removed the tumor, assuring them the cancer was slow-growing and further treatment wasn't needed at that point. "Things went along fairly normally after that," she says.

But about four years later, when Duffy could barely lean over to put on his shoes, Nancy insisted that he go back in to be checked.

"Duffy was a doctor, so his idea of going to the doctor was running into one of his partners in the hall and saying, 'Hey, I don't feel so hot,'" Nancy says. "He would never make an appointment to actually go in and be examined." Sure enough, by the time he did, the cancer had spread to his spine.

It was a staggering setback, but Nancy was not about to give up on him. She'd fallen in love with this strong, vibrant man because he had a spirit of adventure that matched her own. "That bound us together," she says. This would be their next adventure—albeit a scary one.

Over the next four years, she went to all of his oncology appointments, a thick binder in hand. "I took notes, wrote down all the medicines he was on, and reminded the doctors of what they had said before," Nancy says. Together, they decided he should try an experimental treatment. She and their kids, who were now young adults, hung on to the 40 percent chance that it might extend his life.

But the cancer would not relent. Duffy's athletic body weakened and he went into his office less and less. "Not only did he lose his identity as Dr. Hughes, he also stopped being a swimmer, a runner, and a skier," Nancy says. "Having to give all that up was devastating for him. I had to figure out what to do next, support him emotionally, help my kids with what they were going through and sort of pretend that life was normal. It was mentally exhausting."

She was physically tired as well. If Duffy couldn't sleep at night, Nancy sat up with him. Near the end, he could no longer swallow and she'd lie awake listening to the hum of the machine that pumped food into him. When he died in the spring of 2001, "it was almost a relief," Nancy says. "As strange as that sounds, when you've been living with someone with a life-threatening illness for eight years, it's true." By the time he died, "I had already gone through a lot of mourning. It's the gift of having advance notice, of knowing what's coming."

But once she took care of the obvious—things like meeting with the lawyers to settle his estate and thanking all their friends who had brought meals—reality set in: She was a widow at age 58. What would life be like without Duffy in it?

"I had to figure out what to do next," she says. "Once I lost Duffy—and with my kids gone, too—I had to change direction."

That new direction came in 2002, when her son's girlfriend told her she was headed to Playa Grande, Guatemala, with a medical team sponsored by Helps International, a nonprofit that fights poverty in Latin America. Nancy had always wanted to go on this kind of mission, but assumed she was un-qualified because she was neither a doctor nor a nurse. "When I signed up, they said, 'What can you do?' And I answered, 'I guess I can cook.'"

From the very first day of that first trip, Nancy's "mom skills" kicked in. After flying into Guatemala City, then taking a 15-hour bus ride to an aban-doned military base on the northern border, she and the team were famished. "So we made peanut butter and jelly sandwiches—for 125 people!"

That night, she set up her sleeping cot in the kitchen, next to the *pilla*, a laundry tub with a pinhole-sized drain where she and her coworkers had to scrub all the pots and pans. They boiled any water they needed to purify it and depended on dull knives and a single handheld can opener to cook three meals a day for the medical staff—plus any snacks if they got hungry while tending to patients around the clock.

"We worked from the minute we woke up until late, late at night," Nancy says. When she had a free moment, she'd wander into the clinic where the doctors and nurses allowed her a bedside view of their work. "It was fascinating," she says. "I just wanted to help out in any way I could." So she came back to work the kitchen year after year.

But after her third trip, in 2004, Nancy wanted to do more than cook. "I started talking about what I had seen to whoever would listen," she says. "Every time I mentioned Irma, I broke down."

She had heard about organizations that provided fuel-efficient stoves in developing countries, so she wrote her very first grant through her local Rotary Club, where Duffy had been a longtime member. When his college roommates wanted to plant trees in his honor, she steered them instead to her stove project.

"We have enough trees in Oregon," she told them. "I will make much better use of your money." In all, she received funding to buy 100 stoves. "This was my memorial to Duffy," she says.

A year later, Nancy returned to Guatemala, this time to head up a six-person stove team. For ten days, they hiked through fields of corn and up and down the slopes of volcanoes—following directions like "turn left at the banana tree, go until you see the pig and it will be on your right"—to reach the homes that Helps International had selected for the stoves.

As she and her team learned to use rivet guns and screwdrivers to assemble the heavy cement pieces, they also learned that smiles, handshakes, and hugs overcome any language barriers.

"The indigenous people are welcoming, friendly, honorable, lovely people with a wonderful sense of family," Nancy says. "You can go into the poorest home and they will offer you something to drink."

Nancy led several more trips, installing more than 100 stoves at a time, but she began to feel deflated. The stoves had downsides: They couldn't be put in homes with thatch roofs, they were extremely heavy to carry in the mountainous terrain, and they weren't portable, so women were still stuck inside all day cooking. Plus, when she learned that Guatemala alone needed approximately 6 million stoves, "it was overwhelming. What I was doing seemed ridiculous because it was so small in comparison to the need," she says.

Should she just give up? One of the engineers who helped design the stoves wouldn't hear of it. He dropped by Nancy's house one day to give her a copy of the book *Don't Sweat the Small Stuff*—along with a pep talk.

"You can't stop," he told her. "You're very effective at what you're doing. Just keep going." Soon after, she got a call from another stove designer, who said he could create a better stove, one that was portable and didn't need a chimney.

Then about a month later, she opened her mailbox and found a letter from Carlos and Deborah Santana's Milagro Foundation with a check for $10,000. By sheer luck, the sister of the foundation's administrator had seen an article about Nancy in a local medical society newsletter. "It was like a perfect storm of goodness," Nancy says. She had to keep forging ahead.

Since then, Nancy has launched StoveTeam International, which has helped raise nearly $1.2 million so that entrepreneurs could open eight factories in El Salvador, Guatemala, Honduras, Nicaragua, and Mexico. Called the Ecocina, the innovative new stove produces almost no smoke, uses less than half the wood of an open fire, and reduces carbon emissions and particulate matter by more than 70 percent. Even with manufacturing and labor costs, the factories have kept the price of the stove to just $50 or $60. To date, more than 38,000 stoves have been provided to families.

In 2011, Nancy received a $100,000 Purpose Prize, given to social entre-

preneurs over 60 who are working to improve society. And two years later, the White House honored her as a Rotary Champion of Change.

Now 71 and a grandmother of two, Nancy still sees much to be done. She has started a project to lower the costs of the stoves by helping the factory owners receive carbon credits, and she spearheaded a program to open distribution centers to make the stoves available to more people.

As for Irma, she came back to visit the medical team two years after she'd first thanked them. This time, in her beautiful hands she held a baby. If Nancy has her way, dangerous cooking fumes or flames will be something Irma's child will never know.

"People say, 'You have such a passion,' but I didn't start with a passion. I just showed up on the medical team. To find your passion, you have to show up. You have to look around and see what needs doing, and just do it."

Being There

Vicki Sokolik, 52
Tampa, Florida

I n 2000, Vicki Sokolik was standing in the vegetable section of her Tampa grocery store when a fellow mom came up to say hello.

"I've had the worst morning!" the woman lamented, describing how her daughter had thrown a tantrum over a hair bow.

Vicki smiled blankly and gritted her teeth. Oh, what she would have given to have a hair-bow problem. Just the day before, Vicki had returned from a Houston hospital, where she had spent more than three months waiting for doctors to perform surgery on her 11-year-old daughter, Cori, who suffered from a rare form of severe epilepsy.

Now back home, everything and everyone felt surreal.

"Things that once seemed so important were suddenly insignificant," Vicki says. "When I heard this woman complaining, I couldn't put on my usual sympathetic mom face. I was ready to burst into tears."

For Vicki, it had been a long and tough journey. Cori had been wracked with seizures since she was an infant, at one point suffering an episode so serious that she lost all of her memory. ("She had to relearn how to tie her shoelaces, use a fork, comb her hair," says Vicki.) She continued to have as many as 20 seizures a month, and doctors warned Vicki that the cumulative effects would cause permanent damage to Cori's brain.

Then Vicki heard about a procedure that could stop Cori's seizures completely. According to her daughter's neurologist—Dr. James Wheless, a world-renowned expert in pediatric epilepsy—Cori could be a candidate for a rare neurosurgery in which doctors would implant electrodes into her frontal lobe in an attempt to pinpoint the precise spot where the seizures originated. Then they could surgically remove that faulty part of the brain. Dr. Wheless told Vicki she should bring Cori to Houston for the surgery.

It was all very risky, but it promised hope that Cori might live a more normal life. So in October 1999, Vicki and Cori flew to Texas. They were supposed to be there for just two weeks, but those weeks dragged into months. Cori spent every day tethered to monitoring equipment, but the specialists had a hard time determining precisely where the seizures were originating. Then the bad news: Surgery was no longer a possibility.

Vicki was devastated. "We had just spent a third of the school year in a hospital room," she says. "I kept thinking, *Why did I put my daughter through this?*" Several months later, Dr. Wheless called and said there was a new device, a sort of pacemaker for the brain, that was showing good results in adults and he wanted to know if Cori could be one of the first kids to try it. After much debate, they went back to Houston for surgery. "He thought it would help Cori reduce her medications and her seizures, and it did." Remarkably, she was able to get off all her meds.

But through all those months by Cori's side, Vicki had seen things at the hospital that made her realize they were more fortunate than most families. So many of the young patients were alone.

"I'd ask them, 'Where are your mom and dad?' and they'd say, 'At work. And I have brothers and sisters at home, too, so it's hard for them to leave.'

"It broke my heart that these little kids were undergoing surgery and re- covering from major illnesses," says Vicki, "and they didn't have anyone there with them. It also made me sad for the parents who couldn't be there." It was the first time Vicki had come face-to-face with this kind of poverty. She had grown up privileged, and life had remained comfortable: She enjoyed a mar- keting career, married a successful doctor, and was able to leave her job when Cori was first diagnosed with epilepsy.

"My daughter had me by her side, full-time," says Vicki. "It truly opened my eyes to see these other kids. I knew their parents didn't love them any less than I loved my daughter. It was strictly about resources."

So Vicki did whatever she could to right that wrong. In the hospital, she played with the children, and whenever her family visited (her husband, Joel, and their nine-year-old son, Cameron, flew in every other weekend), she asked them to bring toys and electronic games for all of the kids. Her brother even hired a clown.

"All you had to do was look at the smiles on the kids' faces," says Vicki, "and you'd know how much they needed this."

Back in Tampa, after the hair-bow incident at the grocery store, Vicki realized that she couldn't go back to her old life of volunteering at Cori's school, playing tennis, and having lunch with friends. She was haunted by those lonely kids in Houston and their suffering families. She knew she had to find a way to help.

Her first stop was the local hospital in Tampa. She, Joel, and their kids began by regularly delivering baskets full of crossword puzzles, coloring books, and model airplanes. ("I remembered how much those things meant to the kids in Texas to keep them busy," she says.) They also volunteered at a shelter for abused, abandoned, or neglected children, organizing craft activities for Valentine's Day and Easter. Then, as Thanksgiving approached, Vicki signed up with a program through the school system to serve five homeless families for the holidays, bringing them turkey dinners and fulfilling their Christmas wish lists.

But there was one mom Vicki couldn't get out of her mind. Her name was Shelly and she lived out of a motel room with her two young boys. Vicki kept wondering why Shelly, who had held down a steady job for ten years, couldn't afford a real home. The thought kept after her: *How much did that Thanksgiving meal really help this woman?*

"It seemed like a Band-Aid," Vicki says. So two days after she met her, Vicki took the plunge and called Shelly. "Can you meet me for coffee?"

"It all made sense once she explained her life to me," says Vicki. Shelly had been the victim of domestic violence. She'd escaped the relationship for the fifth time, but couldn't bear the thought of taking her kids to a shelter yet again. Her job paid enough to cover the motel room, but Shelly couldn't

Vicki (front left), Cori (behind her), Joel (to her left), and members of Starting Right, Now

come up with the $3,000 she needed for a deposit on an apartment and utilities. So the family had been living in the motel for nearly a year.

"What if I found a way to help you get that apartment?" Vicki asked. "Would you be able to pay the rent?"

"Absolutely," Shelly answered.

So Vicki went out and found a small house for rent not far from the motel, paid the deposit, cosigned the lease, and helped Shelly gather donated furniture to fill her new home.

All went well, until one day, when Shelly mentioned that she needed to dash around town to pay her bills.

"I said, 'What? You don't have a bank account?'" When Shelly admitted that she always cashed out her paychecks instead of depositing them, Vicki told her it was time she opened a bank account. She also taught her how to pay her bills through the mail and how to make a budget. By the end of the year, Shelly had paid all her debts and had even tucked away $1,600 in savings.

"She was filled with pride," says Vicki, "and gratitude."

That year, Vicki helped five more families for the holidays, including a high school sophomore named Gabby who was struggling at school. Vicki soon learned that Gabby was having headaches in class, so she took her to an optometrist who prescribed glasses. She then helped Gabby fill out applications for colleges and financial aid. Two years after they first met, Gabby graduated with a 4.03 GPA and a full scholarship to the University of Central Florida.

By this point, Vicki had recruited friends and neighbors to join her in her outreach efforts, and by 2005, the group was helping 200 to 300 families every year. They brought the families food, even beds—and offered extra assistance to high school students, like a book or school supplies. At one point, Vicki asked her son, Cameron, if he was jealous of the time and energy she was putting into other people's kids.

"Jealous of kids who don't have beds?" he asked incredulously.

By 2007, word of Vicki's efforts had spread to the mayor of Tampa, who called Vicki and proposed turning her mission into a bigger, citywide effort. And that's what happened.

Today, Vicki is the executive director of Starting Right, Now, a nonprofit organization that pairs mentors with homeless high school juniors and seniors. Thanks to its work, Vicki has attended more than 100 graduations of kids who might otherwise be on the streets or in jail.

As for Vicki's own daughter, Cori, she has "defied every odd." She lives in an apartment with a roommate, has earned a bachelor's degree from the University of Tampa, and has launched a career as a hairstylist. Cameron, who graduated from Stanford University in June, recently surprised his mom by nominating her for a service award from Bank of America, which she ultimately won.

In the application, he wrote: "I have set up more beds in stranger's apartments, traveled to more unfamiliar places to deliver dinner, and been reminded of how fortunate I am more times than I can remember, all because of my mother."

"When I read that, I felt like I had already won," Vicki says.

"My daughter's seizures were the worst thing that ever happened to our family but also turned out to be the greatest blessing," says Vicki. "Her remarkable recovery not only brought her back to us, it also led us to these other children, who had incredibly difficult lives of their own. If it weren't for everything we went through in that hospital, I would have never known about these kids, and the blessing you get from extending your hand to help someone else's family."

Flour Power

Jessamyn W. Rodriguez, 36

New York, New York

Jessamyn Rodriguez's entire life changed, and all because she heard something wrong.

Sitting at a conference, Jessamyn heard a speaker mention the nonprofit organization Women's World Banking and misheard the name as Women's World *Baking*.

Even though Jessamyn laughed when she recognized her mistake, the words took her back to the kitchen of her great-grandmother, Minnie Starkman, where, as a little girl, she and Minnie, along with Grandma Perlmutter, would spend an entire, long hot August day baking kreplach, as many as 400 of the small tasty dumplings.

They would roll out the dough; insert ground meat, mashed potatoes, and other fillings; close them up; then freeze them until Rosh Hashanah, weeks away.

"We did this for years," says Jessamyn. "At first, I was little and people had to watch me around the stove. Now my great-bubie is gone, and I am grown and have to keep an eye on my grandma."

For years, the words Women's World Baking stuck with Jessamyn. And in 2006, while working at a high school in Crown Heights, Brooklyn, she thought, *Why not? Why not a place where women from around the world— immigrants like my family, who came to Canada from Romania and Slovenia, and worked in sweatshops—could come together and bake? And not just bake, but learn English, learn to market their skills, learn to run a business?*

This brainstorm wasn't random; it came from a deep place in Jessamyn. The daughter of civil rights activists, she had left Columbia University with a master's degree seeking a career devoted to helping others, which she did in a series of jobs, including one at the United Nations, where her work focused on human rights, education, and immigration issues.

"*Desk-y* jobs," she called them. Too far removed from the people whose lives the policies were actually affecting.

Jessamyn knew that if she was going to make the idea of Women's World Baking a reality, the first thing she'd have to do was learn more about the profession. Taking night courses, she acquired a baking certificate from The New School. Then she spoke to her husband, who is in the wine business; he spoke to the sommelier at Daniel, one of New York's premier restaurants, who spoke to the "chef Boulanger" (head baker), Mark Fiorentio, who invited Jessamyn to interview.

"I told him that I wanted to learn so I could teach others," Jessamyn recalls. "Mark is a benevolent soul. Because there were no women working in restaurant bakeries, he knew that taking on a woman could only improve the industry."

During her 18-month apprenticeship, Jessamyn would get up at dawn, work at the bakery for a few hours, then spend all day at her school job. "I

loved it! I loved the smells, I liked being on my feet and working with my hands, and I liked the people." After the apprenticeship she spent six months working at the bakery, and then took off on her own.

In 2008, Jessamyn launched Hot Bread Kitchen out of her house in Brooklyn, creating a place where immigrant women not only could capitalize on the baking skills they possessed, but could acquire the other skills that would help them and their families escape poverty and move into the middle class. After all those years at a desk, Jessamyn was finally feeling the human connection she'd hungered for.

Starting with five women, Hot Bread Kitchen initially made loaves of bread that were sold in a local farmer's market. Since then, 22 women from 11 countries have come through the on-the-job training program, including two who have moved into managerial positions at Hot Bread Kitchen and two who have taken jobs at Daniel's bakery.

"We have become a United Nations of bread," says Jessamyn. The workers produce more than a thousand loaves of multiethnic breads a day, inspired by the countries the women come from, which are then sold at dozens of outlets in the metropolitan New York area, including Whole Foods. "We have women from Bangladesh, Nepal, Mali, Haiti, Mexico, and Morocco, and we make stone-ground corn tortillas, an Armenian-style *lavash,* and a Moroccan flatbread called *msmen.*" The kitchen also runs English and computer classes for the women.

In 2011, the kitchen expanded its mission, launching HBK Incubates, a program that supports graduates who wish to start their own food businesses and share their knowledge with others in the community. "We rent them space, and later, help them get the licenses they need, learn packaging and marketing, and get started." There are 39 businesses enrolled in HBK Incubates, including a caterer, a cake pop maker, a pickler, an ice-cream maker, a couple who make Dominican-style cakes, and a housewife who makes "sexy novelty bakery items."

As for Jessamyn, Hot Bread Kitchen offers the intellectual stimulation of running a business, the fulfillment of helping others, and the practical happiness of putting on an apron and sticking her hands in some dough.

"Food is the vehicle for sharing and culture, and that's very important to me," she says. "I don't think I'd be where I am today, professionally and personally, without my mother and grandmother—those two strong women—and all of those conversations that happened in the kitchen."

And sometimes it helps if you hear something wrong.

The Giving Heart

Roxanne Watson, 59
Nanuet, New York

My *only chance to live is if someone else dies.*

The thought tortured Roxanne Watson. She tried to push it out of her mind. But in 2010, Roxanne was out of options. She was 56 and needed a new heart.

The transplant team at New York City's Montefiore Medical Center was waiting for a perfect one—strong and healthy—to give her as many good years as possible. That meant it would have to be harvested, still beating, from the chest of a young person whose brain had stopped working. Whatever the cause—a car accident, a gunshot wound—for that person's family, it would be a tragic ending. For Roxanne and her family, it would be a hopeful future.

"That was the hardest part," Roxanne says. "You would never want to be in that position, sitting there in the hospital just waiting for someone to die."

That someone, it turns out, would be a 180-pound, 23-year-old male. Those were the only details doctors were allowed to share with Roxanne

364

about her donor, but they made an immediate connection. A single mother, Roxanne had only one child, a son about the same size as her donor, and only a few years older. "That could have been *my* son," she thought. "What horrific pain was his mother going through? I couldn't even imagine."

Roxanne had been through eight years of deteriorating health that had landed her in the hospital 17 times, leaving her unable to work. "I didn't want anybody else to suffer the way I had," she explains. So when doctors released her from the hospital nine days after her transplant surgery, she had a new heart and a new purpose in life: To tell her story to as many people as possible so they'd sign up to be organ donors and possibly do for someone what this young man had done for her. "That was my mission," she says.

Born and raised in the Bronx, Roxanne had always had a nose-to-the-grindstone attitude that took her from part-time salesclerk at her neighborhood Sears in her early twenties to stints at Sam's Club, Old Navy, and Victoria's Secret. She learned how to open stores, hire employees, and display merchandise, eventually becoming a district manager for KB Toys, responsible for 15 stores and $30 million in annual sales. "I worked like an animal, but I really enjoyed it," she recalls.

In 2003, she took on her biggest challenge yet: Managing a discount designer-goods store called AJWright. "It was in a tough neighborhood and was the dirtiest, nastiest store in the company. Customers were stealing merchandise. Employees were robbing the store. It was out of control."

But in less than a year, she'd turned things around. "I didn't have to fire anyone, but I said, 'Either start working or go away.' When people saw that the store could be successful, they wanted to be a part of that success. They were excited to work." And no one was more dedicated than Roxanne, who put in long hours six days a week for three years.

But the job took its toll: One day, she was out on the floor when she felt like she couldn't breathe and started sweating so badly that her coworkers sat her down in her office, pointing a fan at her face and placing cold towels on her forehead. "I felt like I was going to pass out. I needed air. I was very weak. It was a horrible feeling."

Roxanne had had a heart attack. It was one of many cardiac episodes she'd experience. Even after doctors implanted a pacemaker, she'd find herself slumped at her desk with the same awful symptoms. So she took a four-month leave to try to get back to her old self. But after returning to work on a Monday, she was in the hospital again by Thursday.

"That was it. The doctors told me I couldn't work anymore."

For someone whose drive had taken her from a $70-a-week job to one earning more than $100,000 a year, a forced retirement at age 52 was unbearable. "I was just devastated. I never thought I would not be able to work, especially at a job I loved. I was more upset about that than being sick because I didn't realize how sick I was."

But Roxanne was *very* sick. In fact, her heart was failing, and the next few years were a downward spiral. Not only did she deplete her savings to pay for medical tests and procedures while waiting for Social Security to kick in, but her five-foot, four-inch frame wasted away from 145 pounds to 93. "I was wearing kids' clothes," she says. "I couldn't even look at myself in the mirror."

Roxanne's son quit his job coaching football at Rutgers University to move home to care for her, buying her a Great Dane to keep her spirits up. Many nights, feeling too weak to climb into bed, she'd curl up with the dog on the floor. "I had no strength," she says. In April 2010, her physicians declared an emergency. "We have to get you a heart," they said.

The two-week hospital stay the doctors predicted turned into a month, then two months, then nearly three. "I was the longest in-patient stay in history at that hospital waiting for a heart," she says. "It was 78 days." Three times doctors thought they had the right heart, but each one was ultimately rejected for being the wrong size or not healthy enough. "That's a roller coaster you don't want to ride. Everybody would come to the hospital to say 'I love you' in case I didn't make it through surgery, but then there would be no surgery. It was horrible and I went through it three times."

While she waited, Roxanne, who is black, learned that transplants don't have to take place between people of the same race. So the more people of *every* ethnicity willing to donate organs, the more help for people like her. She also learned that minorities were less likely to sign up to be organ donors. And so, broadening the donor base became a part of her mission.

"Are you an organ donor?" she'd press family and friends who came to visit. Often they'd say they'd never thought about it before, so Roxanne would persuade them to sign up. "It wasn't that they didn't want to. That's when I decided maybe all we really need to do is ask people."

If doctors could find her a heart and she made it out of the hospital alive, she decided, she was going to help others have the same chance.

Finally, on July 15, 2010, just before midnight, she got a call from the transplant coordinator saying, "It's a go."

"It was such a huge relief to me that I wasn't even afraid. But I had always felt that I was going to live."

When doctors opened Roxanne up, her enlarged heart was nearly as big as a football. The new one fit perfectly in her chest, and by the next day, she was sitting up in her hospital bed. Within a week of leaving the hospital, and true to her vow, she had her first speaking assignment: Still wearing a surgical mask to protect her from germs, she was back at the hospital for a Minority Donor Awareness Week, talking about her ordeal.

Although she'd been through major heart surgery, Roxanne was tireless in her new mission. She talked to doctors, nurses, clinicians, and donor organizations; she'd go to health fairs, colleges, and hospitals—wherever she thought she'd find a receptive audience. And if an organization assigned her a table at an event, she'd stand in front of it and corral passersby.

"Are you an organ donor?" she'd ask them, and once she had their attention, she'd tell them her story, answer their questions, and hand them an application. "I love signing people up one-on-one," she says. "They feel more comfortable asking personal questions that may have stopped them from donating before. And whether they sign up or not, most people say, 'Thank you for doing this.' "

And then something very strange happened: Roxanne suddenly had an inexplicable urge to fix up her house. "Out of the blue, I was suddenly attracted to Home Depot and Lowe's. Every time I'd go past one, I wanted to shop. I had a compulsion to do all this crazy stuff I wasn't the slightest bit interested in doing before my transplant, like ripping out all the carpets, repainting the walls, and turning my dining room and garage into home theaters. I thought, wait a minute—could this person, whose heart I have, have been a construction worker? No, that's ridiculous."

But sure enough, while watching a show on the Oprah Winfrey Network one day, in which experts answered viewers' questions, Roxanne wrote to the producers explaining her drive to sign up organ donors, especially minorities, and then she asked a question: "Is it possible to take on the personality of your organ donor?"

Before she knew it, Roxanne was invited on the show, called *Ask Oprah's All-Stars,* and in June 2011, not quite one year after her surgery, she was sitting with her son in a TV studio in Manhattan when in walked her organ donor's family—the father, mother, and three sisters—a surprise arranged by the show's producers.

"We all just started hugging and crying," Roxanne says. One of the sisters said, "My God, you are so beautiful." Another said, "Now we have another sister."

The donor's father beamed as he talked of his only son. "His name was Michael, and they were as thick as thieves," Roxanne says.

He had been a volunteer firefighter who was training to be a helicopter mechanic in the Coast Guard—and, yes, he was a skilled carpenter who had worked alongside his dad to build their family's New Jersey home. "I just knew it!" exclaimed Roxanne.

The more Roxanne learned about Michael, the more she realized how giant his heart was. "Everything he did in his life was service," Roxanne says, "and at the end of his life, he was still serving people. One section of his liver was given to a 5-year-old Hispanic girl, another section to a 69-year-old Chinese man. A 42-year-old Jewish man received both of his lungs, and an 18-year-old black man his kidneys.

"And I got his heart," Roxanne says. "Because of his gifts, there are five of us walking around in the world."

Today, Roxanne continues to share Michael's story with thousands of people, whether she's lobbying state lawmakers to pass organ donor legislation or working with Dr. Oz to create a public service announcement that plays at DMV offices.

Most weeks, she's still in the trenches, passing out organ donor applications. But no matter where she is, she always displays an eight-by-ten photo of a clean-shaven, baby-faced Michael, decked out in his military uniform.

"Wherever I go, whatever I do, I always have his picture. I don't go anywhere without him. I have his heart."

Class Act

Marguerite Heard Thomas, 62
Bainbridge Island, Washington

Quick quiz: Marguerite Thomas is (a) adventurous, (b) energetic, (c) adaptable, (d) curious, or (e) all of the above.

If you answered *e*, then you probably have a good notion why, at age 50, Marguerite was brave enough to leave a successful 20-year career as an architect to try her hand at something new.

Marguerite had never liked staying put. As an army brat, she'd attended "12 schools in 12 years, all over the world," but unlike so many military kids who crave stability, "I loved every part of it—the new experiences, the new challenges." In college, she traveled to South and Central America to work with indigenous populations, and that sense of adventure stayed with her. "Whenever I get an offer to do something new, my response is always: 'My bags are packed! I'm ready to go!' "

Thinking about making a midlife career change, Marguerite had lots of ideas for what she could do next. Should she become a horticulturist? (She was an avid gardener.) Work for a nonprofit? (She loved the idea of giving back.) Go to law school? (She liked the notion of doing pro bono work.)

Marguerite found her answer when a friend mentioned that she was volunteering at a small school on a nearby Native American reservation.

"This woman was even older than me—in her early seventies—and she was telling me how rewarding it was to work with these kids who were struggling to read," Marguerite recalls. "She said their faces would light up when she walked in the door and she loved watching their progress over time. After so many years of dealing with demanding architecture clients and contractors, I was tired of focusing on buildings—I wanted to focus on people. And I don't believe in waiting until you're miserable to take a leap outside your comfort zone."

Marguerite decided to dip a toe into teaching by taking every Monday off to volunteer at the Indian school. "I would read with kids who were way behind their grade level. It was clear they weren't used to getting a lot of individual attention, but by the end of the school year, they'd say, 'I got it! I understand!'

"I thought, *I'm doing this one day a week, and it's my favorite day.* That experience really clinched it for me: I wanted to be a teacher."

Marguerite knew it would be tough making the switch. "Friends said, 'Is anybody really going to hire a 50-year-old teacher?' But I knew I had the energy and enthusiasm to do this, and I didn't want my age standing in my way."

So Marguerite wrapped up the last of her architecture work and enrolled in a teaching certificate program at Antioch University, two hours away in Seattle. "I would get up before five, walk a half-mile to catch a bus to the ferry, ride the six a.m. ferry across Puget Sound to Seattle, then walk two miles to campus." After taking classes all day, "I'd get home around six p.m., make dinner, help my two girls with their homework, then start on *my* homework after they went to bed, working past midnight.

"It was exhausting, but I absolutely loved it. Here I was, a student again after 30 years, going on field trips with my 20-year-old classmates. It was so much fun."

After finishing her student teaching at the same Native American school where she had volunteered, Marguerite worked as a substitute before finally landing a position teaching fifth grade at her daughters' old elementary school on Bainbridge Island.

"Subbing was tough. You don't know what you're walking into every day. And you have to figure out how to manage a class full of kids you've never seen before," says Marguerite. "But once I got into my own full-time class-room, and was able to get to know the kids and exercise my own creativity in planning lessons, everything fell into place.

"Everyone remembers their fifth-grade teacher. It's a rocky age for kids, but they have so much energy and curiosity it's inspiring to see the wheels turning in their brains. And it makes *me* driven to learn new things, too. What's the point of life if you're not always learning?"

Marguerite regularly clocks 11 hours a day in school—plus nights and weekends grading essays and exams. "My husband asks, 'Why don't you just give them multiple-choice tests? They're easier to grade.' But I feel I owe it to my kids to give them more."

And the kids give back. "I ride a motor scooter to work—I love the free-dom of it, the wind in my face—but one day I had an accident and ended up in the ER. The principal said, 'Let me get a substitute,' but I said, 'No, no, I can make it in! I have a big lesson planned today.' So they patched me up, and I went on to school. When I walked into the classroom, with all of my cuts, scrapes, and bandages, the kids started applauding. 'We can't believe you came!' It was so wonderful."

While Marguerite appreciates the students who "you don't have to worry about, who always do their work," she has a soft spot—"an extra measure of patience"—for the tough cases. "I feel like I have to look out for them, give them a little push to succeed.

"I will always remember one boy who had a communication disorder and couldn't connect with the other kids. We were studying the Revolutionary War, and I had broken the class into groups to write and act out scenes about different moments from the war. I knew this boy couldn't work in a group, so I said to him, 'There's a famous speech about liberty that Patrick Henry gave at the time. Why don't you do part of that speech?' He did—and his class-mates gave him an ovation.

"I thought, *This kid will never forget this moment, I'll never forget it, and most of his classmates will never forget it.* He had earned a measure of respect that hadn't been there before."

A few years later, Marguerite was teaching a lesson on poetry when a boy named Brian, who had a similar condition, read a verse he had written about visiting his dad, who had moved to another part of the country.

Extremely hot
a summer day in Arizona
waking up
weary eyes
knowing what I would face
out the window I looked
desert
mesas
pool

Bags were packed
Dad was ready

to his car I went
we talked of great experiences
we were as happy as clowns
I hugged my Dad
a tear drop fell,
a raindrop after a drought
Dad drove
more tears came
When will I see him again?

When he finished, the class was stone silent. "What he had written was so moving. You often don't realize what's inside these kids. His classmates had been hard on him for years, so he had just clammed up. With so many of my students, I *know* they're going to go on and be successful. Then there are a handful about whom I'll think, years later, *I really hope he's doing okay.* And Brian is one of them."

At the end of one recent school year, as the kids in her class were crowding around one another's desks to sign yearbooks, Marguerite noticed one girl who didn't have one—only a blank piece of paper for her friends to sign. "When I asked her about it, she said, 'We couldn't afford a yearbook this year.' This is a sweet girl who would bring me roses from her mom's garden, or show up on Monday with a cookie she'd baked over the weekend."

At lunchtime, Marguerite went to the school office, where she was able to pick up an extra yearbook. "When I gave it to this little girl, she said, 'It's *mine*?' She hugged me so tight, you would have thought I'd given her a million dollars."

"I know that teachers complain about salaries, but on days like that, I sometimes think I should pay the school. How could you not want to experience seeing that change on someone's face?"

On the first day of school last year, Marguerite found a letter in her mailbox from a former student. "He said that last year in my class was the best year of his life and he was going to miss me. He had drawn a picture of a big rock with fireworks coming out, and wrote, 'You rock, Mrs. Thomas!' It's those kinds of things—the notes, the poems, the artwork left on my desk— that remind me that I'm really making a difference in these kids' lives."

Credits and Permissions

P. 12, Lori Cheek: Photograph by Guest of a Guest

P. 21, Natasha Coleman: T Nikole Photography by Tara Allen

P. 53, Heather Femia: Photograph by Malek Naz Freidouni

P. 118, Kerry O'Brien: Michael Sipe Photography

P. 132, Sue Rock: Photograph by Anderson Zaca

P. 150, Susan Porter: Photograph by Aamir Malick

P. 154, Layla Fanucci: Photograph by Chick Harrity

P. 170, Julie Lythcott-Haims: Photograph by Dan Haims

P. 182, Kristine Brennen: Photograph by Alison Caron/Alison Caron Design

P. 188, Mari Ann Weiss Cater: Photograph by Gabriella Valentino

P. 230, Troy Ball: Photograph by Rachael McIntosh

P. 242, Lee Gale Gruen: Photograph by Audrey Stein

P. 268, Veronica Bosgraaf: Photograph by Grooters Productions

P. 277, Laura Treloar: Photograph by Michelle Werner

P. 285, Amy Knapp: Photograph by Alan Gawel/Main St. Portraits

P. 292, Lois Heckman: Lisa Rhinehart/Rhinehart Photography

P. 303, Jennifer Otter Bickerdike: Photograph by Ali Astbury

P. 313, Ofelia de La Valette: Photograph by David Rams

P. 320, Mary Waldner: Photograph by Casey Darr

P. 326, Cinnamon Bowser: Photograph by *Brooklyn Avenue Journal*

P. 343, Robin Béquet: Photograph by Janie Osborne

P. 369, Roxanne Watson: Photograph courtesy of Montefiore Medical Center

P. 375, Marguerite Heard Thomas: Photograph by Annie Thomas

All other photographs in this book were acquired from the subjects of the stories and are reprinted with permission.

About the Author

Marlo Thomas graduated from the University of Southern California with a teaching degree. She is the author of six bestselling books: *Free to Be . . . You and Me; Free to Be . . . a Family; The Right Words at the Right Time; The Right Words at the Right Time, Volume 2: Your Turn!; Thanks & Giving: All Year Long;* and her memoir, *Growing Up Laughing: My Story and the Story of Funny.* Ms. Thomas has won four Emmy Awards, a Peabody Award, a Golden Globe, and a Grammy, and has been inducted into the Broadcasting & Cable Hall of Fame for her work in television, including her starring role in the landmark series *That Girl,* which she also conceived and produced. She is the National Outreach Director for St. Jude Children's Research Hospital, which was founded by her father, Danny Thomas, in 1962.

In 2010, Ms. Thomas launched her website, MarloThomas.com, on *The Huffington Post* and AOL. She lives in New York with her husband, Phil Donahue.